Praise for
Create Marketplace Disruption

"How do you participate in market disruptions which threaten your current leadership status? In this book, Adam Hartung shows how critical it is to break free from the 'Defend and Extend' thinking that blocks adaptation to the new markets and set forth on an 'Attack and Explore' agenda to engage directly with the new market dynamics. This is just the kind of thinking needed to deal with the creative destruction that underlies global capitalism today."

—Geoffrey Moore, Author, *Dealing with Darwin:*
How Great Companies Innovate in
Every Phase of Their Evolution,
Managing Director TCG Advisors, San Bruno, CA

"Adam Hartung presents a fresh perspective and compelling case that demands business leaders harness the courage of an entrepreneur, always pursuing new markets, thirsting for opportunities to disrupt the status quo. Every business should apply Mr. Hartung's principles when hiring—only hiring those individuals prepared to question the Success Formula creating its corporate culture, and vigorously willing to pursue White Space."

—Ken Daubenspeck, Chairman and CEO,
Daubenspeck and Associates, Ltd., Chicago, IL

"Adam Hartung offers courageous leaders a new language system and framework for generating long-term profitable growth. Rich with compelling metaphors, stories, and illustrations, *Create Marketplace Disruption* explains why even aggressive efforts to reinvent an organization's Success Formula will certainly fail unless leaders create Disruptions and design new White Spaces for action. Hartung's Phoenix Principle for overcoming internal barriers provides leaders with practical tools for designing evergreen business models to keep companies ahead of declining results and obsolescence. The book is scholarly and innovative, persuasive and grounded; an easy read, every leader needs to understand Hartung's framework and heed his advice."

—Judi Rosen, Strategic Advisor, former Managing
Director, CSC Index and President,
The Concours Group, Glencoe, IL

"Adam Hartung blends stunning lessons learned from the fallen giants of business with set-you-back-in-your-seat insights that make this a must read for all business leaders of large and small companies alike. *Create Marketplace Disruption* dramatizes why you can't minimize risk without minimizing change and the inherent dangers of perpetuating Lock-in thinking and yesterday's Success Formulas. Hartung provides an intelligent blueprint for achieving what every business craves—competitive advantage and renewable growth. Smart, sophisticated treatment of a topic that no business executive worth his/her stock options can ignore—how to grow and differentiate your business. Adam Hartung's 20 plus years of consulting, innovation, and strategy expertise are powerfully and clearly presented in this gem of a book."

—John Popoli, President Lake Forest Graduate
School of Management, Lake Forest, IL

CREATE MARKETPLACE DISRUPTION

CREATE MARKETPLACE DISRUPTION

HOW TO STAY AHEAD OF THE COMPETITION

Adam Hartung

NACD *Board Leadership Fellow*

www.AdamHartung.com

Published by: Content Laboratory, Inc.
2272 Horizon Light Ct.
Henderson, NV 89052
Www.MyContentLaboratory.com

content
LABORATORY

First Printing July, 2008
Second Printing October, 2018

Library of Congress Cataloging-in-Publication Data is on file.
This product is printed digitally on demand.

ISBN-13: 978-1-7328074-0-2

To Alex, Grant, and Spencer.
May you vigilantly keep your eyes open to Challenges,
never fear Disruptions,
and always maintain White Space in your lives.

Contents

Foreword

A hundred years ago, no smart businessperson would have produced bath products—only one in five houses had bathtubs, and women washed their hair once a month. No shrewd financier would have invested in the telephone, which cost more for a three-minute call than the average person made in a week. No prudent distributor would have considered the California market because of its physical remoteness and tiny population. A manufacturer was more likely to release version 3.0 of the horse carriage than to retool for the new automobile or aero-plane, both new and dangerously unsafe.

In retrospect, the foolish short-sightedness of such mindsets is obvious. We don't stop to think of how many companies of that era *did* go out of business because they could not see the *new*. They were locked in by historical thinking, by defending and extending what had worked before, by perceiving their market as relatively stable, static, and safe. Any number of businesses missed the shift from the Agrarian Age to the Industrial Age. Even more have missed, or have been slow to join, the shift to the Information Age, as Adam Hartung describes in *Create Marketplace Disruption*.

Today's business leaders, managers, consultants, and educators have the same blinders (to continue the horse-and-buggy conceit) as our forebears. We think our technology is "advanced," yet the internal combustion engine has not fundamentally changed for a hundred years, the Internet Age is no further along than automobiles were in 1920, and our major medical treatments continue to be slicing people open with knives, bombarding them with deadly radiation, and infusing them with poisonous chemicals. A hundred years from today, carbon-consuming engines will run only in museums, the Internet will be seen as we now see the telegraph, and our barbaric medical practices will be an ancient, sorry chapter in human biology. Historically, we are as primitive and short-sighted as anyone before us.

How can we step outside ourselves to perceive such shortcomings in our business thinking today, rather than wait until history books are written—or our company's obituary? Hartung offers both a change in mindset and a change in behavior, with a "Phoenix Principle" that is both academically sound and pragmatically do-able. He doesn't just wave his arms and talk about the importance of change. He explains how every company can make it happen every day.

Of course, we all believe that we are "change ready." From some perspectives, we are. It seems natural that we went from Kitty Hawk to the moon in 66 years—less than the lifetime of an average person—and use a lot of the derived technology in everyday life. We appreciate our ability to travel to any major city in the world in hours instead of days, to make, buy, sell, and service products globally, to communicate instantly. We are grateful that modern medicine has eliminated most childhood diseases and is gaining on cancer. During the working life of any senior businessperson, digital technology has transformed business and given rise to multiple new industries. In a historical instant, we have seen the rise and fall of the mainframe, the rise and fall of the minicomputer, the rise of the PC, and the rise of connectivity and an array of digital gadgets that will destroy as many technology companies as it will give birth to.

Change is great when it benefits us as consumers or happens to somebody else at work.

We are curiously resistant to change within the confines of our business lives. It's as if the physical walls of our cubicles and offices create mental walls impervious to market signals. Or maybe we're too busy to think because we're responding to email, talking on our cell phones, or texting friends and colleagues (all technology that will appear quaint to our grandchildren). The simple fact is, business teaching, business thinking, and business execution is locked in to the past, to what has worked before—or in many cases, has *not* worked before, but we fail to see the truth. As avant garde as we think we are, we're as much in our own cocoons as our predecessors were when they missed the shift from hard labor to cotton gins, automated looms, and mechanical threshers.

How did Kodak and Polaroid miss the shift to digital film? How did Sony miss the shift to digital music? How did existing makers of small aircraft miss the shift to composite materials so that most of them went bankrupt? How did IBM miss the shift to smaller computers—twice? How do airlines *continue* to miss the real reasons they struggle—the fact that they overcharge their best customers and provide the worst service of any business that ever existed?

Create Marketplace Disruption takes on this profound problem in which businesses lock in to the practices that gave them their initial successes and seek to defend and extend their current products and markets against all comers—including their own employees with new ideas—all the way to their demise. The problem begins in academia. We continue to teach the same business mindset, disregarding the statistics showing that Fortune 500 companies have no more than a 50-50 chance of staying at the top of their game for even ten years. Hartung points out that once companies fall into the "Defend and Extend" mindset, only seven percent will ever grow consistently again, and fifty-five percent will remain in permanent decline. Yet academia keeps teaching the "basics" that will repeat this formula for failure.

Businesspeople, who ought to be more practical than academia, are just as blind. Hartung gives many examples in which companies sabotage new thinking and approaches through management indifference or hostility, by organizing new projects for failure, by hamstringing resources, and by outright "cooking" of financial analysis to reconfirm that it is more sensible to continue a weak or failing strategy than to take a risk on something new.

Fortunately, Hartung does more than critique the status quo (or describe the many subtle techniques of the Status Quo Police). He also provides many examples of companies from multiple fields that have broken away from locked-in thinking. There's the router maker that obsoletes itself as fast as possible. The workstation manufacturer that got into film. The PC maker and coffee shop that got into music. The music maker that got into airlines. And many, many others. This book is replete with examples of companies that not only disrupted their own business but redefined entire markets. He takes the added, and usually overlooked step, of describing how companies can bring along their customers, who are also locked in to the old way of doing things and prevent vendors from moving ahead.

More than the interesting case studies (which are valuable enough), Hartung describes specific steps that every business can take to create disruptions in thought and action. He shows how businesses can build in strategies and techniques for disruption and constant rethinking, reevaluation, and new action, rather than relying on rehash and re-action (the latter usually an effort to cut costs rather than raise revenue). He gives numerous specifics about the future that companies should be acting on now. How has your business disrupted itself to take advantage of universal connectivity, biotechnology, nanotechnology, green business, the demographic changes in the United States, or the burgeoning economies of China and India? These are things *we know* will create the markets of tomorrow. Hartung covers them all.

If you want to teach or conduct the business equivalent of the flat-earth theory, look elsewhere. If you want to keep doing the "same old, same old" because it's easier, if less productive, than disrupting your product development, look elsewhere. You can be like Hartung's farmer, who beats on the hen house to improve the laying of his hens. Not because it works but because he always has. Or you can be like the vendor who showed farmers how new products would reduce fuel and water consumption and improve profitability. The vendor disrupted its own business to develop new products and sales approaches and disrupted customers by changing how they understood and responded to costs. Everybody won.

Create Marketplace Disruption shows businesspeople how to create results rather than complete processes. It shows practical ways to use short-term disruptions to generate long-term profits. It's a valuable tool for any businessperson who wants to go where the market will be tomorrow instead of remaining where it is today.

Collins Hemingway
Business author, marketing consultant, executive coach
Coauthor, *Business at the Speed of Thought*, with Bill Gates

Acknowledgments

When *Create Marketplace Disruption* was nothing more than a set of concerns about how we manage, Mark Youngblood was my confidant and contributor for taking rough ideas and helping craft them into a cohesive set of thoughts. I thank him for his early contributions and conviction that this project was worth pursuing.

Alan Weyl and Charles Searight contributed extensively to many of the most valuable concepts underlying *Create Marketplace Disruption*. Neither tired of pursuing solid foundations for the concepts or contributing extensive insights while challenging the ideas. Both were lighthouses providing direction to my efforts.

For their considerable assistance on my journey, I acknowledge and thank all three.

About the Author

Adam Hartung has been a successful entrepreneur, executive in three Fortune 100 companies, and business consultant with leading firms such as Boston Consulting Group, Coopers & Lybrand, and Index. For 30 years he has created growth through innovation and breakthrough strategy in positions from middle management to CEO. Currently a strategy consultant and public speaker, he is Managing Partner of Spark Partners strategy and organizational transformation consultancy. He holds an MBA with Distinction from the Harvard Business School. He lives in suburban Chicago.

Preface

The Phoenix Principle: Those actions which allow any organization, group, or individual to overcome obstacles to achieve perpetual growth.

Those who understand and follow The Phoenix Principle overcome Lock-in to past practices and behaviors by utilizing internal Disruptions and White Space to keep their Success Formulas evergreen.

The Phoenix Principle gives businesses a clear vision of their future problems and the tools to address these problems—or avoid them altogether in today's highly dynamic marketplace. The Phoenix Principle overcomes previously static business planning approaches so businesses can compete more effectively—growing revenue and profits that create and sustain success.

PART I

Understanding How We Got Into This Mess

Overcoming Schumpeter

Is there no overcoming Schumpeter's argument that businesses are unable to achieve long-term success?

Who Is Schumpeter, and What Did He Say?

Joseph Schumpeter was an economist born in Austria in 1883. Atypical for economists, he was first educated as a lawyer. A very good student, at age 36 he became the Finance Minister of Austria and at age 38, President of the privately-owned Biederman Bank. It was in this latter role that he learned firsthand the concepts of competition and business risk, given that the bank failed in 1924, leaving him impoverished. Schumpeter spent the rest of his career in academia, most notably as an Economics professor at Harvard from 1932 until his death in 1950.

Professor Schumpeter was a maverick. Rather than believing Adam Smith was the premier historical economist, he revered one of Smith's teachers—the far less well-known French economist Jacques Turgot, who professed (among other things) that societies pass through cycles of growth followed by cycles of conservatism that lead to ruin. Turgot wrote that human progress sows the seeds of its own demise.

Schumpeter expanded Turgot's thinking and is best known for the popular text *Capitalism, Socialism,* and *Democracy* in which he introduced the concept of "Creative Destruction." An avid fan of capitalism and free markets, Schumpeter adored entrepreneurs and wrote that they were the most important element of a vital capitalistic economy. He expanded on the long-wave cycles introduced by Russian economist Kondratiev, in which over periods of 50 to 75 years innovation drives waves of economic growth. According to Schumpeter, innovation that is brought to market by entrepreneurs creates economic vitality. Then over a long period of time, economies falter as innovation grows stale and entrepreneurship dwindles. To Schumpeter, entrepreneurs were the kings of innovation, and thus they drove all economic benefit.

But Schumpeter saw this process of innovation and renewal as extremely destructive as well, hence the term, Creative Destruction. Innovation unleashed by entrepreneurs often causes a vast amount of inventory, equipment, and skills to become obsolete, causing existing businesses to flounder and fail, while new businesses drive a resurgent economy. Entrepreneurs in their creative drive unleash a torrent of destruction upon existing competitors and generate a wake of destroyed business in their aftermath—thus companies cannot expect to have a long life. Creative Destruction wipes out historical competitors as new innovations come to market.

Schumpeter is considered the father of "Evolutionary Economics." Businesses are born into an environment, grow, mature, and die. As players in a larger environment, they have a particular, and not easily adapted, role. This concept of business evolution is so far-reaching that we no longer even recognize how embedded it has become in our thinking and our lexicon. While business leaders frequently refer to Darwin, it was Schumpeter who started managers talking about companies as if they were an animal species that emerges from competition, grows in strength, and then matures and eventually dies. This sort of thinking has become widespread, even though there is nothing evolutionary about companies or business organizations.

Businesses are abstractions created by people to serve a purpose, and they have no inherent evolutionary cycle. A business is not born; it is a legal and organizational construction. There is no maturity timeline. There is no requirement that it "age" or that it even "die." Yet it is from Schumpeter and his notions of Creative Destruction that we developed these concepts upon which many business assumptions are built.

What Is Business Success, and What Creates It?

For most business people, success is achieving planned goals. Business leaders plan to grow revenue and profits, and by meeting those plans, they are considered successful by themselves, their investors, their employees, their suppliers, and usually their customers.

How to achieve future projections is the fodder of hundreds of management books, countless business gurus, and the content of almost all MBA classes.

A common set of themes emerge from reviewing this enormous volume of business education.

- *Hard work.* Those who put in considerable hours and build organizations that are highly industrious are considered more competitive and therefore more successful.
- *Diligence.* Constantly paying attention to key barometers and working to improve performance is considered a hallmark trait for success. Like the tortoise racing the hare, the diligent performer is considered to have the greater likelihood of success.
- *Persistence.* Never giving up is part of demonstrating the ability to compete. By having employees who work hard and long, businesses can expect to find themselves partnered with success.
- *Setting goals.* Jim Collins, in his best-selling book *Built to Last,* talked about creating a BHAG—Big Hairy Audacious Goal— around which the organization can rally to tremendous success. Variations of this thinking abound, all oriented toward the notion that goals provide motivation for success.
- *Planning and execution.* Volumes have been written on the importance of creating a plan to achieve goals and then executing those plans. Management literature is filled with doctrine about planning your way to success and then merely being disciplined to execute the plan.

Few business leaders would take exception to this list as a set of core elements for business success. Yet, the press is filled with stories of companies that simply do not succeed. Every quarter there is a long list of publicly traded companies that fail to achieve their forecasted goals. Some of these companies miss goals for several quarters.

Over the last few years General Motors, one of America's largest employers and a member of the Dow Jones Industrial Average, has shown a complete inability to maintain market share or improve margin. GM management has made decisions and taken actions, but results indicate these behaviors have been directed at something other than long-term success, given company long-term performance.

In the early 1980s, AT&T was launched into the deregulated telecommunications marketplace with a near-monopoly of long distance phone service. AT&T had enormous resources and deep industry knowledge unavailable to any other competitor. No competitor had the people, assets, or money AT&T had and none knew anywhere near as much as AT&T about long distance. Yet management ran the business for 25 years with declining sales and margin erosion and eventually sold out completely to one of the companies they had previously spun-off, SBC.

We could add to these stories those of Polaroid, Xerox, Ford, Montgomery Ward, PanAm, Sears, Fannie Mae, KMart, Kodak and many others. While each story might have unique particulars as to why sales and profits waned, are we to believe that these companies were simply being led by management that did not understand the critical elements of success?

Or could the answer be that the definition of success is more complex than we previously assumed? On the surface, achieving results seems like the most natural definition of success. And that definition certainly fits with economists' notions that we all behave rationally within a competitive market. Each player must achieve results, or he will be eliminated in favor of a better performing competitor. But if management has demonstrated repeatedly that decision-making by educated and trained leaders often does not achieve goals, and yet those decisions and behaviors are repeated, then perhaps a new definition of "success" is necessary. One is needed that explains why businesses do what they do, even when their decisions and actions have shown little likelihood of achieving desired results.

The Sad Tale of AM

Addressograph-Multigraph (AM) was a very successful company. An early pioneer in printing equipment, the company grew quickly in the early twentieth century. As the industrial revolution dawned, AM had the right printing equipment and supplies to help businesses with their emerging printing needs. Through acquisitions, international product sourcing, and new product development, AM became the global leader in printing solutions for in-house print shops and a standard-bearer for quality in small, offset printing equipment.

In the 1950s AM grew by opening offices globally. The company hired its managers from top business and law schools, as well as the ranks of leading management consultancies, such as McKinsey and later The Boston Consulting Group. In the 1960s, AM was compared with IBM by analysts and considered likely to have a more illustrious future than the younger and smaller office products company. After all, AM had a global sales force reaching into practically every substantial company, a global manufacturing and distribution organization keeping costs low and inventories well supplied, and a global service organization well trained and capable of keeping customer equipment running around the clock.

Company return on sales, return on assets, and return on capital were all above average, giving AM an above-average stock price to earnings multiple. Product development had been robust, generating an excellent growth rate for over a decade, and the company showed no signs of slowing its market leadership.

It was in the early 1970s that AM missed its first revenue and profit forecast. The stock price declined as investor confidence declined. So the company hired external consultants. No stone went unturned in the effort to put the company back on track. Immediate actions to cut costs and focus on core customers and markets included the following

- Manufacturing was streamlined; some plants were closed, and management consolidated work into others. Some manufacturing was outsourced to new partners in Japan and Europe.
- Distribution was overhauled, slashing inventories and freeing cash.
- Sales was reorganized, and several reps were laid-off.
- Equipment service was reorganized, and enhanced dispatching technology was added, allowing for service technician lay-offs.
- Accounting and procurement personnel at AM's headquarter's were cut, lowering overhead.
- New product development costs were slashed as the company turned to outside vendors for new products in what was perceived as a slower-growth environment.

- Marketing costs were almost eliminated as the company relied on its brand name and market share.
- Forecasts were lowered, given new expectations about underlying industry demand.
- Customers were classified into groups, and sales resources were targeted at larger customers.

As a result, within a year AM was back on track to making forecasts. The company had weathered a storm, management had taken significant action, and leadership was hopeful to regain the previous P/E (price/earnings) multiple. In discussions with investment analysts and the press, AM brimmed with confidence that management had righted the ship. Future results would soon resemble those of the past.

At the same time, a leading consulting firm prepared a strategic report for AM management that said that its market was under attack by Xerox. The consultants predicted that printing equipment sales would decline as users switched to copiers. Although there were a range of cost and quality issues complicating the economics of which equipment was optimal, there was no doubt that copiers were far easier to operate and Xerox was making rapid inroads into the AM customer base.

AM quickly developed a series of competitive maneuvers. New pricing schemes lowered initial equipment cost, similar to the per-page pricing Xerox initiated. AM harped on its ability to print in color and published technical documents demonstrating lithography's superior quality. And AM produced charts showing traditional printing's cost advantages.

But by the 1980s it was clear to management that the ease of use of the copier made it preferable for most customers. So AM reacted by sourcing copiers from IBM to resell under the AM brand. These IBM machines were comparable to current Xerox machines, and AM took them to customers with aggressive marketing and pricing programs intended to meet the competition head-on. AM used its best managers and hired premier consultants to advise them on strategies and plans.

Unfortunately, AM's copiers never took off—sales achieved less than 10 percent of forecast. With sales weakening, their traditional products and their failure to succeed with copiers, AM horribly missed revenue and profit forecasts and management announced they would make a "strategic" decision to file for bankruptcy. Given protection from creditors, leadership was convinced AM could regain competitive strength.

After a year, the company reemerged from bankruptcy. The company was smaller and had lower costs. AM announced it was again focusing on its core corporate printing market. Additionally, AM intended to utilize cash flow from traditional markets to aggressively develop new opportunities.

But, AM did not return to meeting forecasts. Inconsistently, AM met and at times missed both its revenue and profit results. Leadership repeatedly pointed out that its traditional market was being overtaken by copiers, and thus investors should not expect substantial growth. Profit misses were brushed off as pricing problems, which AM hoped would resolve themselves when competitors disappeared and the company's consolidated position improved pricing power. New markets proved fleeting in their technology solutions, never allowing AM time to establish a firm position or profitably grow market share.

By the late 1980s, AM again filed for bankruptcy. The executive ranks were completely overhauled. A new Chairman and CEO were installed, as were new in-house legal counsel and, CFO. New division presidents were hired, and new management teams populated the divisions. New personnel were again recruited from top business schools, management consultancies, and the ranks of successful Fortune 50 companies. Promises of substantial bonuses were tied to turning around the company, linking compensation to performance. And another round of employment cuts and operational reorganizations across the company were intended to improve performance.

Equity investors were wiped out. Bank loans were reorganized, and a Mike Milken junk bond was issued to provide the cash for implementing a turnaround. Nearly half the equity was placed into an Employee Stock Ownership Plan (ESOP), financed via an investment of all the old employees' pension plans, tying employees' retirement to company performance.

A new Board of Directors was installed, including the famous Harvard Business School marketing guru Arthur Levitt, as well as CEOs from famous and high-growth companies such as Avery Label.

By the early 1990s AM was again a new company. One division president, a West Point graduate, Stanford MBA, and McKinsey alumnus, who regularly arrived for work at 6:00 a.m. and started meetings by 7:00, typified leadership. Managers, many young and banking their careers on company success, worked long hours. Expenses were slashed—gone was free coffee. Travel and sales expenses were kept to a minimum. When employees had lunch meetings, everyone paid for his own.

Employees were part of the planning, with all-employee meetings happening monthly. Quarterly meetings with field sales personnel provided the pulse of customers. Team efforts were pushed, and everyone was encouraged that reaching goals required individual success as well as company success. A new Total Quality Management (TQM) program was implemented by an experienced quality guru to improve product and service quality, as well as quality in all areas of overhead (marketing, accounting, procurement, and so on).

Goals were set for every part of the organization. The company had ambitions to be #1 in not only equipment but also printing supplies. AM also intended to leverage its sales and distribution skills to become a leader in new markets for emerging digital printing technology. A vision was set to leapfrog xerography and be the leader in a range of new products and technologies just coming to market via start-ups with digital printing and reproduction expertise.

But by the late 1990s, AM was gone. The company turnaround never happened. Management filed again for bankruptcy protection in the mid 1990s, and eventually the assets were acquired first by a competitor and later by a private equity firm. Most top managers of the company never again held substantial positions in any large organization. For most of them, this was the painful end of their careers. Most equity investors, including the ESOP (and pension) were wiped out. And bondholders received a fraction of their investments.

AM Is Not Alone

On the surface, Creative Destruction reared its head, and Schumpeter would have predicted AM was doomed. While AM was wiped out, Xerox, Sharp, and other competitors benefited greatly during the AM downfall. Copier growth was high, creating a raft of new jobs in companies bringing to market new innovations. Copiers quickly led to innovations in desktop printing—such as laser printers—and other digital printing solutions created yet more revenue and more jobs. While AM was faltering, the number of printed pages was certainly not declining. In fact, they were growing at a rapid pace! Total printing equipment sales exploded as traditional press and platemaker sales declined.

The AM story is all too familiar. Good, often "great," companies fail. AT&T, Bethlehem Steel, Polaroid, Digital Equipment Corporation (DEC), Compaq, White Hen Pantry, Brach's Candy, PanAm, Eastern Airlines, Montgomery Ward, and KMart are just a short list of companies that have been unable to effectively compete despite incredibly successful histories. And the list of companies that have had enormous setbacks but haven't faltered to the point of bankruptcy or market elimination, includes names such as Xerox, Kodak, Sun Microsystems, Sears, and Tribune Company—who were big winners just a few years ago.

Foster and Kaplan, in their book *Creative Destruction*, provide substantial statistical evidence of the fact that companies "built to last" regularly and systematically underperform in the market. Looking at just over 1,000 of America's largest companies, they discovered that from 1962 to 1998 only 16 percent remained in the top 1,000. Of the Forbes 100 in 1917, America's best resourced and most capably managed organizations, only 39 survived into 1987, and only 18 remained in the top 100. And only 2, yes only 2, earned above average rates of return. And since 1987, one of those has declined horribly.

Of the S&P 500 in 1957 (the peak year for babies in the Baby Boom), only 74 remained in 1994. Only 12 had gained in position on the list. Less than one-third of these companies survived a mere 25 years. Had you been so prescient as to invest in the "winners," your returns would have been less than an index fund. And probably more concerning, almost no one can expect to have his employer survive the length of his working career.

But relying upon Schumpeter's Creative Destruction would indicate that business managers have no say in the future of their organizations. Schumpeter's thesis implies managers are mere automatons doing day to day what they previously had done without thinking about how to adjust to changing requirements. Are these executives and managers simply incompetent? Are they simply arrogant and unwilling to listen to their marketplace? Do they lack diligence and persistence? Do they fail to set goals—or ignore the need for detailed plans? To accept these answers would be illogical, for in almost all cases the leadership held most of the traits described earlier as important for achieving success. And we know that the best minds from the best business schools and advisory firms are plotting strategies and tactics to help these companies succeed.

When market changes are obvious to outsiders, and simple, important actions seem clear, we find it inexplicable that management does not take what we see as necessary actions. But this simplistic outsider's view is naïve and self-serving because we presume none of us would ever find ourselves in such a difficult situation. Almost all managers *will* find themselves in exactly the problematic situation as described at AM once, if not more than once, in their careers. And few will behave much differently than the management at AM.

Something more is afoot—something that allows, possibly even promotes, decision making and behavior which *appears* to be the right thing and yet results in unsatisfactory results. If we can accept that there is a rational explanation for management's misbegotten behavior, then possibly we can determine how to overcome the circumstances that seem to support Schumpeter's view that capitalism depends upon Creative Destruction—causing so much pain to investors, employees, customers, and suppliers.

A New Explanation for What Goes Wrong and How to Fix It

A considerable amount of business education, and the activities undertaken by managers as they advance their careers, is dramatically removed from implementing, or even understanding, innovation. The history of business education largely began as industrial engineering post-WWII and focused on how to operate manufacturing plants more effectively and efficiently. Over the years, finance, marketing, and eventually information technology all came to greater prominence in business education. Yet the focus still remains largely on how to do better what was previously done.

Business education is steeped in optimizing execution as opposed to managing innovation. This focus fit the business world's needs from 1940 into the 1980s well, but times have changed. Markets are now global, and they have become increasingly dynamic via lower trade barriers and enhanced technology for communication and transportation. Market leadership via consolidation and domination is increasingly giving way to increased flexibility and access to resources. What produced good results in 1970 or 1980 does not create the same results today. What's needed is a new approach for managing that produces positive results.

Very few executives make their way to the CEO position or any other senior position by following the route of entrepreneurship or innovation management. By and large, most advance by managing a group as good or better than their predecessors. Consistent performance is praised, and small incremental benefits are valued. Managers advance by better optimizing the performance of their teams.

This leads to *Defend & Extend Management*. D&E places, as the manager's first priority, understanding the existing business and working to defend and extend what has previously been done. By *focusing* on core capabilities, core customers, core services, core assets, core functionality—whatever is considered *core*—and first defending that core while seeking incremental opportunities to extend it, followers of this doctrine believe the future will successfully take care of itself. Avoiding mistakes is absolutely critical. Those who don't screw up are more likely to succeed than those who take chances.

One result of Defend & Extend Management is that practitioners are always late to new innovations. They are late to market challenges. Innovations are threats to *core*, and it is most important to defend against these potential attacks. Further, it is costly to adopt and implement innovation—much more costly than extending what is already considered core by adding new, but similar products, similar new services, new functionality to existing products, or by entering an adjacent and similar market segment or taking the business without change into a new geography. These actions are simple and straightforward and relatively low-cost. If they don't produce desired results, not much is lost, and it is reasonably easy to retrench.

But businesses that adopt Defend & Extend Management doctrine early in their life cycles quickly fizzle. Early breakthroughs do not develop into robust solutions with significant markets when management stays intent on optimizing existing technology or current business model. That is why pioneers often fail. They attempt to Defend & Extend into a large business what worked in very early stage implementations. And competitors find it easy to out-innovate the early innovator.

Businesses that adopt the Defend & Extend Management doctrine later in their lifecycles find themselves incapable of addressing market challenges, whether they result from technology or business process innovations. For these companies, Defend & Extend is like a bomb fuse. Protective behavior slowly burns toward detonation from a competitive failure they cannot overcome.

AM fell into the trap of Defend & Extend Management. While it recognized a market challenge was developing in the form of xerography, the company primarily acted to

- defend its existing market position in traditional products,
- defend its business hierarchy and structure,
- defend its manufacturing and distribution assets,
- defend its sales organization and brand,
- defend its service organization,
- defend its existing large customers from intrusion,
- extend its position into additional geographic regions,
- extend its existing position with new products for the traditional market, and
- extend its existing business model into xerographic equipment.

AM failed as a result. It never really adapted to changing market dynamics, and competitors used innovation to creatively destroy the company.

AM largely followed best management practices while it found itself waging war with Xerox, Sharp, and a slew of upcoming competitors in both analog and digital printing equipment. But those practices were not oriented toward adopting and implementing innovation. They were designed to protect historical assets. And those assets were rapidly dwindling in value as a result of new technology and innovative changes in business processes they provided customers.

Understanding Defend & Extend Management gives us the first insight to "success." For most people and organizations, success is *not* about achieving goals. Success is defending and extending each day, each week, and each month what was done in the past. Operationally, success is not about the result, but rather about the doing. And successfully doing is all about defending what exists and seeking out extensions to prolong what was previously done.

Everyone has heard of a story where a business manager pioneers a breakthrough for his company and is still let go. Despite producing results far beyond expectation, his activity took the business away from what it had previously done. Although this manager exceeded goals, he did not Defend & Extend the business. And the company reacted not with gratitude and advancement, but with admonishment and concern for breaking cultural norms and structural procedures. Performance was not evaluated upon what he accomplished, but rather how he did it. He did not Defend & Extend, and thus he found himself without a role.

Likewise, everyone is familiar with the manager whose results never greatly exceed expectations. Despite consistent mediocrity, the manager enjoys a stellar career. His ability to Defend & Extend the organization, while supporting its behavioral norms and structural practices, allows him to be perceived as an important contributor. Resulting company performance is not even factored in.

Quite frequently, possibly more often than not, *success is not about the results*. CEOs who do not achieve desired results remain in their jobs, as do their Boards of Directors. The executive team makes little contribution toward improving company return on capital, revenue growth, or cash flow enhancement, yet it remains almost completely intact. There is little punishment for not achieving the defined success target, as various explanations are offered for how the expected results were simply not achievable.

People in senior positions are usually considered successful merely by having the position, not because they can demonstrate superior results achievement. And some companies are considered successful just because they once were—and have not yet failed. The CEO at General Motors commands considerable respect, and so does his executive team, despite the fact that sales, market share, profits, and return on capital have declined precipitously over nearly two decades. This is because what we think of as defining success, the achievement of results, is not the success actually being sought. Instead, most "successful" behavior is that which Defends & Extends the past for one more day—without failure...yet.

Also not well understood are the assumptions about what creates business success. Americans love a Horatio Alger story about hard work and dedication that leads to success, even though Mr. Alger is a fictitious character. As we explore the road to achieving results, it is important we watch for myths that pervade our assumptions.

The flip side of Foster and Kaplan's statistics are those companies that have defied the statistics and been successful long-term. What distinguishes them? Why were they able to avoid or escape Defend & Extend Management? How did they overcome Creative Destruction and survive—even *thrive*? What helped the winners to earn long-term high rates of return? What makes them exceptional?

These better performing companies implement The Phoenix Principle. They utilize Disruptions and White Space to unlock themselves from repetitive Defend & Extend behavior and seek out new Success Formulas that create evergreen performance.

Schumpeter observed patterns of innovation that lead to failure. But Schumpeter does not condemn us to repeat these behaviors with predictable results. It is within our power to understand why we Lock-in to behaviors that create failure or choose to embrace alternative decisions and behaviors which will allow much better future managerial performance.

I

The Myth of Perpetuity and Lifecycle Realities

Does anyone really believe his or her business will last indefinitely? If not, why do we act like it will? What is the reality of business lifecycles, and how do lifecycle myths help us fulfill Schumpeter's predictions?

The "S" Curve Theory of Business Lifecycle

Anyone who has ever read about business growth has read about "S" curves. "S" curves are very popular, in part, because they do a great job of describing many biological systems. Business theories that reflect what we see around us in everyday life are easy to accept and need only have a few good analogies to be wholeheartedly believed. However, businesses are not biological systems, and they are not required to behave like them.

Most of the pioneering work on "S" curves was done by biologists who were describing the behavior of viruses. Even Jonas Salk, inventor of the Salk vaccine for polio, wrote extensively on "S" curves as a descriptor for how viruses compete and mutate to propagate and succeed. This laid the groundwork for business academics and professionals to use "S" curves as tools for describing business behavior. After all, businesses compete and desire to propagate, which is similar to viruses, so shouldn't the analogy hold true?

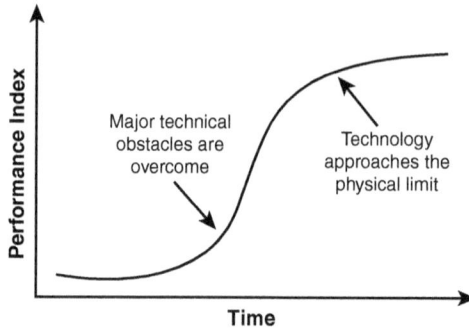

Figure 1.1 Traditional "S" curve

According to the "S" curve theory, businesses start with a very slow growth rate, taking substantial time to demonstrate business efficacy. Early on, growth is challenged by the need to find a customer or two willing to consider the new business. Eventually, growth explodes as customers find the solution more valuable than other solutions. In a relatively short time, revenue begins to exceed expectations. However, this rapid growth does not last forever because new competitors enter, making what once was valuable less so.

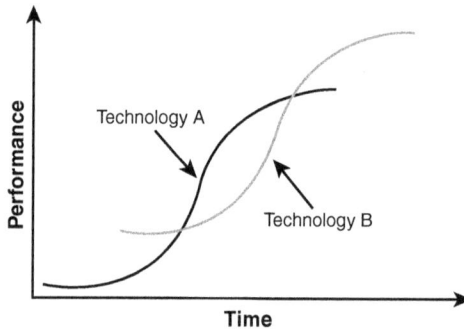

Figure 1.2 Jumping the curve

So what should a business do once the "S" curve starts to become level? Introduce something new, of course! A new product or a new version of an existing product creates a new curve. This new curve, built on the first-generation solution, means revenue doesn't start at zero. Instead it continues to grow.

According to the "S" curve theory, as shown in Figure 1.2, no business need ever decline. By maintaining a constant stream of replacement products, businesses can generate continuous growth. Multiple curves can blend into a nice northeasterly line of increasing revenue. A business could live into perpetuity this way!

Over the last 30 years, there have been many articles and books that offer management guidelines for utilizing "S" curves. They present a number of multiple theories and often include case studies that describe how the researchers applied the "S" curve concept. Each theorist claims that using multiple curves allows for "jumping the curve," which means to jump out of curve A and into curve B before the business starts to observe a revenue decline.

The Myth of Perpetuity

The "S" curve concept for business growth has been around so long that it is now accepted as dogma. It's not whether a business *can* jump the curve, but *how* it is going to happen. The fact that there are few examples of actually building a business this way, especially in the last 20 years, is conveniently ignored. After all, the concept itself has been demonstrated in the physical, biological world. And it does seem to make sense. This logic allows leaders to take the "S" curve concept to its limit and expect their businesses to go on forever.

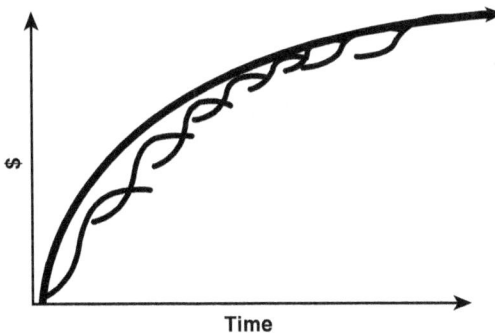

Figure 1.3 The Myth of Perpetuity

According to the "S" curve lifecycle theory, in its early days, a business should introduce new variations, products, and technologies quickly, resulting in more curves per time period with faster growth. These build upon each other to maintain a high growth rate. Later, the number of variations decline as there is less need for and less capability to produce meaningful enhancements. It is accepted that the technology will start reaching its limits, customers will achieve high levels of satisfaction with fewer products, and the number of competitors will decline. This leads to fewer curves with less growth in each. Eventually a market "shake out" occurs as competition turns from new products to cost management. Scale advantages should lead to fewer, larger competitors that operate at lower cost and offer a lower price yet maintain an acceptable margin.

As the lifecycle curve flattens, however, results do not worsen. According to the theory, fewer competitors, and each of those being larger, grants much more market stability. Competitors learn to protect their positions, and there is less competitive intrusion as competitors protect their market shares and rates of return. It takes much greater investment for a new competitor to enter the marketplace, and this higher investment rate makes it practically impossible for newcomers to achieve an acceptable return. Existing large competitors have so much volume that their costs are far lower than anything achievable by a new entrant.

The "S" curve lifecycle theory then states that as growth slows, investment rates also slow. So return on assets and equity remains acceptable. The market is at this point considered "mature." Employees and executives begin focusing on market share maintenance and cost control. And the business can begin paying out increasing dividends to shareholders or repurchase shares to drive up investor value. Late in the cycle, the big payoff happens. New products are far less necessary, given that the technology is more mature and market shares are more stable and defended by high-volume large investments. It's time to pay back investors for riding the curve. And there is no discernable end to how long this should continue. Thus, very mature companies should be great places to work and to invest in because they have become predictable and produce lots of cash.

There has been a great deal of work done by academics and consultants to support this theory. The Boston Consulting Group became famous for its pioneering work on experience curves where volume from market share leaders created long-lived cost advantages. Experience curves led to the growth/share matrix, which defined high market share companies in low growth markets as "cash cows."

Great examples of companies that followed this theory to powerful success in the 1940s to the 1970s were General Motors, AT&T, Polaroid, and DuPont, to name just a few. All these companies achieved market domination. When looking at the pattern of the era, it appeared that the largest companies were those that followed this lifecycle plan.

It's too bad that most of these example companies later got into trouble. They took advantage of the unique post-WWII U.S. economy to grow rapidly in an industrial era with huge demand. But once markets shifted to greater competitiveness, more differentiation, and higher information content, these companies found themselves unable to use "S" curves to find perpetual success.

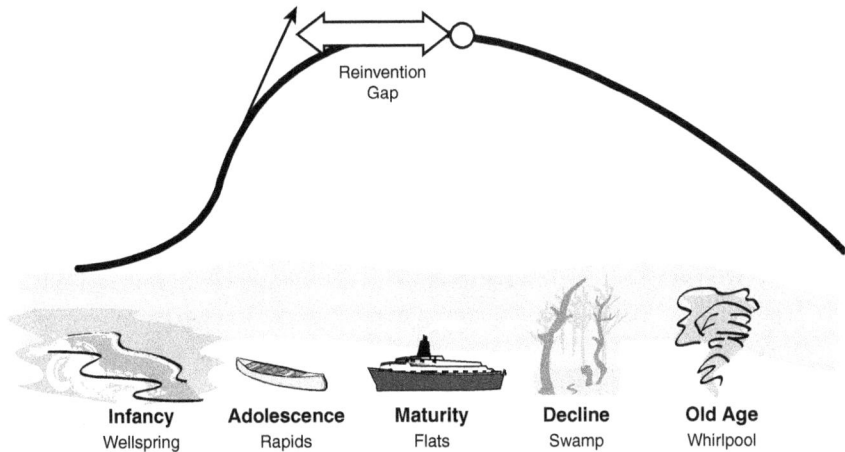

Reinvention
Gap

| Infancy | Adolescence | Maturity | Decline | Old Age |
| Wellspring | Rapids | Flats | Swamp | Whirlpool |

Figure 1.4   Business lifecycle reality

In reality, few businesses "jump the curve." The vast majority of businesses follow the pattern in Figure 1.4. On the lifecycle river, after initial growth, they simply decline and fail. Their time spent in maturity is surprisingly short—and getting shorter in today's competitive environment. Even for the largest companies, much more time is spent in decline and failure than in any other part of the lifecycle.

The Wellspring—Find Something that Floats

Businesses are started in the Wellspring of ideas. For entrepreneurs, the goal is to find initial customers and figure out how to make a profit. Though much has been written on the Wellspring, there is no predictability as to how long a business will spend here, nor whether it will ever emerge into the next phase. Venture capitalists often say that only one in ten businesses ever really break out, and they invest broadly to distribute risk and create more predictable returns.

Wellspring behavior is largely exploratory. The focus is finding a customer. In the Wellspring, discussions are not about developing a marketplace or competing for share. They are about finding one customer who will buy the product and then finding a second. It's about proving the product, service, or business idea is viable and then figuring out how to make a profit at the price initial customers will pay.

The Rapids—Paddle Fast and Stay Afloat

Companies that emerge from the Wellspring enter the Rapids of high growth. The business has found a way to add value to customers, and there are a lot of customers looking for that value. The high growth rate covers a multitude of sins, as revenue expansion either produces great positive cash flow or there are investors more than ready to throw money at the business. The business uses this cash to further define and refine its products and services to continue meeting customer needs.

Most businesses thrive in the Rapids. New products are generated quickly and expedited to market. New services are launched. To keep the growth rate high, lots of customer analysis is undertaken to determine the most critical needs. Simultaneously, the technology and offerings are focused on the customer value proposition. The organization keeps looking for ways to ride the market growth and extend their position. Mostly, amidst the chaos of white water in a fast growing market, it's about staying alive by growing faster than everyone else.

The business press and gurus love to talk about businesses in the Rapids. Ford in the 1920s, Woolworth's in the 1930s, General Motors in the 1940s, Coca Cola in the 1950s and '60s, Polaroid in the 1960s and '70s, KMart in the 1970s, Apple Computer in the early 1980s, Cisco Systems and Dell in the 1990s, and Google today represent companies loved while in the Rapids. AM was in the Rapids during the 1940s through 1960s as businesses exploited the small offset lithographic printing presses and low-cost printing supplies made and sold by AM. In the Rapids, life is good. Even when things go wrong, such as bad product launches or lousy acquisitions, growth allows the business to prosper.

The Flats—Don't Run Aground

Eventually the Rapids slow, and usually much earlier than management predicts. The market growth rate is *perceived* to slow—frequently significantly. Maturing is a wonderfully pleasant euphemism for what is actually an unpleasant growth slowdown.

In the Flats, it's common for businesses to hire new managers who are more "experienced" and considered more "professional" to replace early management from the Wellspring. The mindset of business leaders changes dramatically, as the focus shifts from high growth to greater predictability and the focus on revenue shifts to costs. P&L management receives a lot more attention as new leaders begin jettisoning activities that are deemed unable to generate sufficient profitability.

By saying that *market* growth has slowed, business leadership is able to deflect the most critical problem in the business—its own slower revenue growth. Because investors and employees are conditioned to view maturation as acceptable, and even desirable, any overwhelming worry about future business viability is swept away. Believing in the Myth of Perpetuity, it is accepted that in maturity costs will decline and the business will turn toward producing more security for investors and employees. All that's needed is a different perspective on the part of management—less focus on revenue and more on profits.

Sheer size is seen as the greatest protection for the business. By being large, leaders believe the business can protect itself from competitors. Even though growth is slowing, competition is intensifying, and results are not as good as before, an enormous amount of faith is placed on size as protection, which is exactly what management is led to believe by the "S" curve lifecycle theory. This is despite the fact that a brief look at history shows many failed businesses were once extremely large. Size, at one time, did offer various protections, but in today's Internet-enabled world, size can be as much a negative as a positive.

Believing maturity is good, or even acceptable, is a deadly assumption that sets the stage for failure. By assuming that lower growth can be compensated for with better cost management, the entire business is thrown into jeopardy. As leadership turns to cutting costs, the word "focus" takes on much greater importance. The business starts spending much more time on larger customers and dropping smaller ones as it reduces headcount. It is deemed acceptable to lop off entire product lines—sometimes in profitable niches—if they don't meet criteria for size and sales to large customers. To generate a more predictable and consistent profit stream, usually at a lower return on sales, serving existing customers becomes more important than finding new ones. And leveraging existing products becomes more important than new launches. Both of the former activities are much cheaper than the latter, and it is considered better to defend what the company has always done than seek out new opportunities.

For example, in the 1800s there was a thriving market for whale oil to fuel lamps. Returns were high for whalers and their crews. Then crude oil distillation created a competitive product called kerosene. Kerosene was much easier to make and considerably cheaper. The demand for lighting fuel grew exponentially. But not a single whaling company stayed in business, as they determined that the *market* for whale oil rapidly matured and declined. These companies all could have seen themselves as participating in the market for fuel, but instead they accepted the maturation of *their defined* market for whale oil.

Recalling AM, the market for printed pages exploded in the 1970s and continued to grow at double digit rates through the rest of the century— there was no maturing of demand for printing. By stating that the *market for lithography* had slowed and then undertaking a series of cost cutting actions to better manage the P&L, AM management drilled a series of holes in their boat. They were slow to evaluate new printing solutions, such as xerography, and even slower to make changes to market these solutions. Their first reaction was to manage for maturity, the Myth of Perpetuity, and accept lower revenue growth while reducing costs.

When a business enters the Flats, it begins creating a "Reinvention Gap." This is the gap between what the marketplace wants and what the business sells. The market continues to grow, sometimes even faster, but the business does not participate. Rather than quickly admit there is a new technology, a new product/service, or some type of solution that is replacing them in the marketplace, management starts looking for ways to capitalize on history. They stop looking to the future and begin trying to recapture the past. The longer management tries to Defend & Extend its old business, the larger the Reinvention Gap becomes. The larger the gap, the less likely a business will ever cross back over it.

For many business leaders and investors, the Flats are considered good—but this is a myth based on believing in the old lifecycle theory.

In believing the Myth of Perpetuity, leadership views its existing sales force, distribution, brand image, service expertise, manufacturing volumes, tightly knitted supply chain, or other capability as "entry barriers" which protect them from new competitors. Business decisions become oriented toward protecting these "entry barriers."

Entry barriers were an enormously valuable concept when introduced by Harvard's Michael Porter in his groundbreaking 1980 book *Competitive Strategy*. At the time, looking back at the industrial economy, large companies had often successfully created and defended entry barriers. But in the information economy, entry barriers are proving far more difficult to not only erect, but to defend. Using widely available and very cheap computing resources, along with the Internet, entry barriers are increasingly easy to overcome.

OVERCOMING ENTRY BARRIERS

- Today, globally connected financial institutions provide access to large financial resources cheaply and extremely quickly.

- Access to financial resources means that "scale" manufacturing plants can be built in months, often in countries with lower cost labor or fewer regulatory requirements.

- Learning curve effects are captured in knowledge databases, which then become available to everyone almost instantly via the Internet. Competitors achieve learning benefits even at small volumes.

- Large sales and distribution organizations are circumvented by Web sites with volume pricing.

- Service organization knowledge is replaced by online service manuals and training available to small distributors and clients.

The Reinvention Gap is completely ignored by the business as it tries to improve its relative position with *existing* customers against *historical* competitors. Frequently, the most threatening *new* competitor is not even addressed. As the business increasingly talks only with historical, large customers, it loses any vision about where the market is still growing.

In the 1980s IBM pioneered the personal computer through a small development team in Florida. The PC became a wildly popular product, portrayed on *Time's* cover as the "Man of the Year" in 1982. Yet when IBM interviewed its primary computer customers, data center managers, IBM did not perceive a high demand for PCs. Data center managers were clamoring for better and cheaper hardware and software used on their IBM proprietary mainframe and mid-range computer systems. Many of these customers chastised IBM for bringing PCs to market because PCs disrupted Information Systems Directors' plans. Several of these customers were actively anti-PC. As a result, internally the PC was not seen as a threat to IBM's large and profitable computer business, and IBM downplayed the product. Before the end of the decade, IBM was one of the earliest companies to exit the PC business.

At AM, Xerox's early entry was ignored because AM was busy selling lithographic products to print shop managers in client basements. Copiers were being sold to office managers who controlled typewriters used on the office floor. AM did not even track Xerox sales because Xerox was not seen as a competitor in the print shop where AM dominated.

Because management is making forecasts using financial models from the Rapids, it does not recognize that most of its assumptions are wrong. Rather than having an easy time generating margins at lower growth, the business finds it is chronically struggling to maintain customers, price, and competitive costs. Lower volumes start to drive costs per unit up rather than down (despite focusing on procurement and supply chain expertise), and greater competition intensity among remaining rivals— as well as the new competitors—makes price maintenance impossible as per unit revenues decline. Missing forecasts becomes too common.

Given all the dangers of the Flats and all the problems that develop in this phase, it is startling that business leaders seek to operate here. According to The Conference Board, hitting a revenue stall is deadly. For publicly traded companies, after hitting the Flats, seven out of ten companies will lose more than half their market capitalization. Only 7 percent will ever again consistently grow at a mere 2 percent per year, and nearly 40 percent will have a future with virtually no growth. Even worse, 55 percent will have a *negative* revenue growth rate—a persistent decline!

Sustainable Growth Plunges

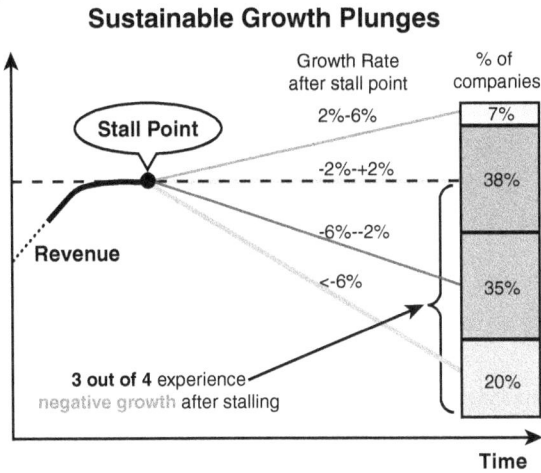

Figure 1.5 Business stalls are deadly

Market Capitalization Destroyed

Change in Shareholder Wealth

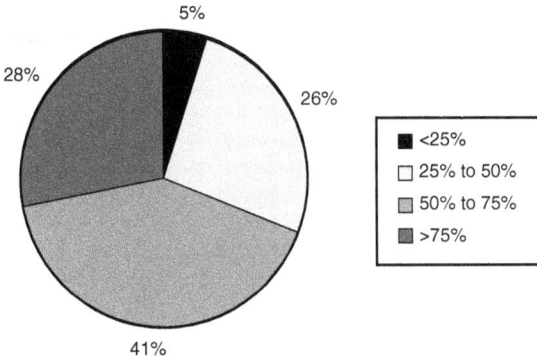

7 of 10 lost more than half their value after stalling!

Figure 1.6 Destroying economics value

According to Foster & Kaplan in their book *Creative Destruction*, even for large companies the odds of maintaining a business are not good.

- Of the S&P 500 in 1957 (a big year for baby-boomer births), by 1998 only 74 still existed (15%).
  - Of these, only 12 gained in position (2.5%)
- Since 1962, of the 1,000 companies that were largest by size in the U.S., only 160 (16%) managed to stay in this group.
- Less than one-third of companies in the S&P 500 survive 25 years

The Flats is the riskiest position on the business lifecycle.

The Swamp—Trying to Get Unstuck (While Fighting Alligators and Mosquitoes)

When interviewing business leaders, the vast majority will describe their businesses as being in the Flats. They know they are not in the Rapids, and they don't want to think they are in the Swamp. But, truthfully, most are well into the Swamp.

The Swamp is characterized by limited growth. No growth means no current to the water. Any forward movement has to come from paddling. Unfortunately, the Swamp is full of competitors that behave like alligators, constantly trying to eat you and your boat. At the same time, swarms of new competitors are buzzing around like mosquitoes looking to suck all the blood out of the business.

Modern business has a basket of tools to use for hiding low growth. One of the easiest for a public company is simply to start buying back shares. Management uses cash in the bank or money from issuing bonds (often low grade/junk) or from selling a division or other assets to buy back shares. Management starts focusing on earnings per share (EPS). EPS goes up not because earnings rise, but because the number of shares goes down, and position in the Swamp is hidden.

Another good Swamp-hiding management technique involves acquisitions. Company A agrees to buy some or part of Company B. Prior to acquisition, the revenue of A is $5 million and the revenue of B is $4 million. A year later, Company A announces it has revenue of $7.5 million and declares a 50% revenue increase!

This technique is extremely beneficial for leaders that believe in the Myth of the Perpetuity because it reinforces the assumption that troubled businesses will benefit from competitor consolidation to drive down costs. It's also a nice way to hide declining growth.

There are a myriad of opportunities to use Generally Accepted Accounting Principles (often times referred to as GAAP Accounting) to modify published financial results. In any given year, a company can simply shift the handling of how taxes are booked, changing expenses this year, last, or next. Or by altering accounting for pensions, an extremely complex issue that is handled deep in the footnotes and is not even a line item on the P&L, earnings are adjusted. By simply underfunding the pension plan or even raiding it for resources, a business can look better purely at the expense of the company pension fund.

Other financial machinations used in the Swamp include reclassifying expenses into capital items to improve short-term profitability or changing the focus of management reports to analysts from net profit to a higher margin line in the P&L and then shifting cost problems down into "non-recurring expenses." These are supposedly one-time events but often seem to never let the business return to old net profitability levels. When discussing weakness in current results, management frequently turns to discussing "pro forma" (or future prediction) numbers where they discuss "synergies" intended to improve revenue and lower costs. This is despite the fact that there is no way to track such synergies by outsiders, and most academic literature says these synergies are rarely found.

Of course, all these manipulations must be spelled out in the footnotes of the financial statements. But footnotes are not where emphasis is placed when evaluating management. Analysts and investors, customers, vendors, and employees focus on the P&L itself. Even with pages of footnotes, including supporting schedules, financial machinations get little attention. For people who believe in the Myth of Perpetuity, such actions are often viewed as good management decisions being implemented by smart executives who are utilizing all available tools to increase the apparent strength of the company!

One favorite tool of businesses deep in the Swamp is bankruptcy. Leaders will declare that there is really nothing wrong with the business, but due to some sort of unexpected circumstances (of course they were unexpected—if they were expected, we are to presume management would have dealt with them!), the company is unable to meet its obligations. As a result, the business is in a "technical" default.

For example, after the year 2000, several of America's largest airlines, including United, declared default due to union contracts and particular clauses in their financing instruments. Leaders did not describe their problems as a bad business model, unlikely to ever make money and unable to deal with almost any competitive shock, nor did management admit it was unable to price its product appropriately to cover its costs or that it had made assumptions when signing labor contracts which proved overly optimistic, running the business utilizing those assumptions until bankruptcy loomed. The problem creating bankruptcy was described as a "technical problem" with union contracts and financial agreements that had to be resolved by the unions and the banks.

And of course bankruptcy was a "strategic" move taken to protect the airline. By characterizing as strategic, this action was positioned as sensible for smart executives. How declaring financial failure is "strategic" is less than clear.

Amazingly, demand for air travel has continued growing year-over-year since deregulation, so it was not insufficient demand that plunged United and its counterparts into bankruptcy court. And somehow Southwest managed to avoid this problem altogether. Both facts imply that the problem causing bankruptcy is not an industry problem, but instead something directly related to the particular companies stuck in the Swamp.

Once bankruptcy is undertaken, management does not portray the action as a failure. The fact that debt holders are forced to take a loss, that suppliers are never repaid in full, or that employees see their pay or benefits reduced is just part of the "strategic" overhaul that management wanted to do for a long time but could not implement due to legal restrictions. Management will often blame investment bankers for loading the company with too much debt or too high an interest rate. Or state that the employees, through their union, simply are unrealistic in their demands for the business. Or claim that regulators made it impossible for the business to succeed.

In reality, bankruptcy is never a tool used by healthy, growing companies. Only companies that are in the Swamp and struggling to understand their growth problems find themselves in bankruptcy court.

TRUE STORIES: YOU KNOW YOU'RE
IN THE SWAMP WHEN...

- The CEO sends out an e-mail to all employees chastising them for using color printers in the office, due to the cost, and instructs them to switch all printing to black and white.

- The Division President e-mails the company that the business is having a tough quarter, so all use of overnight shipping is suspended.
- Employees receive a memo from the HR vice president that all business auto rentals are being downsized by one vehicle type.
- The business owner takes time at the all-employee meeting to tell everyone that he is appalled by the wastefulness of people, throwing away paper clips along with used paper. He then demonstrates the proper way to dispose of paper by removing the clip.
- The CEO describes a recent quarterly loss to employees as caused by a downturn in customer business, having nothing to do with company operations.
- Top management asks all management personnel to participate in two weekend days of inventory auditing without pay to complete the task at lower cost.
- A vice president lauds employees for coming into the office over the weekend and painting their offices themselves—the first time these offices had been painted in nearly 20 years, and he recommends all leaders have their employees do the same.
- Company travel is suspended to meet quarterly profit projections.
- The company installs a centralized headquarters system to control the heating and cooling of all facilities.
- The Vice President of Marketing tells analysts that a competitor growing at more than double his rate is unimportant because that company is so much smaller.

No business leader ever says, "Our company has misjudged the direction of the marketplace. We have missed what our customers want. We are in deep trouble, and we're getting so far behind new competitors that we will probably never compete effectively in our markets again." Management never admits they are in the Swamp. But they are.

The Whirlpool–Paddle Like Crazy

Eventually, competition simply becomes too intense. New solutions, born out of Wellsprings or competitive Rapids, overwhelm the company's attempts to stave off disaster. The company's product or service is so costly or competitively ineffective that it becomes impossible to maintain a profit. And the business spins into the Whirlpool from which it never returns.

Some companies simply disappear in a bankruptcy court, such as Polaroid, with all remaining assets sold in liquidation. But this is the rare dramatic case. Instead, businesses are more likely to begin a long but consistent route of selling off assets, such as Eastern Airlines, Montgomery Ward, or Wang. A slow liquidation occurs where each sale brings in a little more cash to keep the company alive a little longer until eventually there is simply nothing left, and the business disappears. Its brands, products, customers, technology, product designs, intellectual capital, and equipment find their way into a myriad of other companies through a series of small sales.

Some businesses are acquired. Another competitor, itself usually stuck in the Swamp, acquires the deeply troubled business in an effort to improve its own lot—such as when Compaq, struggling to compete in the PC market, acquired Digital Equipment. Often, within just a few months, the acquired company simply disappears.

A similar fate befalls some companies acquired by private equity or leveraged buyout firms. Here a private entity takes over the failing business, strips it of all possible costs, and sucks whatever cash it can out of the business to invest elsewhere. This is the direction KMart and Sears have taken the last few years under the control of Chairman and CEO Eddie Lampert.

We Keep Repeating the Same Cycle

The lifecycle river is very familiar to all businesspeople, largely because everyone can think of *so many* examples. Yet management keeps repeating it as if there is no other option to the cycle of breakout, then grow, then *decline and fail*. While management gurus and academics talk about "jumping the curve" from one "S" to another, it simply doesn't happen very often.

While businesses enjoy being in the Rapids, very few return to the Rapids after hitting the Flats. And practically none return to the Rapids from the Swamp. (When these do occur, such as the turnarounds at IBM and Apple Computer, they get an enormous amount of attention.) As a result, we become sanguine about Schumpeter's forecasts of business failure—as if it is simply destined to happen.

Most business leaders have the will to turn their companies around—they are globally savvy, hard working, and smart. They have enormous desire to leave a legacy of success, and they are willing to demonstrate their will and their sacrifice by undertaking painful management actions, such as employee lay-offs, reducing benefits and pay, cutting executive ranks and perquisites, slashing expense budgets, and enforcing draconian vendor cuts and under-funding employee pension plans. They take these actions because they truly believe it is the right thing to do, often telling everyone the businesses are accepting the pain for the long-term good of the enterprise.

Many of these leaders will turn to outsiders for help. They seek experts at law firms, accounting firms, investment banking, and management consultancies in downsizing, outsourcing, and strategy. Yet, the vast bulk never find the Rapids again. When they find themselves in the Flats, they remember the theories surrounding lifecycle management developed 50 years ago and take actions that yield more than a hundred Polaroids for every Apple.

It's time to understand why it is so hard for businesses to undertake a different set of recommendations. It's time to look at how we develop *Success Formulas*.

2

The Value and Power of Success Formulas

How do businesses produce really good results?
Why do some businesses achieve above-average returns
and grow so quickly?

Companies Rise in the Rapids on the Strength of Their Success Formulas

We all have Success Formulas. Success Formulas help us navigate through each day with confidence in our behaviors and decisions. They help us operate quickly and efficiently, replicating behaviors, which helps us reach our goals. Each of us have individual Success Formulas, work teams have Success Formulas, functional groups have Success Formulas, business units and companies have Success Formulas, entire industries have Success Formulas, and even economies are built on Success Formulas.

So what is a Success Formula? Success Formulas are much more than simple "business models." They are the combination of

- Our Identity—who we are
- Our Strategies—what we do
- Our Tactics—how we do it

A *Success Formula* is a self-reinforcing cycle of assumptions and behaviors which early on creates desired results. Creators of business models place most of their attention on Tactics, with occasional discussion of Strategies. They rarely address Identity, which is the most assumption-laden part of the Success Formula and plays a critical role in Strategies and Tactics. A linked Identity, Strategy, and Tactical set which helps to produce desired positive outcomes developed early in the life cycle becomes self-reinforcing as it is implemented, continuing to produce more desirable results.

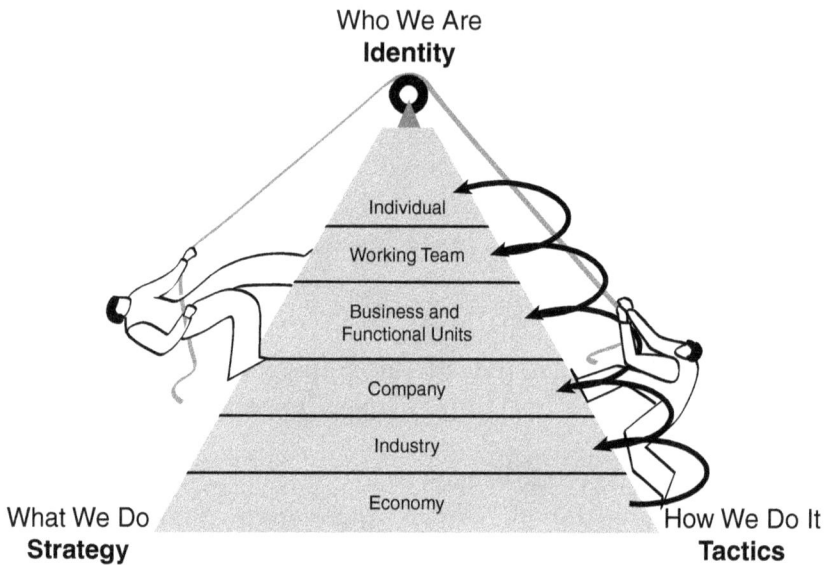

Figure 2.1 Success Formula Pyramid

"Who are we?" whether spoken or not, is one of the first things a business asks itself. Long before a business has figured out how it will attract customers or make money, founders apply their personal experiences to determining *who* the business will be. Identity is full of assumptions of what is considered good—or not good—and is built up over a lifetime. Within Identity are the strongest beliefs about what works and what does not.

There are virtually no books on strategic planning or operational execution that discuss Identity. Identity is assumed, but Identity actually must be developed. It does not originate out of thin air. It is created, often carefully crafted, by the leaders of the organization to reflect long-held assumptions about everything from what industries and markets to include themselves in, to what activities should be performed, to who should be in the business and how these individuals should behave.

As previously mentioned, businesses are nothing more than legal abstractions. It is Identity that sets the initial boundary conditions for the business. And Identity circumscribes what Strategies are developed and what Tactics are executed.

Take for example Sun Microsystems. Sun was founded in the 1970s by engineers taking advantage of distributed computing architectures using a new operating system called UNIX. Sun pioneered the use of UNIX when innovating applications operating in what it called "network architecture." This architecture was usually cheaper and more powerful than competitive solutions at the time using mainframes and mini-computers sold by IBM, Digital Equipment, and Wang. Sun solutions were especially popular for engineering tasks, graphics, and other computationally intensive work. Eventually, Sun machines running UNIX challenged supercomputers from companies such as Cray by performing many functions at far lower cost.

As businesses built internal networks, then external wide-area networks and eventually adopted the Internet, network computing became far more prevalent. Sun was a primary beneficiary of this change away from mainframe data centers toward distributed computing. In the mid-1990s Sun invented a new software language (Java), which became extremely valuable to developers of Internet software solutions. This new language enabled many new features, making the Internet far more valuable as a business tool, and earned Sun a very positive reputation among software developers and Internet mavens.

One of Sun's early employees was Scott McNealy, who rather quickly became CEO and Chairman. Across his colorful career, when asked what business Sun was in, Mr. McNealy would talk about selling hardware. And, indeed, Sun started by selling boxes full of computer hardware. Early in its lifecycle Sun had even been a leader in developing powerful microprocessors called Reduced Instruction Set Computing (RISC) chips, available only in its computers. While Sun's great advantage had always been its leadership in distributed computing, McNealy and his leadership team always focused on selling boxes.

Sun loaded their computers, largely using hardware developed outside Sun, with considerable software which Sun developed. This included operating systems, eventually many software applications, and later network software. Sun had an entire division devoted to software, named SunSoft, which employed hundreds of engineers. But few customers ever bought Sun software independently. Well over 95 percent of SunSoft's revenues were to Sun Microcomputer Company, the hardware division of Sun. To utilize its software, practically all customers had to buy a Sun workstation or server.

After developing Java, the company was conflicted about how to make money on the product. Java did not require a Sun box to be useful. So Sun provided Java to the computer community at practically no cost, supporting rapid Internet growth, in a market where Sun sold lots of servers and workstations. One of the great early Internet product innovations became free largely because it did not fit into Sun's Identity as a seller of computer boxes.

During the early days of Sun's growth and well into the latter 1990s as Sun Internet server revenue exploded, Mr. McNealy loved to say that Sun sold "iron." He utilized automobile analogies comparing Sun's "big iron" with Detroit muscle cars of his youth. As it happens, Mr. McNealy is the son of an automotive executive. Sun's Identity, like Mr. McNealy's, was closely aligned with selling big, fast boxes.

After 2000, Sun hit a very rough patch, and company revenue growth stalled. Company valuation fell precipitously. Interestingly, the great threat to Sun's revenue was Microsoft's enhancements to its operating system (as well as applications Microsoft supported) and the emergence of Linux. Linux is an operating system which supports distributed computing, many network functions and applications, and utilizing hardware from varied manufacturers. As Sun's box sales languished, its software sales did the same because users switching to the other software solutions purchased alternative, usually lower cost, hardware from other vendors.

Sun's Identity, tied to selling hardware, severely limited management's view of its options. Sun's software could have been have been sold independently and made to run on other hardware. But Sun's Identity kept it from thinking of itself as a software or networking company (such as Cisco Systems).

Strategies and Tactics Come from Identity

From Identity, Success Formulas develop a Strategy. Strategy is about *what* the business will do. Strategy connects Identity to the marketplace. Consider Wal-Mart, a company with a strong Identity tied to low prices. Sam Walton started the business in rural Arkansas, and he was able to compete town-to-town by always pricing just a little more aggressively than the existing general merchandiser. This led to a Strategy focused on supply-chain management. The Strategy of being number one in supply-chain expertise allowed Wal-Mart to fulfill its Identity as the low price leader.

After Strategy is set, a Success Formula puts in place its Tactics. Take for example McDonald's. After acquiring a unique hamburger restaurant from the McDonald brothers, Ray Kroc focused his company on selling hamburgers. He saw how limited product offerings supported a simple value proposition, generating high store volume and revenue. Although Kroc had been a milkshake machine salesman, McDonald's Identity, from the beginning, was tied to hamburgers and volume.

To grow quickly, McDonald's pioneered a franchising Strategy. Franchising allowed McDonald's to grow much faster, building volume quickly, than could ever happen via building all its own stores. Making sure the company could execute its franchise Strategy led McDonald's to define its Tactics around consistency as the definition of quality. Making the same food, every time, everywhere allowed McDonald's to replicate extremely fast. And this Success Formula built McDonald's into the premier restaurant operation of the 1900s.

Identity, Strategy, and Tactics become interwoven and tightly linked. They support each other in helping a business succeed—hence, the term "Success Formula." These elements become self-reinforcing as Identity drives Strategy, which is supported by Tactics, which then fulfills the Identity.

Despite claims about the need for Strategy and Tactics in entrepreneurial businesses, Success Formulas are not born in the Wellspring. In the Wellspring, businesses have only an ill-defined Identity. At that point they are searching for customers and searching for a Success Formula as they sell early customers and hope to turn a profit.

It is by profitably delivering value to customers that a business moves into the Rapids. It is in the Rapids where a business defines its Success Formula. Strategies and Tactics are the added pieces that help the business fulfill its Identity, solidify it, and achieve growth plus positive returns. Strategy and Tactics are needed during rapid growth and thus are defined in the Rapids.

Winners Create Success Formulas in the Rapids

In the Rapids, businesses solidify Success Formulas into valuable tools. By specifying Identity, Strategy, and Tactics, businesses can grow rapidly. Leaders need to hire new employees, bring on new vendors, and identify as well as capture new clients. No longer can the founder/CEO close every sale or lead every new product development. Success Formulas must be made explicit for customers to know who they are dealing with. Investors want to know why they should give the company money. Employees and vendors must be able to react rapidly to new opportunities. It is the Success Formula that serves as a guide for growth. Although tweaked and adjusted, Success Formulas are very powerful for any company hoping to achieve breakout performance and remain in the Rapids.

Take, for example, Dell Inc. Founded by college student Michael Dell, the business quickly focused on selling low-cost personal computers using off-the-shelf components assembled cheaply and rapidly for small Texas businesses. Much bigger manufacturers, such as neighboring Compaq, had a firm grip on computer retailers and Value Added Resellers (VARs), so Dell used the telephone and advertising to attract new customers directly. Higher volume lowered cost, so Dell priced lower than rivals Compaq or AST and shipped faster. Dell rabidly pursued its Strategy of direct-to-consumer sales. Bypassing the traditional distribution organization, Dell was able to save money and reinforce its Identity as a low-cost personal computer supplier.

Soon, all Tactics were focused on how to drum up new business with direct-to-buyer advertising and promotions. Dell became #1 in catalogs, far outpacing traditional retailers and resellers of other manufacturers' gear. Dell was an early adopter of Internet selling and advertising and standardized on low-cost components from high-volume supplier companies, forsaking R&D in favor of assembling what others created. Dell exclusively utilized the Microsoft operating system and application software, meeting the vast majority of customer needs. Supply-chain Tactics became critical as the company sold computers as fast as it made them, keeping its inventory investment at nearly zero.

As demand for PCs soared, so did Dell's growth. Its Success Formula guided all parts of the company from sales and marketing to new product development and procurement. Customers, new employees, and vendors all knew what Dell did, and the Success Formula augmented rapid growth as Dell quickly rose to #1 in desktop PC sales and later laptops.

Success Formulas are not new. DuPont, a member of the veritable Dow Jones Industrial Average, was founded on the banks of the Delaware River over 200 years ago as a gunpowder manufacturer for the Revolutionary War. The company used chemists to create several new products over the years, which promoted rapid growth. Prolonged growth and avoiding costly manufacturing accidents created a culture of safety at DuPont. The company's Identity related to making things with chemicals, its Strategy of using R&D to develop new products internally for growth, and its Tactics around safety led to a very consistent culture, which for many years produced very good results.

This Success Formula still dominates DuPont. The company tag line in the 1980s was "Better Things for Living," which was a shortened version of the original "Better Things for Living Through Chemistry." Today, the tag line remains "The Miracles of Science," reinforcing the tight Identity DuPont has with chemistry and its dominant Strategy of spending heavily on R&D to create new products.

DuPont also maintains its focus on safety. Long after the gunpowder mills are gone, and most manufacturing is done by people in clean rooms with white lab coats, everyone at DuPont receives many hours of safety training. Even finance and marketing employees receive training and measure safety records. While DuPont's markets, products, and customers have radically changed over 200 years, the Success Formula still dominates what happens. What once helped DuPont grow and augmented DuPont's rise in the industrial era to the top of American business is still a guiding mechanism for behavior today.

The source of Identity is not always obvious. Earl Tupper was an ambitious young fellow born in 1907 who wanted to be rich before age 30. He tried several ventures but was not successful. In 1937 Tupper went to work for DuPont, where he learned about plastics, and then left in 1938 to form his own company. Tupper's company was only modestly successful, primarily making products for DuPont and acting as a supplier to the war effort. Although he developed and patented several plastic innovations, including the tightly resealable lid, Tupper's products simply did not sell well in retail stores, and the company had limited growth.

In the late 1940s Earl Tupper noticed that he was selling an unusually large amount of product to two individuals. One, Brownie Wise, was a single mother from Florida who had previously been a Stanley Home Products salesperson. Where Tupper's products were languishing in traditional retail, Ms. Wise was able to sell considerable product directly to homemakers. This appealed strongly to Earl Tupper because at age 10 he had made a considerable contribution to his family's nursery business by selling products door-to-door. Quickly, Earl Tupper was ready to accept that his company's success would not lie in plastic inventions, but in direct selling. By 1951 Wise was running company sales, and 100 percent of Tupperware product was moving through in-home parties.

Tupperware's Identity lay in direct selling. The people who moved Tupperware into the Rapids were Wise and Tupper, and both not only believed in direct selling but achieved their lifetime goals, in the face of adversity, by implementing it. Tupperware's products, first plastic housewares and later many other types of products, were tied to its Strategy of offering exclusive products to the direct sales organization. Tactics were all linked to helping direct sales people generate more revenue through in-home parties.

As mentioned earlier, Success Formulas are formed in the Rapids, not in the Wellspring. Success Formulas are valuable for helping a business create and then replicate its behaviors to first grow quickly and then maintain that growth. Without a Success Formula, no company can become a rapidly growing business, the kind we like to discuss in magazines and books and emulate in our organizations.

Vertical Success Formula Alignment Leads to Great Results

Success Formulas do not exist only at the company or business unit level. They are, in fact, linked up and down the pyramid. Vertically, Success Formulas intertwine between individuals, work teams, functional groups, and the company. Meanwhile, the company's Success Formula becomes connected with the industry and the economy. Across the pyramid, Success Formulas tie people together with the type of work they do, fellow employees, suppliers, competitors, and the marketplace.

For a business to succeed in the Rapids, not only must its Success Formula meet a market need, but it must fit within the industry and economy Success Formulas. When businesses grow rapidly, these Success Formulas all align vertically up and down the pyramid, and positive results are notable.

What generates rapid growth in one economy does not work well in another. Over the last 120 years we've seen a shift from an agrarian economy to an industrial economy to an information economy. In the agrarian economy, land ownership led to great success. The term "Landed Gentry" referred to their great wealth creation during the 1800s.

As the long wave of technological change shifted us into the Industrial economy, value shifted from land ownership to the means of production. Great wealth came from creating or owning industrial products and manufacturing plants. The empires of industrialists Henry Ford, Cyrus McCormick, and Cornelius Vanderbilt, as well as industrial financiers such as Mellon and Rockefeller, came by augmenting production. The shifting economy, from agrarian to industrial, shifted the source of wealth creation.

Recently, the economy has shifted again. Today, businesses that augment the creation, management, and flow of *information* are generating enormous wealth. Modern day empires are being created by the owners of Microsoft and Google—as well as MySpace, YouTube, and Facebook. Meanwhile the value of industrial production is faltering.

Economies have a Success Formula. Each has an Identity—as described in land, then manufacturing, and most recently, information. Different Strategies led to success, from maximizing land use to improving productivity and now generating, moving, and using information. And wildly different Tactics supported execution of these Strategies across all three types of economies.

All Success Formulas inherit the properties of lower layers. Microsoft could not have succeeded in an industrial economy (IBM did). Nor could Microsoft succeed had the computer industry not created dozens of component suppliers, supporting rapid development of powerful, smaller, and cheaper computers. Positive results-producing Success Formulas must align with the economy. No business can enter the Rapids or maintain itself in the Rapids if it is not aligned with the current economy. A new idea brought to market too early or too late will not produce great results. Businesses today that do not adjust to the information economy cannot hope to prosper.

Industries must align with the economy Success Formulas to grow. The American steel industry did very well for most of the 1900s because it aligned with the industrial economy. As this economy grew, steel's use exploded. Industry Strategies extensively utilized vertical integration to greatly increase production and mirrored the industrial economy Success Formula. Tactics focused on volume helped integrated steel providers grow. But today transportation, inventory, just-in-time delivery, and quality are much more critical to tightly designed information-intensive supply chains. Vertical integration is less valuable, and more nimble steel suppliers, such as mini-mills and fabrication shops, are capturing more value than the old behemoths.

Once company Success Formulas align with the Economy and Industry, it is important that *functional* Success Formulas align. In the Industrial Era, when production was critical, it was important that human resource (HR) Success Formulas hired people capable of increasing output. Tying compensation to production and implementing policies so workers showed up together when needed were hallmarks of great HR. As economy demands shift to information, it is far less important to manage when workers show up and to tie compensation to volume. More critical is hiring people who can utilize technology or information to find new insights and being able to bring those insights to bear on customers, thus increasing value. HR Success Formulas have to align with the requirements of more fundamental Success Formulas.

Work teams and individuals also have Success Formulas, and these too must align with those lower in the pyramid. When individuals join a company they frequently ask, "What leads to success around here?" This question is intended to understand the inherited Success Formula with which they must align. "Valuable" employees are those who share the Identity, Strategies, and Tactics of the business. The faster teams and individuals align themselves, the faster their results meet expectations and the greater their perceived contribution.

Reflecting again on AM, the company was in the Rapids when the industrial economy needed high volume and fast printing. The printing industry responded with small offset lithographic technology, which met needs for improved communication at low cost. AM tied its Identity to building small, low-cost offset printing presses and low-cost supplies. Its high-volume Strategies in manufacturing and distribution allowed the company to flourish as its Tactics lowered manufacturing costs while adding functionality and improved utilization. Every functional group in AM focused on improving AM's ability to make, distribute, and sell more offset products—especially their manufactured machines. Its workforce was filled with expertise in machine manufacturing, distribution optimization, and offset printing. These aligned Success Formulas allowed AM to grow fast.

Success Formulas Are Very Good Things– and Define Success

Success Formulas are critical to the success of any company that makes it into the Rapids. Without an aligned Success Formula, a business will remain in the Wellspring, unable to produce breakthrough results that create value for investors, managers, and employees. Even if it achieves early success with a customer or two, without a Success Formula, it will not replicate effectively to grow in the Rapids.

It's a wonderful time living in the Rapids—enjoying a Success Formula that produces good results and tweaking execution as the business rides on a river of positive returns.

Success Formulas in the Rapids also change the definition of "success." Once in the Rapids, for almost all businesses and the people who work in them, the operating definition of "success" is no longer merely achieving goals. After a Success Formula is created, "success" becomes *operating the Success Formula*. Results, good or bad, are the *outcome* of operating the Success Formula. Ironic as it appears, even though managers take credit for growth, it's the aligned Success Formula that produces superior results, not the managers themselves. And when growth falters, it's the Success Formula as well. Yet managers define success as operating the Success Formula, regardless of the results.

When the Success Formula is defined, managers put all available energy into operating it. Leaders can be very comfortable with result shortfalls if they know they are working hard at implementing the Success Formula. Managers *assume* the Success Formula will produce the same results it did early in the Rapids, and short-term troubles are expected to go away, allowing old results to return. Managers create a break between their actions, which are about operating the Success Formula, and their intentions—which are achieving results. And this break creates Re-Invention Gaps.

3

The Power of Lock-in

"Lock-in" is the foundation for Schumpeter's claim that businesses cannot transition to new technologies and business models like markets can.

Why is it that even after a business knows it is well along in its life cycle and realizes it is not doing well, managers continue undertaking actions that do not effectively address known problems? What drives management to keep doing what it always did?

Businesses Use Lock-in to Implement Their Success Formulas

Lock-in comes from economics and means committing to a behavior, structural process, or cost element to achieve a perceived benefit. For example, if a construction company always uses the same concrete supplier, the company knows the type of concrete it will receive, the type of trucks used for delivery, the reliability of the delivery, the talents of the drivers to unload the concrete close to where it's needed, the price it will be charged, and the billing method including terms. The contractor "Locks-in" on the concrete supplier because it benefits him to do so.

Similarly, corporate information technology (IT) groups frequently Lock-in on a single platform. During the 1990s, many IT groups forced all employees to utilize similar personal computers using the Microsoft operating system and business applications. By Locking-in on a single platform, IT shops were able to lower their costs of equipment and software acquisition as well as user support. They were also able to improve understanding of Microsoft products to achieve maximum utilization, thus improving business capabilities more rapidly at lower cost. Locking-in to the "Wintel" (for Windows + Intel) platform made IT shops more efficient and augmented rapid platform education as well as improved capability to maintain revisions and upgrades.

When Xerox brought the 914 copier to market, it was not priced the way traditional office equipment had been priced. It allowed customers to acquire the machine at a low price and then pay Xerox a fee for each piece of paper put through the machine. Pricing was mostly what users called "click fees," referring to each click on the copy counter. Customers loved acquiring the machine cheaply, and the per-use fee worked well for them. Customers Locked-in on Xerox because they loved the pricing model, which bundled together service, toner consumption, and the equipment cost.

Everyone utilizes Lock-in. It reduces potential options, speeds the decision-making process, and lowers cost. By Locking-in on a previous analysis and its results, we improve performance through repetitive use of that decision. We build upon Lock-in to focus on other decisions. Lock-in allows us to move through a host of decisions without having to analyze them multiple times. Although we all carry a raft of potential options for any decision, for most decisions we maintain a Lock-in to the previous decision (and thus the previous analysis and previous approach), which once yielded the best results.

RECOGNIZING PERSONAL LOCK-IN

Everyone comes face-to-face at a personal level with Lock-in when visiting a foreign country.

- Breakfast in Japan is fish and rice.
- In India or Spain, you would not typically eat lunch until 2:00 p.m. and dinner often after 10:00 p.m.
- In Europe people take their dogs into restaurants.
- Traditional toilets in Asia and India are "flush" with the floor.
- It is very common for French or Italian teenage youth to have wine with their parents at dinner, and in Germany it's not uncommon for teens to have beer with their parents.

- In Germany prime-time television programming includes fully nude adults and soft-core pornography.
- Outside the U.S. there is almost never tax (sales tax) added to the price at time of sale.

These differences expose Lock-in to American expectations and can be unsettling!

Like a Success Formula, Lock-in is a good thing. If we didn't have Lock-in, our efficiency would be so bad we wouldn't get anything done. There would be no "standard operating procedures" for us to follow. Lock-in is the first step in automation, which yields tremendous productivity in everything we do.

Lock-in supports our Success Formula. We don't Lock-in on things that produce bad results. We Lock-in on things that help us achieve our goals. As we build our Success Formula, we not only observe what Tactics support our Strategy and Identity, but we identify mechanisms that promote repetition. These Lock-in mechanisms help our Success Formula operate over-and-over without reanalyzing what we want to do or why we want to do it. They act as guide rails to keep our Success Formula on the road.

The better our Success Formula works, the more we Lock-in to it. As we succeed, Lock-in prunes away options which might lead to lesser results. Our interest in exploring different decisions declines because tinkering with the Success Formula might make it less effective. We like the results, so we do more of the Success Formula to get more of those results. We Lock-in to repeating activities and exclude other options.

As new people are added within organizations, management works hard to reinforce Lock-in. The stronger Lock-in, the faster a business can indoctrinate new folks into the Success Formula and make them productive contributors to their expected future results. In the *Rapids*, that thriving time of high growth, businesses not only work hard at defining their Success Formulas, but they also figure out how to lock them in. Leaders want to maintain high growth, and the most effective way is with strong Lock-in mechanisms that indoctrinate employees and vendors to the organization's way of doing business.

Looking again at Addressograph-Multigraph (AM), management used several techniques to Lock-in how things were done:

- AM maintained a training department for printers. Everyone at AM focused on lithographic printing skills and ignored other printing technologies.
- Sales commissions were highest on printing presses, second highest on printing press supplies, and lowest on non-lithographic products.
- AM paid much higher commissions on sales of its manufactured products than products sourced from vendors.
- When AM's profits faltered, the company adjusted depreciation schedules, altered accounting for the pension plan, and changed its handling of tax adjustments to improve earnings.
- For many years, everyone in the company had a printing background. People talked about having "ink in their veins" and "under their nails." People with specialized printing expertise were given prominent positions.
- All investments passed a stringent risk-adjusted ROI process that discounted revenue from non-lithographic projects. Projects that increased plant utilization used a streamlined process to speed approval.
- All R&D and new product development were exclusively directed at lithographic technology, where the company had a history of inventions and improvements.

Additionally, AM, like all companies in the Rapids, created "Status Quo Police." The Finance department maintained an iron grip on all spending and investments at AM. Practically no decision, from a price change to a new hire to travel or a marketing program, could be implemented unless approved by the CFO. All spending evaluations revolved around their ability to generate additional margin by selling printing equipment and supplies—preferably manufactured in AM plants.

New products that detracted from printing equipment sales were assigned "cannibalization charges" to compensate for anticipated future lost margins from lost lithographic equipment sales. Finance would not authorize hiring new technology trainers because ramp-up time for new training programs had lower ROI than incrementally staffing existing lithographic training programs. Finance preached plant utilization at every employee and management meeting. The decision evaluation system operated by Finance was designed to keep AM focused on manufacturing and selling lithographic products.

Success Formulas Are Locked-in Behaviorally and Structurally

Lock-ins are used by organizations to help themselves rapidly grow. They make certain necessary tasks are accomplished efficiently, and they effectively promote doing more of what worked in the past. However, for all Lock-ins there are risks.

There are Several Ways Organizations Lock-in Behaviorally

The following are some primary ways organizations can Lock-in to their Success Formulas from a behavior standpoint:

- Rigid adherence to an historically defined market
- Sacred cows (often not even seen)
- "Not invented here" mentality
- Rewarding farmers while punishing explorers
- Hierarchy
- Financial machinations

Rigid Adherence to an Historically Defined Market

Adhering rigidly to an historically defined market is a frequently utilized form of Lock-in. How often have you heard someone say, "We are in the _____ business," where you fill in the blank with a product? When a business defines its Identity and Success Formula around a product or service, it leaves little room for doing anything else.

Consider McDonald's. McDonald's defined its business around hamburgers. This Lock-in helped the company develop clear standards, and it grew very fast. Keeping the product line simple helped everyone—from vendors to customers—know exactly what McDonald's was all about. Product Lock-in contributed tremendously to McDonald's becoming the world's largest restaurant company.

However, by Locking-in their business to hamburgers, a monumental challenge was created for any other product. The company took great pride in promoting the Big Mac and the Quarter Pounder. Yet, as mad cow disease threatened the business and as consumers opted for other products, McDonald's struggled to succeed with anything beyond hamburgers. Most recently, McDonald's has been challenged to introduce a salad line that could attract new customers. Instead, salads have been mostly a defensive move to protect the hamburger business from losing entire families when one person either doesn't want or can't eat a hamburger.

Sacred Cows

Maintaining sacred cows Locks-in a business to its Success Formula. The interesting thing about sacred cows is that no one admits having one. Leaders uniformly state they will not tolerate sacred cows. Yet they do have them—and they exist because managers are unable to see them.

MY PERSONAL EXPERIENCE WITH SACRED COWS

On a trip to India, I was greatly delayed arriving at a meeting by a meandering cow that brought traffic to a standstill, causing miles of back-ups. I asked my taxi driver, "With all the new wealth in India, why don't you put fences along the roadways or possibly have workers stand on the roadway to keep animals off the roads and thus allow traffic to flow freely?"

The driver looked at me with a puzzled expression and asked, "Why would we do that?"

I replied, "To help improve traffic flow." And then he said, "I don't understand your question."

I finally understood what a "sacred cow" really meant. It was impossible for this driver to understand my question because to him the cow was sacred. The cow had the right to wander onto the roadway. My alternatives for bovine control were nonstarters because the cow was sacred. Thus it was impossible for the driver to imagine fencing off the cow or keeping her off the road by any physical interference. Although my goal was to preserve the cow—to increase its safety while simultaneously achieving other worthy societal goals related to traffic flow—my options could not be considered.

It is blindness to alternatives which creates a sacred cow. To those for whom it is sacred, there is no consideration of options. The sacred cow might be seen, but it is never seen as the cause of a problem.

Sacred cows can be wide ranging. Some can appear almost trivial to an outsider, such as the previously discussed DuPont conviction for safety. Nonetheless, that commitment to safety keeps everyone in the company aligned with the Success Formula. Other sacred cows can be completely dominating. Kraft's ongoing commitment to invest in and promote cheese through legacy brands, such as Velveeta, even while other consumer products and brands have grown much faster and have had higher margins, highlights the company's "sacred cows." Saying "America spells cheese K–R–A–F–T" promotes commitment to the sacred cow and does not have changing customer tastes as a goal. Kraft has kept its focus on Velveeta, while selling off high-growth brands such as Altoids.

Businesses often cannot move forward simply because change would interfere with a sacred cow. Even though Xerox knew their market for large copiers was under attack by desktop printers connected to computers over local area networks, and Xerox had pioneered much of the technology for this solution at its R&D facility called Xerox Parc, Xerox was unwilling to look past their sacred cow of selling end-of-hall large copiers priced on clicks. Instead of launching laser printers and supporting products, Xerox brought to market a 914 on steroids called Docutech that never came close to meeting the 914 success—nor the success of desktop printers.

"Not Invented Here" Mentality

A "not invented here" mentality strictly Locks-in organizations to engaging with only those technologies, products, markets, distributors, customers, and so on that produced past success. DuPont built the Experimental Station in Wilmington, Delaware, as one of the most advanced R&D facilities in America. But ties to historical research areas and links to legacy businesses impede the ability of such a well-funded and well-staffed facility to embrace anything not developed within. By continuously investing in the Experimental Station, DuPont reinforces the mentality that the company can invent all its own products, a cornerstone of the Success Formula upon which products such as nylon, Teflon, and Kevlar were created—even if only one per decade or so and even if those innovations are becoming dated. Think of *The Graduate*, when Dustin Hoffman is given the one-word career advice, "Plastics." It's unlikely that would be the primary guidance for today's recent matriculator.

For decades Motorola was known as a preeminent electronics engineering company. It successfully developed, marketed, and profited from radios, starting with those used in automobiles and homes and then moving into two-way mobile radios used by police and fire departments. Motorola successfully developed many electronic components, including the microprocessor brains in the Apple Macintosh—a design considered superior to Intel's chips for many years. And Motorola was a pioneer in developing mobile telephony, from handsets to infrastructure products on towers.

But Locking-in to developing its own products has also significantly harmed Motorola. The company was late recognizing customer shifts from Apple products to Microsoft platforms and saw its share in microprocessors erode from 70% of 16 bit machines and 20% of the entire market to low single digits in both. The company fell in love with its own satellite telephone system, Iridium, and lost billions of dollars before recognizing the market was miniscule and would be supplied by conventional cellular technology. Preoccupation with advancing its own analog cell phone handsets made Motorola woefully late to the digital handset business and caused a dramatic 1990s company downsizing.

Rewarding Farmers While Punishing Explorers

This type of behavior Locks-in people to preserving the Success Formula. While leaders ask sales people to find new customers, compensation systems are designed to make sure existing customers buy as much each year as they did the previous year—rather than have the business invest in missionary sales work to develop new customers or promote new products. Sales people who miss revenue targets while seeking out new customers for new product launches are often put on "review" as they are pushed to rapidly get sales volume back up. Sales people at AM who tried selling new OEM copiers from IBM saw their compensation fall and then their jobs put at risk due to declining press sales.

People creating new uses for old products, such as selling into new international markets, are rewarded. Those who try to bring new products to old customers are chastised if their efforts create cannibalization of legacy sales. When Mr. Nasser was promoted to the top spot at Ford, he was lauded for his ability to increase profits in Europe, not for developing a small car that appealed to Europeans but that was not interesting to U.S. consumers (and sold for a lower price than the average U.S. car or light truck). Consequently, Ford did not leverage its European small car strength into America—or take a leading edge in hybrid cars.

Hierarchy

Hierarchy is a necessary requirement for life in the Rapids. No company can move from the Wellspring into the Rapids if it cannot implement a hierarchy allowing more people to be engaged and guided in the direction of doing what works. Hierarchy is critical to making sure that the Success Formula is followed. Those who manage the hierarchy are responsible for making sure that everyone is marching in the right direction. Hierarchy allows the U.S. Army to mobilize thousands of troops quickly to areas requiring national defense. Hierarchy allows soldiers to undergo strict indoctrination in operating methods to quickly understand their roles and proper behavior when given orders.

Simultaneously, hierarchy Locks-in the Success Formula, making organizations resistant to change. Leaders who plan new strategic direction for their companies or divisions and then publish their vision to their organizations with the command to "march" often end up woefully disappointed. Organizations are designed to operate their old Success Formulas and are completely incapable of simply shifting toward new decisions. Inside the hierarchy, individual parts can only see one step forward and one backward. It is impossible for participants to design their way out of old Success Formulas because the hierarchy was designed with the specific intent of making sure such activity could not occur! The deeper the hierarchy, and the more strictly it is monitored, the more successful it will be at Locking-in the Success Formula.

In 1997 Xerox brought in former IBM executive Richard Thoman to be its CEO. He was charged to turn around declining sales, which resulted after desktop printing and small copiers decreased demand for large Xerox copiers. Mr. Thoman questioned internal manufacturing and began telling the organization to use more outsourced manufacturing as well as external technology. He also established a vision for selling smaller products, leveraging more of the technical advances from Xerox Parc. Unfortunately, he ignored the hierarchy, and by 2001 Mr. Thoman was unceremoniously dumped. He was a victim of vision confronting hierarchy, and hierarchy clearly won. All the historically great Industrial Era companies were experts at establishing and utilizing hierarchy to achieve company goals. Often modeled on the military, businesses such as General Motors, Ford, Chrysler, Bethlehem Steel, IBM, Kodak, and Sears had powerful hierarchies that made sure Success Formulas were carefully followed.

Financial Machinations

Financial machinations are a superb tool to Lock-in a Success Formula. Any auditor or investment analyst can describe the differences when implementing Generally Accepted Accounting Principles (GAAP) across industries. But why do these differences exist? Why do different industries and different companies need different depreciation rates? Why do they need different R&D capitalization rules and amortization schedules? Different policies for incurring revenues or deferring expenses? Different methods for adjusting tax schedules or for pension accounting? Because in each instance the industry and company have a Success Formula, and they use the accounting system to both reinforce and protect that Success Formula. It is not external factors from investors or customers that drive the accounting differences—but rather decisions made by executives who wish to portray their financial results in the best light given the assumptions built into their Success Formulas.

Structurally, Organizations Have Several Lock-in Mechanisms

Along with behavior-based Lock-in, there are many structural mechanisms that support and propagate Lock-in:

- Strategic bias
- Correlating decision size with strategic value
- People practices
- Architecture
- Best Practices
- Resource allocation

Strategic Bias

Strategic bias Locks-in a business to its Success Formula. When decisions are needed, analysts do not treat all options similarly. Strategists are biased toward using historical data. What's well-known and well-documented is given more attention because reams of data support assumptions. But this data is *history*. Data volume reinforces the notion that decisions in known markets will be better, when in fact most data is little more than extrapolation of historical assumptions. In a changing world, this offers no assurance about future results! More data might *imply* better decision making, but in reality most data is biased toward extending past decisions.

Imagine two managers are seeking funds to develop a new product. One product is a variation on an historical product. The manager forecasts an uptick in revenue based on past sales. He forecasts product costs using component prices from previous products and adjusting downward for higher anticipated volume. He is confident in his margin forecast because he extended previously known numbers.

The second manager identifies a new solution to a well-known customer problem. He is unsure of the market size, so sales estimates are little more than guesses. His solution utilizes new technology, so his cost estimates are based on other companies' costs and new vendor proposals. His margin forecast is shaky, although he has considerable customer market research supporting the new technology's efficacy.

Who gets funding approval? The mere use of internal data that extends known products pushes decision making toward the Locked-in Success Formula.

Worse is using "core competencies" or "core markets" as decision criteria, including "focus" as a priority for business strategy. Strategists using these parameters will define opportunities as either supporting or not supporting what is "core." By defining "core" and "focus," strategic opportunities which are not "core" aren't even reviewed! Only those things supporting Lock-in are considered "core" and thus have the potential to be approved.

Jim Collins promotes focus in his best selling books *Built to Last* and *Good to Great*. In both he offers his list of "great" companies. He talks about company-wide BHAG (Big Hairy Audacious Goal) adoption and "getting everyone on the bus" to implement approved programs. Companies identified in his books as "great" are those with clear Success Formulas and as described, clearly Locked-in. For these companies strategy becomes a way to "wash the cottage cheese"—an analogy he uses to describe how one intensely competitive bicyclist literally washed his cottage cheese to remove unwanted fats. Collins recommends companies wash away everything from their diets except those things absolutely critical to single-focused strategy.

Collins' "great" companies, unfortunately, have been no better than average performers since they were highlighted in his books. Why has recent overall performance of these firms not matched Collins' historical analysis? At least one important reason was change in their competitive environment. But in a dynamic world, shouldn't all strategy prepare for competitive change?

Collins likes to use sports analogies. But in sports—unlike business—rules are clearly known and unchanging during competition. Those that perform best within the rules win. In business rules are not nearly as clear cut as in a marathon, bicycle race, or basketball game. The environment is constantly changing, as new entrants and substitute products change the playing field, and competitors can literally change the rules. By applying intense focus, Collins' "great" companies missed important market changes and opportunities to consider alternatives that would have helped them compete more effectively.

Correlating Decision Size with Strategic Value

Correlating decision size with strategic value is another strategy-based Lock-in. By definition, most big investments are tied to the Success Formula. Acquisitions and mergers are almost always linked to Success Formula continuation. Large R&D and new product development investments continue past product technologies. Large capital investments are usually plant expansions or new plant construction—or for IT to better manage the existing business. Mislabeling large decisions as "strategic," rather than tactical optimization of an existing Locked-in Success Formula, lends itself to doing more of what's being done. Real "strategic" decisions are about modifying Success Formulas, not building large monuments to the existing ones.

When J.P. Morgan Chase acquired Bank One, the company and the press called the transaction "strategic." But all this really did was extend the retail Chase bank into a new market—Midwestern U.S.A. A big acquisition, yes—but was it strategic?

People Practices

The policies and practices set in place to handle human resources often Lock-in organizations very effectively. Frequently, HR personnel will define the "right kind of person" that they believe would do well in their business. These definitions link success to specific educational backgrounds and industry experience. As a result, most people in the business start looking a lot alike. How will this lead to developing new and different opportunities?

In the latter 1980s, DuPont's charismatic Industrial Products Department leader decided a significant opportunity existed in digital imaging. DuPont had succeeded for years selling polymer films for analogue imaging in uses like printing and x-rays. But this executive vice president predicted film's future revenue was threatened by computers capturing, displaying, and managing images. As a result, he began hiring a new wave of managers who were steeped in electronic device and equipment sales. He hired a successful manager from General Electric as Division Director.

Very soon there were difficulties between the new Electronic Imaging Division's leadership and the DuPont Executive Committee regarding investments. As time passed, difficulties worsened. Distressed, one of the executive committee members said to the Division head, "We are chemists. We understand people who talk about chemistry. We don't understand the leaders of this division." Those leading DuPont were very uncomfortable with the backgrounds of the newly hired individuals. Shortly thereafter an effort was made to sell the Division. It was dismantled, and the top managers moved on. They did not "fit in" at DuPont.

Hiring and promotion are sources of Lock-in and can turn the HR function into the Status Quo Police by implementing tight recruiting and advancement controls, making sure new hires and "high-potential employees" are similar to those who "grew up" in the company and helped define the Success Formula. When evaluations include reviewing how well people conform to behavioral standards, the review system becomes a Lock-in mechanism, assuring only those who promote the Success Formula survive. We can measure this Lock-in by tracking the weightings assigned during reviews to assess how well people "fit in" when deciding who gets to stay, who gets promoted, and who gets compensation increases. When being "well thought of" is as important as achieving results, Lock-in to the Success Formula is reinforced.

Architecture

Particularly in the last decade, architecture has become an effective tool for Success Formula Lock-in. For many years, Information Technology was used largely to automate paper processes, such as payroll or accounts payable. (Do you remember when IT was called DP—for Data Processing?) But since the early 1990s IT, particularly in the form of "enterprise" applications such as enterprise resource planning (ERP) has become a tool for managing decision making. Now Oracle and SAP dominate corporate IT software budgets, particularly in large organizations.

Growing companies now frequently turn to ERP systems quite early as a way to Lock-in their Success Formulas. These applications tightly control how data is used and what decision options are even possible, and executives enjoy the tracking and decision-making consistency these applications provide. These systems are bought and implemented even though they are known to be extremely expensive and cumbersome to implement as well as operate.

For years, data processing reported to the top finance person and was usually a cost-reduction tool for an old manual process. As IT emerged with more robust applications and capabilities, supported by increasingly powerful and lower-cost computers connected over high-throughput networks, spending rose dramatically. Many CFOs decried runaway IT spending and difficulties measuring return on investment.

But not so with ERP applications. Although extraordinarily expensive, these applications allowed CFOs to wire together the business decision-making apparatus in a way that made it hard for employees to do as they wished. ERP systems promoted common processes, common behaviors, and common, pre-designed, decisions. With an ERP system in place, no marketing manager could sneak an ad through a new journal because the ERP system would mandate a review. No purchasing agent could cut a purchase order for a new vendor without a thorough vendor review.

Well-documented, most ERP installations take much longer than planned (frequently months or years longer) and most often cost much more (multiples of budgeted project cost in some instances) than budgeted. Yet, the majority of CFOs have steadfastly supported implementing a tool that helps them monitor and promote Success Formula Lock-in. Executives who deride high new plant construction costs, over-budget distribution systems, or even kill expensive Customer Relationship Management software projects often find ROI to be less important when the project achieves consistent behavior and decision making across the organization.

Executives pursuing Lock-in mandate using large "core" systems, whether ERP, procurement, accounting, or supply chain applications. Even small start-up operations inside larger businesses are forced to accept the high cost and extensive employee training required for these complex applications. Acquired companies are usually forced to rapidly adopt these systems, and they become a tool for maintaining Lock-in to the old Success Formula, even when the original objective was doing something new!

Best Practices

Best Practices are another effective form of structural Lock-in. The theory behind adopting Best Practices is that you can find a process which someone has used and if copied will assure positive results. Best Practice followers find someone else's practice and then Lock-in to it, hoping results improve. But a business that applies Best Practices finds itself constantly behind competitors because instead of creating *real* Best Practices, it is working to become as good as some other business was three years ago when it created that Best Practice! Best Practice users hope their efforts will sustain a Success Formula—but how can they?

When important *knowledge* is immobile, contained within a small group of people, it Locks-in the organization to comply with the wishes of these people. Top executives or key managers will utilize knowledge to force those lower in the hierarchy, or dependent upon them for resources, to adhere to Lock-in. These knowledgeable people can become Status Quo Police, as decisions become dependent on them, and they withhold approvals unless they confirm Success Formula adherence.

At DuPont, business managers frequently had ideas for new products. Competition helped them identify new technologies and products they wanted to adopt—and adapt. But DuPont frequently required new technology investments be vetted by the powerful R&D organization within the heavily funded Experimental Station. These bright technologists and scientists were considered "experts," and they held veto power over many investments. This created substantial difficulty for external technologies and products to become part of DuPont's offerings—and this hurdle killed many good ideas.

When only individuals or small teams can access the knowledge needed to do their jobs, they become Locked-in to their roles. They become just one step in Success Formula execution, without the ability to influence it. Results become dependent on the work process and hierarchy, not the people. While this reduces business risk, it also Locks-in the process. Work processes Lock-in a Success Formula. No one can change the Success Formula without changing the entire process, affecting multiple people and often multiple functions.

Resource Allocation

One of the strongest structural Lock-in tools is resource allocation. Finance academics will say *sunk cost* (past investments) are irrelevant when making decisions. To academics, the only important costs are future costs. It's not important how much has already been spent when deciding whether to spend more. But saying that to a company president with a large manufacturing plant on his balance sheet and significant depreciation charges on his P&L might well get you fired! Once a business builds a large plant or distribution center (DC) or buys a big IT application, options that do not promote asset utilization are simply not considered. These big asset investments are made intentionally to Lock-in a plan and limit flexibility to do anything else.

Fixed cost investments do have benefits in the Rapids. Anticipating higher revenue and volume, it is sensible to incur more fixed costs to lower variable costs. Simultaneously, variable cost increases lag revenue increases because you cannot bring on cost as fast as revenue grows. This cost lag creates additional profits, benefiting the P&L during rapid growth. Locking-in costs via fixed investments is great *while demand grows.* "Scale" improves margins.

Once a distribution center is built, leaders think about the money spent and ask managers, "Isn't there some way to make greater use of this DC?" Incremental costs of using the asset are low. Justifying the new DC requires higher volume, and higher volume requires operating the Success Formula. The organization Locks-in on contribution margin toward the fixed costs and commits even more deeply to the Success Formula when seeking volume. Over time, profitability can disappear as everyone focuses on creating contribution margin toward an unproductive asset not meeting customer needs!

Obsessive cost accounting within the business and its resource allocation process makes it impossible to spend money on anything that doesn't strictly adhere to the Locked-in Success Formula. The only approved costs are those designated as supporting the Success Formula, and the Status Quo Police (usually finance personnel) chase down all non-approved costs and hold up the spender for senior personnel review.

Punishments for non-approved expenditures can often be significant, including termination.

Likewise, large supply chain or outsourcing deals help the resource allocation process Lock-in the Success Formula. These deals generate long-term returns only if their use is strictly enforced. Long-term agreements span multiple years and cover large volume requiring the business operate within the confines of the deal.

Some monuments that promote Success Formula Lock-in aren't so obvious. Headquarters buildings, corner offices, executive perquisites (like company airplanes or upgraded travel) lure employees and executives to Lock-in on what used to work in an effort to maintain and achieve these success symbols. They can even become sacred cows to employees and executives with personal identities tied closely to the company Success Formula.

Understanding the Status Quo Police

As mentioned previously, in every organization there are Status Quo Police. Their role is to enforce the Success Formula. The Status Quo Police controls the most powerful Lock-ins, and they use their power to make sure the Success Formula is followed when critical decisions are made. They view their role as minimizing risk by minimizing change.

To identify the Status Quo Police, look for the most critical Success Formula elements. The protectors of those elements are the Status Quo Police. They wield dictatorial control over decisions that touch these elements. Any person or proposed practice or procedure that attempts to conflict with the Success Formula will never get past the Status Quo Police roadblocks. They are well armored and have the guns to back themselves up.

IT performed this role in the 1980s at Pizza Hut. Pizza Hut did 100% of its IT internally, including payroll. Payroll printed checks for all employees in corporate headquarters and overnighted them to individual stores nationwide. If a manager wanted to hire someone, the new person had to be set up in a system. If a store manager wanted to buy pepperoni from a vendor, that vendor had to be set up in a system. If a regional manager wanted to pay an electric bill on a new store, that store and vendor had to be set up in a system. And nothing was set up in a system until both the IT Director and his CFO boss agreed. Therefore, because no decision could be implemented unless it was set up in the computer system, IT was the Status Quo Police, making sure all decisions fit the Success Formula.

Mid-1980s, Pizza Hut set up a small team to evaluate competing with the newly emerging Domino's. The team was told it could implement whatever necessary to compete. However, Pizza Hut's executive team set up this project before agreeing that they were committed to home delivery. Some just wanted to experiment with options.

The home delivery team developed evaluation store concepts and created an approach that showed great promise. The executive team liked the approach but was not unified about whether Pizza Hut should deliver. However, observing Domino's rapid growth, the executive team was unwilling to stop the effort. When the home delivery team attempted to set up payroll for its store openings, it asked IT to implement a new employee category called "Driver." The Director of IT simply said, "I don't have approval to set up an employee code in payroll for Driver," and the entire project was kept on hold for weeks by an effective Status Quo Police doing its job of protecting the existing sit-down restaurant Success Formula. The executives didn't have to say yes or no; they merely let the Status Quo Police hold up the project.

The newly hired DuPont Electronic Imaging leadership developed a growth plan including an operating budget. After much wrangling, the budget was approved. That budget included funding to hire new managers and technical people critical for growth. However, when division leadership went to Human Resources to spend their budget, they were told no approval had been given to increase the headcount. Yes, the budget existed for the positions, but the headcount was not approved. HR, in the role of Status Quo Police, kept anyone from hiring new positions that conflicted with the DuPont Success Formula, regardless of budget.

Inside AM sales managers would meet their revenue and margin goals, but Finance maintained a line-item budget for sales. Even if sales managers met their overall goals, if revenue fell short for manufactured equipment or supplies, the Finance managers would reduce bonuses for failure to sell enough of the old stuff. Finance was the Status Quo Police, making sure salespeople kept selling the products closely tied to the Success Formula.

All companies have Status Quo Police. They could be product development, R&D, or manufacturing managers who dictate the technology to be used for new products, regardless of what customers request, maintaining adherence to a preferred technology. Manufacturing managers can dictate which plants or which vendors will supply a product regardless of customer requests, regional requirements, or even cost objectives to maintain Success Formula commitments within the supply chain. And procurement managers can dictate vendors, regardless of price or availability, in order to enforce Success Formula compliance.

Lock-in Is Good in the Rapids

Lock-in is deliberate and considered good management when driving Success Formula replication. In the Rapids, *Lock-in is a good thing*. When the Success Formula is making money, Lock-in helps growth, as it creates and amplifies positive returns. By optimizing the Success Formula, Lock-in produces the most returns with the least effort.

Lock-in, however, also creates blinders to what's happening outside the Success Formula—activity which is not considered important to Success Formula execution. Optimization efforts and ensuing efficiency is the goal, so little if any attention is paid to what happens outside the Success Formula. That is why Locked-in organizations fail to see emerging technologies, competitors, and environmental changes which threaten Success Formula results. So Lock-in is a good thing because it helps companies in the Rapids grow. But it is more often a hindrance, blinding companies elsewhere on the lifecycle to critical options.

MISSED OPPORTUNITIES DUE TO
LOCKED-IN SUCCESS FORMULAS

- Apple missed the market for PDAs after pioneering the Newton because it was Locked-in to selling Macintoshes.

- Xerox missed the desktop printer market, even though it's own R&D department played a major role in developing the product, because it was Locked-in to selling large machines for copying high volume priced on a per-page-copied model.

- IBM practically invented the personal computer industry by pioneering the product. But IBM exited the business because it was Locked-in to its mainframe and mid-range computer business, projected limited sales, and felt PCs conflicted with data center customer goals.

- AT&T was late to mobile phones and data networks because it was Locked-in to thinking of itself as a landline long distance provider.

- Kodak pioneered digital photography technology and products but arrived at the marketplace extraordinarily late due to its film market Lock-in.

- Sun Microsystems led the marketplace in network computers and developed a critical software product for the Internet with Java but missed the market for network software, hardware, and services because it was Locked-in to selling workstations and servers.

As long as the future closely approximates the past, Lock-in helps businesses efficiently succeed. If the environment doesn't change, managers can expect results won't change. Leaders can tune Success Formulas to improve growth within existing environments, optimizing historically profitable processes.

But what happens when the environment changes? In biological systems, the competitor at greatest risk from environmental change is the one most optimized to the existing environment. Quite literally, the most successful competitor is usually the most disastrously affected by environmental change. Even small changes can spell ruin due to tight links between competitive behavior and the environment. Today global warming (regardless of the cause) is likely to be the demise of penguins and polar bears because they are very highly adapted to their northern climate and require polar ice.

As businesses Lock-in to their Success Formulas, they Lock-in to the environment upon which their Success Formulas were built. Everything from how the economy works to industry models, tax rates, acceptable competitive behavior, pricing, cost and margin assumptions, leadership skills, team customs—and more—is rolled up into the Success Formula.

The better a Success Formula's results, the more it is Locked-in and the tighter it becomes wedded to its environment.

What Lock-in exchanges for its pursuit of growth and efficiency is adaptability. Dinosaurs once ruled the earth and were highly adapted to their environment. And they remained successful, eating smaller animals, right up until the last dinosaur died—due to a change in the environment, which made their Success Formula obsolete. Environmental changes meant small, furry animals were better adapted to the new, colder environment. They not only survived, but flourished. Similarly, large companies often eat small, new competitors. But if the environment changes, size alone will not protect these large businesses. The better-adapted, new competitors will flourish and overcome old competitors.

All businesses risk obsolescence from environmental change. *Success Formulas are dependent on the initial state when created*, so changes to the initial state are deadly. Long after the initial state has passed, Lock-in keeps organizations behaving as if that initial state remains. Vulnerability to initial state changes explains the poor performance of businesses compared to markets, as identified years ago by Schumpeter.

YOU MIGHT BE LOCKED-IN IF...

- Travel or hiring is frozen in order to meet an upcoming quarterly profit estimate.
- Most of the top executives have degrees in the same field, went to the same school, or spent more than ten years in the company.
- Recruiting notices require candidates with current industry experience.
- Most newly hired managers or executives came from competitors.
- The Board of Directors has not changed for five years.
- Internal accounting rules have been changed for pension funds, tax adjustments, depreciation, or amortization.
- Earnings have been restated for any of the previous three years.
- The current P&L is taking charges for future reorganizations.
- The business reports "special charges."

- Competitive technologies are discounted because they have no patent protection.
- Evaluations of plant performance, material costs, or productivity do not benchmark outside the existing industry.
- Smaller competitors are ignored, regardless of their growth rate.
- Executives talk more about how big the business is than how fast it is growing.
- A new ERP system is being installed.
- Leadership recommends raising prices or cutting services to small customers.
- Vendor consolidation becomes a "strategic" activity.
- M&A focuses on buying competitors.
- The business has not sold any significant assets for three years.
- The number one growth initiative is entering a foreign market.
- Most new product launches are existing product variations.
- R&D budgets are being cut.
- Marketing and advertising budgets are focused on historical products.

The Really BIG Environmental Shift

As mentioned in the Part I Introduction, "Overcoming Schumpeter," Russian economist Nicolai Kondratiev postulated in 1925 that economic shifts happen in long waves of 50 to 75 years based on technology shifts. And as we see in Chapter 2, "The Value and Power of Success Formulas," his theory provides an explanation for the shift from an agrarian economy to an industrial economy in the early 1900s, and more recently the shift to an information economy. Scholars may argue exactly when we shifted into an information economy, but practically none argue that the shift has happened.

The industrial economy underpinned almost all management practices used by today's business leaders. From Henry Ford's assembly line to Frederick Taylor's Scientific Management using time and motion studies to Henry Fayol's Modern Management (plan, organize, command, coordinate, and control) to the Harvard Business School's

Hawthorne Studies documenting productivity improvement, all of these advancements in management education were based on an industrial economy. During the popular rise of business schools, it was improving performance in an industrial economy that dominated curriculum.

But now that we are fully into the information economy, Success Formulas and management tools must adapt. Industry, company, business unit, functional group, work group, and individual Success Formulas all must realign to the requirements of this historically rare, but very real, change in the base of the Success Formula pyramid. Unfortunately too many businesses have not made these changes. Leaders still try to execute Success Formulas tied to economic assumptions that no longer prevail. And that's why today's business climate seems so unsettled, so uncertain, and so difficult for so many managers— especially those over 40 and those in older businesses.

Think about the economic value of corn. In the 1800s, value went to landowners. With over 50% of Americans employed in agriculture, it was common knowledge that you either owned the land, or you worked for low wages making money for landowners. America's great western migration was people seeking land in an agrarian economy.

But the move to an industrial economy shifted value creation. Those improving production, such as Cyrus McCormick and John Deere, captured the greatest value from corn. For the next 80 years America's "family farms" diminished as land ownership saw its value transfer to those who managed larger farms that used more mechanization. Only highly mechanized large farms survived the great rural shakeout of the 1970s and 1980s. By 2000, fewer than 1% of Americans were employed in agriculture. Meanwhile, equipment manufacturers flourished.

Today, enormous corn fortunes are made in Chicago's future trading pits. Traders who own no land and have no means of production make hundreds of millions of dollars trading nothing more than contracts representing the eventual transfer of real corn. These traders capture tremendous wealth as value has transferred from those who own land, grow corn, or provide equipment to those who use information about corn.

As the base of the Success Formula evolves, Success Formulas that created value in earlier economies lose most of their value. Value transfers to those who have Success Formulas built on the new economy foundation. This does not mean no one makes any money in farming or supplying equipment. But competing in these businesses requires changing the Success Formula.

Modern farmers not only own land and operate large, mechanized businesses, but they use satellite information to micro-manage acreage production. They also must become as skillful at trading commodities futures as they are at selecting seed, fertilizer, and financing both land and equipment. Equipment manufacturers must become skilled at information-laden supply chain practices, including using futures contracts to manage steel and other material costs. Earning high rates of return requires using information better, not simply owning assets or utilizing them productively.

Most people think of evolutionary forces as linear. We now know that is not the case. Most competitive environments are stable for a long time—many years or even decades. Then something dramatic happens. The environment doesn't change slowly and gradually, allowing for easy adaptation. Instead, the equilibrium remains, even if shaky, for a very long time and then suddenly, seemingly overnight, there is a dramatic shift to an entirely new equilibrium. In this "punctuated equilibrium," the river suddenly changes course.

Business gurus refer to the information economy shift as "the new normal." This language is intended to help managers recognize there has been a sudden, dramatic environmental shift. What was once normal no longer exists, and a "new normal" has arrived. Between 1995 and 2005 we passed through a punctuated equilibrium from living in an industrial economy to living an information economy, creating an entirely new competitive environment.

Every industrial Success Formula now has to shift. The base of the pyramid has changed. Locked-in Success Formulas can no longer be considered valid. Every single business and every Success Formula has to be modified, or it will eventually fall victim to Schumpeter's "Creative Destruction."

4

The Dark Side of Success—Defend & Extend Management

Why do business leaders claim success even when rates of return are not acceptable? Why do we have so much business failure? Why don't business leaders, knowing their practices are not producing acceptable results, change business practices? Why haven't we gotten any better at managing businesses for long-term success?

As recently as the 1980s, most U.S. college graduates thought they could work their entire careers for one business. This implicit employment contract is gone forever, a victim of adaptation to changing market conditions. Private sector union participation has declined by more than 50% since the 1980s, and lay-offs—blue collar and white collar—appear almost daily in business newspapers, no longer a recession rarity.

Actually, it's unlikely any employer will survive the 40 years most of us work. Again, using statistics from *Creative Destruction*, we can determine that a Fortune 500 company has only a 50/50 probability of remaining among the top 1000 businesses for a mere decade. The largest, and ostensibly most stable, 500 companies have a viable employer half-life of only 10 years. Survivability for 20 years has a probability of less than 40%, and 40 years survivability is only 25%. Declining job maintenance is increasingly due to shortened business longevity, rather than worker skill, capability, or desire.

Percentage of Fortune 500 Remaining in Fortune 1000

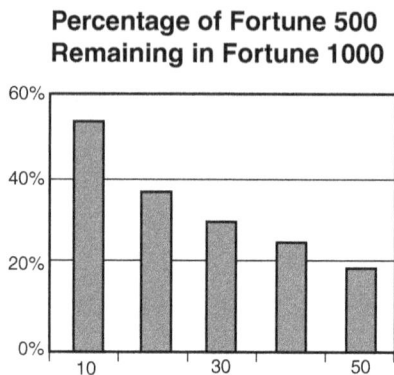

Figure 4.1 Percentage of Fortune 500 remaining in Fortune 1000

After years of few publicly traded company bankruptcies, as we entered into being an information economy in the late 1990s the number skyrocketed. From a 1980s average of only 25 bankruptcy filings per year, by the early 1990s the number jumped to more than 75—a tripling. By the end of the 1990s, filings soared to more than 250 in 2001, and early in this century the number remained well over 150—a 6-*fold increase* in only 20 years.

Chapter 11 Filings-All Public Companies 1985-2003

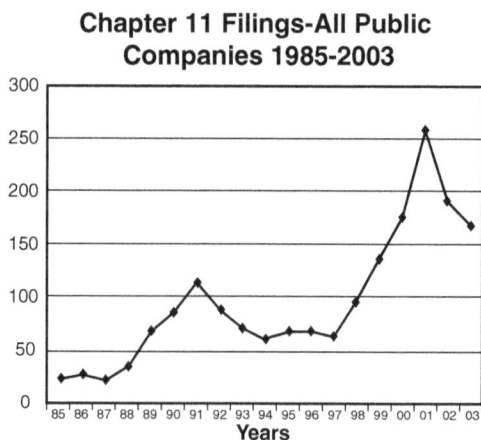

Figure 4.2 Chapter 11 filings—all public companies 1985–2003

Looking at large companies, the number of public companies with assets greater than $1 billion declaring bankruptcy from 1985 to 1987 was 6. But between 2001 and 2003, that number jumped to 105—a staggering 1,750% increase in two decades. In the years 2001 and 2002, 8 of the 10 largest bankruptcies in history occurred.

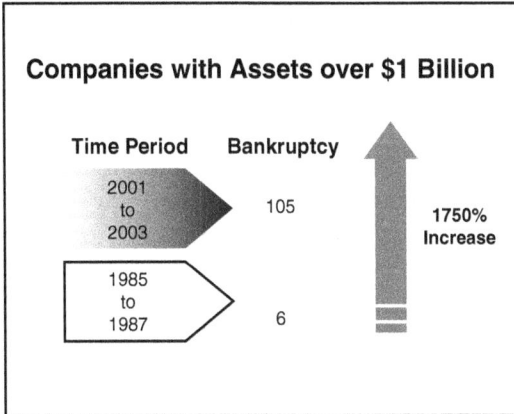

Figure 4.3 Bankruptcies of companies with assets over $1 billion

By the 1990s an MBA degree had become a staple for those seeking management advancement. It was no longer an advanced degree for liberal arts majors seeking to improve hirability. Undergraduates from all disciplines, and even professionals from accounting, law, and medicine, were applying to MBA programs. Even midcareer managers in varied functions, from IT to sales, were going back to get an MBA.

But the performance of publicly traded companies would belie an MBA's value. While some have dubbed this the era of the MBA executive, and for the first time an MBA made his way to the U.S. Presidency, it's not at all clear that leaders manage better than before. Given changes in long-term employment outlook and pensions, as well as the high rates of business failures and restructurings, there is ample evidence indicating long-term business value creation is worse than it was 40 years ago.

Given advancements bragged about in management education and all the money invested in business schools, why hasn't performance improved rather remarkably? As we added to our knowledge in medicine and engineering, there are multiple examples of how much better we are at everything from saving lives to transportation and construction. These disciplines can point to longer average lives, more people traveling more miles with fewer incidents, and taller buildings being built faster and more safely. But we cannot say that businesses today are better at achieving long-term survivability and rates of return than they were before all this investment in business education.

Could we possibly have taken the wrong road somewhere along the way?

The Focus on Defend & Extend Management

As discussed previously, most management dogma was created based on our participation in an industrial economy. It's also true that most business education is focused on defining a Success Formula and then locking it in.

One of the first business school strategy questions is: "What business are we in?" Posed as the critical question every CEO and his or her management team must answer, this question is another way of asking to define a Success Formula. "What worked? Where was the business successful with customers? What demonstrated an ability to compete effectively? Where does the business make money?" These questions help a business start writing down its Success Formula.

Recent texts focusing on "core" have continued promoting defining a Success Formula. When C.K. Prahalad and Gary Hamel in their successful book *Competing for the Future* encouraged business leaders to identify their core competencies and then figure out how to leverage them, they asked leaders to specify elements of their Success Formula. More recently Geoffrey Moore's book *Living on the Fault Line* claimed creating economic value came from identifying a business's core, creating value for that core with early customers, and then driving internal focus on that core while outsourcing everything else. These approaches helped leaders identify and Lock-in their Success Formulas.

Management education next turns to optimizing the Success Formula. Focusing and optimizing are key themes in popular business books from management gurus such as Jim Collins, Michael Hammer (*The Agenda*), and Yale's management school Dean Jeffrey Garten (*The Mind of the CEO*). Lou Gerstner, describing IBM's resurrection (*Who Says Elephants Can't Dance*), promoted focus, as did Larry Bossidy, former Chairman and CEO of Honeywell, in his book *Execution*. It is considered a waste of business resources to chase small markets when resources can be utilized in larger markets. Pruning unproductive technologies or services makes sense when customer demand is not fully understood.

Pruning occurs in the Rapids because leaders must put resources toward unmet customer needs. Resource shortages create option limitations. When they reach the Flats, most leaders believe continued pruning makes even more sense. They recognize pruning worked in the past and jump to the conclusion it will continue adding value. First they prune to Lock-in the Success Formula, and then they continue pruning to lower costs and maintain it.

Most business leaders have been trained through education and career advancement to focus and prune—to operate within the Success Formula. Managers who don't challenge Lock-ins and demonstrate consistent, if minor, improvement via pruning and cost cutting find themselves moving up the organization. Managers who challenge Lock-ins or the boundaries of the Success Formula are perceived as unprepared for corporate stewardship—even when they produce spectacular results. Perceived as taking too many risks and being unpredictable, they aren't considered good "executive team members."

The IBM team that created the Windows + Intel personal computer left shortly after their dramatic breakthrough introduction. They weren't considered "high-potential" managers. Although the PC was spectacularly successful, it was not developed within the IBM process, nor did the product easily fit into the IBM portfolio. Phenomenal success was not the road to the top for those who invented the PC, but rather a short trip out of the organization.

Deep indoctrination in finance skills, including cost and return on investment (ROI) analysis, is often seen as a prerequisite for top management. Utilizing finance to implement strategic bias, as well as fulfill the Status Quo Police role, is seen as vitally important for top leaders. It's considered "disciplined" (a popular moniker) to prune options and kill "risky" projects. "Tough" is a positive adjective describing managers who are good at pruning, including outsourcing and layoffs.

Focus, optimizing, and pruning is *Defend & Extend Management*. Defend & Extend Management is the practice of reacting to business challenges and threats through the lens of historical practices. D&E managers utilize Lock-in to seek rapid profit improvement and then attempt to solve all business problems within the historical Success Formula. All problems are viewed as external, and all solutions are expected to reside internally via improved Success Formula operation.

The Success Formula is never the cause of a problem, but is considered the solution.

For most business leaders, D&E Management is the road to personal success. D&E Management begins at hiring, where as candidates they figure out how to pledge to protect the employer's Success Formula. Candidates do not challenge the Success Formula, Lock-ins, or the Status Quo Police. D&E Management reinforcement continues throughout their careers, as D&E skills are actively encouraged and rewarded with pay increases and advancement, regardless of results.

WHY WE KEEP HAPPY HARRY

If all of a business's employees aren't "high potential," how do organizations decide which ones not on the advancement list to keep?

Happy Harry is successful because he very clearly understands the Success Formulas of the business, his functional group, work teams, and leaders. He knows the Lock-ins. And Happy Harry never challenges any of these. Although his performance is never spectacular, possibly rarely good, he is considered a "good and loyal" employee, and he swims through every performance review unscathed. Happy Harry "fits" into the organization and makes everyone feel comfortable, so he is kept and even promoted.

Happy Harry might get caught with his hand in the cookie jar, fudging expenses. Perhaps he violates a company policy. But Harry slips by with a slap on the wrist because he explains how his behavior might have been a technical violation, but it was done protecting the Success Formula. And he was trapped into it by some Lock-in.

As organizations become filled with Happy Harrys, leadership wonders why performance and results struggle to improve.

An unpleasant D&E Management side affect is rampant organizational politics. When performance measurement shifts from results to protecting the Success Formula and operating within Lock-ins, it affects everyone. Work teams and individuals (including bosses) have Success Formulas. When reviews are affected by how well a Success Formula was defended or extended, D&E managers get raises or promotions despite performance. Realizing that pay and promotion can be improved by supporting the Success Formulas and working within Lock-in, employees will spend less attention on results. Quickly the road up the hierarchy and pay grades becomes politicized as personal success comes from Defend & Extend machinations.

We have trained and rewarded a legion of managers in D&E Management. Is it any wonder this practice has become today's primary management method?

The Road to D&E Management Acceptance

All businesses find Lock-in advantageous for growth. But why do businesses continue utilizing old Lock-ins when growth slows and D&E Management no longer produces desired results?

THE ARMADILLO SYNDROME

Armadillos have a very tough shell that provides their primary defense. When under attack the Armadillo allows predators to batter his hard exterior to no avail. Later the Armadillo rises and continues his journey.

This works great until the Armadillo is crossing a west Texas road in the dark. Seeing an automobile charging toward it at 70 miles per hour, the Armadillo relies on Lock-in and sits down in the roadway. Only he's destroyed by the unsuspecting car because it's unable to avoid the lonely Armadillo in the dark at high speed.

What appeared to the Armadillo as a good Success Formula became life-threatening. The Armadillo's threat response was based on how well it previously worked, not how well it would work given the immediate threat. To an observer the Armadillo should have scurried off the highway. But the observer is not following Defend & Extend Management.

Well-meaning leaders frequently seek D&E Management as the preferred way to manage in all circumstances. After a professional lifetime educated in D&E Management principles, it's easy for any manager to become so comfortable with Lock-in, and preserving it, that D&E becomes very desirable—no matter its effectiveness. Although

Lock-in is beneficial only in the Rapids, most managers apply Success Formula Lock-in to improve performance in all lifecycle stages.

After observing how well Lock-in aids early growth, many managers Lock-in on Lock-in! They desire conformity and automation, assuming both always produce better results. So Lock-in is considered good, *all the time*. Defending and extending Lock-in becomes the paramount task. Looking at an early win, they quickly Lock-in and start eliminating other options. They consider limiting options "good management" even when new solutions may be necessary to improve results.

Pruning can go wild. The D&E manager perceives that long-term success comes from rampant short-term pruning—every single quarter. "Take care of the short term, and the long term will take care of itself" is his point of view. Believing Lock-in will solve all problems, these managers start pruning everything they can, convinced there is no end to the benefits of pruning. Never mind that taken to its limit, eventually the business would be pruned down to one customer, one product, and one employee!

For too many managers, the belief in D&E Management and the power of Lock-in is so powerful that they cannot wait to use it. While still in the Wellspring, before moving into the Rapids, they define their Success Formula—and identify Lock-in. They don't allow the marketplace to define Lock-in during the Rapids; instead they select it. They document this in their business plans and promise to use the best skills of D&E Management to exert discipline and "drive" success.

Although Success Formulas and Lock-in are very beneficial tools in the Rapids, applied in the Wellspring they are primary sources of early business failure. The allure of D&E Management, frequently prompted by investor requests to define how the entrepreneur will apply D&E, entices too many leaders to Lock-in too early and kill a great idea before the marketplace can shape it into a viable high-growth business.

Consider the entrepreneur who identifies a high-traffic restaurant location in a rehabilitated section of a major city. Realizing that gentrification is bringing in new wealth, he commits to a lease. Reading that vegetarian food popularity is growing exponentially, especially among younger people, and being a vegetarian himself, he writes a business plan for a vegetarian restaurant and raises funds.

After opening the restaurant, however, he struggles. There aren't enough patrons. He stands out front and offers free samples to passers-by as an enticement to come in and dine. He adds new menu items, lowers lunch pricing, and develops a low-price entrée selection for evenings, obtains a liquor license and adds a full bar, buys radio advertising, and places direct-mail ads to local residents. But despite these excellent business practices, the restaurant fails.

While accepted as Best Practices for a start-up, unfortunately these were D&E actions undertaken to save a flawed Success Formula. The entrepreneur will probably tell investors failure was due to bad luck or bad timing. Actually, his error was Locking-in on a cuisine type that wasn't popular enough for that location. Rather than maximize the location's value by changing the Success Formula (his plan), the entrepreneur continued promoting his restaurant until it failed. Shortly after closing the doors for good, a barbecue restaurant opened in the same location and flourished despite limited marketing and no advertising.

Where D&E Management really draws press attention is when a high-growth business hits the Flats. After a string of successful results, leadership suddenly has to deal with insufficient growth. A popular reaction, especially for publicly traded companies, is to replace the original, entrepreneurial management team with "professional management." Not understanding that Lock-in has led them into a dead-end tributary, the Board of Directors looks for a new leader who will address the poor results, not necessarily the market challenges which led to the results shortfall.

Executive recruiters and the Board look for someone who will immediately make changes to "re-right the ship" and get back on the profit growth curve. Leadership reacts to weak results, rather than the market challenge. They want someone who will immediately improve the results. And the fastest way to do that is D&E Management. There is no faster way to improve profits than by stopping something, and D&E managers with their great skills at pruning are excellent at stopping things. D&E managers quickly dismiss long-term projects and cut advertising, marketing, as well as product development. D&E managers rapidly outsource to vendors, promising cost reductions. Recruiters and hiring personnel seek someone who will prune fast to regain previous results *without* changing the Success Formula.

There are other reasons we accept D&E Management. Most managers and work teams enjoy Lock-in. When a D&E manager shows up, options are limited, and decisions happen faster. Efficiency goes up. Although arguments may ensue as to whether the option selected was a good one, undeniably productivity improves. For those remaining, the environment is less complex. It's easy to blame the decision maker for problems, while putting their destiny in someone else's hands. All managers have to do is *execute*, and they can absolve themselves of responsibility for results.

Our brains' wiring is attracted to predictability. We fear ambiguity, some of us more than others. For most of us, fearing the unknown is far greater than fearing failure. Living with an uncertain outcome created by an uncertain set of conditions is more stressful than a known environment offering a limited chance of success. Although we would rather not admit it, most of us would prefer to know what we are going to do and know it's likely not to meet our goals than jump into an alternative where we have no guidelines and no idea of the outcome. We love D&E managers who create a "vision" and provide clear operating principles.

AMBIGUITY AVOIDANCE

Daniel Ellsberg is best known as the Rand Corporation analyst who released *The Pentagon Papers* in 1971, divulging the U.S. military's internal account of the Vietnam War. But prior to this he was an economist famous for the Ellsburg Paradox that described *ambiguity avoidance*.

Imagine you are shown two urns. You are told each has 100 balls inside. The first has 50 red balls and 50 black balls. The second has red and black balls, but you don't know the ratio. You will receive $1 if you pull out a black ball. Which urn are you likely to select? Because the second urn might have 100 black balls, or 100 red, or any mix, mathematically you should be indifferent. But, the vast majority of people will select the first urn with the 50/50 distribution.

Next you are told that if you select a black ball from the first urn you will receive $.90. But if you select a black ball from the second urn you will receive $1.00. Mathematically, you should select the second urn because you don't know the distribution, and the second urn pays better. But most people will select the first urn, with the known 50/50 distribution. They make a less good choice.

In fact, even when told the first urn has 49 black balls and 51 red ones, most people will still select the first urn. Under almost all scenarios, people will select the urn with the known distribution of balls over the ambiguous urn.

After many revisits of this experiment, ambiguity aversion is largely attributed by scholars to accountability pressure. Concerned that they may later have to explain their selections, people select the urn about which they know the most—not because it offers the best odds of success but merely because it is better explained.

Despite our best efforts, we do not operate fully at a conscious level. Assumptions affect how we interpret our world and how we react. *Confirmation bias* causes us to accept stimuli that reinforce our Success Formula while overlooking input that might counter our assumptions. The results are mental blind spots and denial in the face of evidence that would recommend an alternative approach. Confirmation bias allows us to pick out facts that reinforce our willingness to defend and extend, even when a sea of conflicting data surrounds us.

D&E Management is based on Newtonian thinking. Newton proved *with all other things remaining constant*, we can predict how an apple will fall from a tree. We tend to ignore that *all other things don't remain constant* very often. Because they are moving, we need a theory of relativity to explain behavior compared to other moving things. Nowhere is this more true than in business. Almost nothing remains constant in business—especially since the advent of the information economy.

The Myth of Perpetuity was built on expectations of stable markets, with stable competition. All other things being the same, the largest competitor should be able to control price and competition. But we now know that as fast as a manager can make a decision, something can change in the environment. Things don't remain constant. Trying to defend and extend past decisions when the assumptions, practices, and relative differences between the players are in perpetual motion becomes a never-ending game of "cat and mouse." In a relative world, applying static, Newtonian solutions leads to falling performance.

D&E Management also appeals to leaders' desire to control variables. When so many pieces are moving, it is tempting for a leader to decide he or she will hold constant the internal pieces. By limiting options, through aggressive pursuit of Lock-in, there are far fewer variables in play. This leads to unfounded comfort that somehow things will work out for the better. Although the market may swirl in an entirely new direction, the D&E manager feels confident he is in control of the ship. It may sink, but it is under control.

Functional leaders prefer the predictability of D&E Management to the complexity of managing to market expectations. It is far easier for an IT manager to remain dedicated to his or her systems, limit the use of other systems, and then manage toward up-time and accessibility of that system than attempt to judge the value of IT by what it contributes to the business revenue or its bottom line. HR managers feel much more comfortable with tightly designed job descriptions, rigid compensation structures, fixed benefit plans, and rigid employee rules that define behavior than developing more loosely organized roles, work teams, compensation plans, and reporting structures. Although competitors as well as workers in today's economy often find greater productivity in a less structured environment, it is much easier to develop clear lines of behavior and codes of conduct that can be more easily enforced. Managers would often rather be held to an historical role, defined by Lock-in, than the performance of that role in meeting or exceeding competitive requirements.

Investors, employees, bondholders, vendors, and even customers look to investment analysts for business reviews. Analysts clearly prefer that leaders describe their businesses simply, supporting analysts' development of computer forecasting models. Using elaborate models full of voluminous historical data hides the obvious fact that small changes in assumptions can make the largest computerized forecasting worksheet worthless. Nonetheless, management teams that can help analysts build extensive worksheets for predicting future performance utilizing relatively few assumptions are given higher marks.

Furthermore, investment analysts are far more interested in predicting three-month performance than one- or two-year performance. And D&E tactics are very predictable—especially short-term. An immediate headcount reduction, a product line sale, or abandoning an advertising campaign can be run through a spreadsheet for impact fast and with high accuracy. Other tactics, like entering a new business, are far less accurately forecasted and are thus given less favorable analyst review. More unknown variables and longer timelines reduce forecast accuracy—and it is accuracy analysts want. When an analyst's forecasts turn out accurate, he or she is perceived to be good, regardless the forecast. Thus, D&E managers who provide predictability and consistency are liked much more than managers who are more experimental—regardless of results.

Remember, almost all academic studies have shown that it is a rare investment analyst who can beat a monkey throwing darts at numbers on a wall when predicting equity price movements. All that information may remove ambiguity, but it has not demonstrated improved investment performance.

The Outcome of D&E Management

Because D&E Management reinforces conformance to Lock-in, businesses breed innovation-killers. The financial person who is imbued with Status Quo Police authority will consistently talk about the risks of a new idea and the more assured returns promised from traditional investments. Who is not familiar with hearing, "That's a great idea, but you'll never get it approved by finance" (or HR, or legal, or product development, and so on)? Being inwardly focused makes it easier and faster to reinforce the Success Formula by cost cutting and doing more of the same than looking externally for opportunities and new ideas. Prolonged pruning of R&D, product development, and marketing eventually removes the capacity for innovation. And as lower sales lead to fewer salespeople, it's not long before no one's left discussing innovation.

Once started, cutting those who promote innovation becomes self-reinforcing. Immediate profit improvement is so direct and predictable that it's like crack cocaine. The more a business reduces its R&D staff, the fewer projects are created for investment. The more advertising people are pruned, the fewer advertising programs are recommended. Short-term benefits of pruning reinforce themselves, leading to rampant—even draconian—pruning as the Success Formula is less challenged.

After Addressograph Multigraph (AM) found itself in bankruptcy, the Board predictably changed management. Out went the people in charge when AM hit the Flats. In came new managers focused on cost reductions and efficiency improvement. Gone were the print-focused executives, replaced by MBAs with experience improving P&Ls. Within months, the P&L showed higher profits. It took years for revenue declines to eventually kill the company.

At AM, new projects were slashed, enhancing cash flow. R&D was shuttered as new executives pronounced printing technology "mature" and therefore not worthy of additional development. Because AM had the largest market share and was the best known brand, advertising was no longer considered necessary and was eliminated. A careful analysis revealed that the top 20% of customers yielded 80% of company revenue, so the sales force was consolidated (a euphemism for slashed by 50%) to focus on those customers, leaving the bottom 50% of customers with no support. Analyzing top customers revealed they purchased a select group of products, so lower volume products were eliminated, leading to layoffs in sourcing, manufacturing, and marketing. These fast D&E actions yielded an immediate improvement in profits and cash flow and a significant reduction in future opportunities for AM.

D&E Management leads exclusively to sustaining investments, as described by Clayton Christensen in *The Innovator's Dilemma*. Nothing disruptive is even considered, given that all activity is focused on sustaining the old Success Formula. Lock-ins are not challenged because that would impede rapid cost improvement. This is one reason private equity investments yield such a rapid improvement in cash flow. New owners simply turn back the investment spigot for anything that isn't sustaining. These new owners are interested in maximizing cash flow, not disrupting a market to improve competitive position.

Sears was once America's largest retailer and also its most innovative. Sears pioneered the catalog mail-order industry. It pioneered one-stop financial services through its credit card, banking, and insurance units. And it was a leader in the American shopping mall movement, understanding that it could share real estate and marketing costs by having stores in malls rather than as free-standing units. But in the 1970s Sears Locked-in on its general merchandise mall stores, and over a span of 20 years lost its pre-eminent retail position to discounters such as Wal-Mart and Target.

Ed Lampert acquired Sears after buying the bankrupt remnants of KMart. But his post-acquisition plan was not to re-energize Sears into a highly competitive retailer. Instead, he attempted to milk the business of cash. Since the acquisitions, KMart and Sears have closed stores, laid off workers, consolidated into fewer markets, and sold real estate. Under Mr. Lampert Sears has discontinued several offerings, such as Sears Hardware Stores. Although total sales have declined overall, as have sales per store, Sears has increased cash flow. As a devoted D&E leader, Mr. Lampert has claimed victory. But Sears' future as a general merchandise retailer is easy to predict. Under new management, the Sears retail chain has plunged further toward the Whirlpool.

D&E MANAGEMENT KEEPS BUSINESSES FROM SEEING NEW OPPORTUNITIES

- Tupperware never moved its product into retail stores. Although retail sales of plastic housewares soared, Tupperware steadfastly refused to amend its Success Formula. By defending and extending the home-party Lock-in, Tupperware avoided investing in inventory, new salespeople, and advertising that the retail channel would have required. The company avoided long-term revenue growth as well.

- Pizza Hut completely missed the market for home-delivered Pizza. Focused on defending and extending the "red roof" sit-down units, management pushed carry-out instead. It also pushed delivery customers to Domino's.

- Krispy Kreme realized it was saturating the market for doughnuts, so it expanded into China. Rather than adding other products to expand the sales per customer and sales outside morning hours, management defended the Success Formula and extended it to a foreign market. These actions extended Krispy Kreme into bankruptcy.

Management sees the impact of market challenges. Leaders know that technology, new products, and substitutes are making inroads into their markets. But for D&E managers, these facts make little difference. Their objective is to defend and extend the Success Formula. That is their dogma and their only plan to improve the business. Through the lens of D&E Management, challenges are threats to the Success Formula, not potential opportunities for renewal.

D&E Management makes a business a much easier target for competitors. Once the Success Formula is Locked-in, and management is clearly defending and extending that Success Formula, competitors can easily predict what the business will do. In a dynamic market, no target is more vulnerable than the one standing still. And D&E

managers cause their businesses to be sitting ducks for other, particularly new, competitors.

Let's look at Southwest Airlines' success. Major airlines entered the deregulated market asset-rich, well-funded, having deep experience, and holding gates in all major cities. But Southwest benefited enormously from knowing exactly how its primary competitor, American Airlines, would behave. And as Southwest expanded into each new market, it knew how each competitor—United, Delta, or Northwest—would behave. The "major" airlines were all so thoroughly committed to defending and extending their Success Formulas that Southwest had no problem cherry-picking the best routes and building a successful business right under their noses.

It wasn't long before Southwest was the most profitable airline in the industry. But D&E managers at larger airlines were so committed to their Success Formulas that they refused to follow Southwest's lead. As each major airline struggled with profitability, and some failed outright whereas others sought bankruptcy protection or brushed perilously close, Southwest continued quarter after quarter expanding routes and increasing both revenue and profits. Southwest did many things right, but it also benefited because it could so accurately predict the behavior of its largely unprofitable D&E competitors.

Similarly, digital camera pioneers never had any real concerns about Kodak. Although Kodak developed considerable digital camera technology, the D&E managers at Kodak made it obvious the company was more worried about cannibalizing film sales than developing the digital market. When Kodak launched fast processing centers, film processing kiosks, and one-time use cameras in its effort to defend and extend film sales, the company made it easier for early digital entrants, Sony and Hewlett Packard, to stake out a beachhead. Kodak's D&E practices telegraphed their behavior and made Kodak easy prey for competitors dedicated to unseating Kodak from its dominant position in amateur photography.

The Lock-in Cycle

D&E managers get trapped in a vicious cycle. Initially, they benefit from Lock-in as a tool for improving growth. But eventually a problem develops. This might be the loss of a big customer or the quick obsolescence of a key product or a price war in a high-volume product line—something causing a significant, deleterious change in performance. When this happens, D&E managers switch from focusing outward to focusing inward. When problems develop, D&E managers start searching for ways to operate the Success Formula better, faster, or cheaper in hopes of improving results.

Performance declines are created by *market challenges*. Something changes in the marketplace that creates an internal problem. Perhaps a new competitor enters the market with a superior technology. Or a competitor finds a way to dramatically lower costs—and passes on some of that cost savings to customers with lower pricing. Or maybe a substitute product comes to market, making existing products less valuable. These are market challenges. But D&E managers overlook these challenges, often seeing them as beyond their control. Instead, they focus on the *problem*—the sales, margin, or profit shortfall. All energies are put toward fixing the *problem*.

Defend & Extend Management first *denies* there is a problem. Popular management denials include "We have been subjected to a one-time event..." or "Although we've seen a short-term price change, we are convinced customers will soon recognize the value in our product and return..." or "Recent cost increases are expected to abate shortly..." or "We expect economic downturns that have affected our market will reverse." All these statements mean that "We believe our Success Formula is still operating effectively, and we expect it will return historical results soon."

Next D&E Management attacks someone for creating the problem. Popular comments from D&E managers include "There was a problem in our supply chain, and we have replaced the Vice-President of Operations..." or "Due to unexpected price changes implemented by our Vice-President of Sales, who has been replaced..." or "Accounting irregularities found under the auspices of our recently replaced CFO..." or "Due to supply shortfalls from vendors under the guidance of our previous Procurement Director..." These phrases mean "Our Success Formula is still in great shape, only it was mismanaged by someone, and we have replaced that person. So you can expect historical results to return shortly."

Third, D&E managers address a problem by *justifying* performance in the face of bad results. In this case management says: "Although our results did not meet expectations, there has not been time for future plans to begin..." or "It was impossible for management to have foreseen these unanticipated, dramatic changes..." or "Everyone in our industry was surprised by..." These comments mean "Our Success Formula does not need to change because whatever caused the bad results really wasn't our fault. You can't hold us accountable for these recent shortfalls because we were operating the Success Formula correctly."

And fourth, D&E Management addresses a problem by *stalling*. For example, comments might sound like "Sales are down due to a recent rise in interest rates, and when rates abate we can expect a performance recovery..." or "Management expected that recent market changes would not occur until next quarter, and new products in the pipeline will address these market shifts..." or "Our pending reorganization will address recent performance changes..." Phrases that mean, "If you just wait, I'm sure the Success Formula will once again produce old results."

Problem "fixes" are expected to come from inside the organization— and they come in four flavors: *More, Better, Faster,* and *Cheaper,* the four most deadly words an employee or investor can hear from a D&E manager. No matter the problem, D&E Management is sure they can fix problems if they

- Do *more* of what they had been doing, such as continue a plant or sales consolidation project, or continue longer or deeper with a discounting program—most likely already having only marginal success.

- By doing what they've done *better,* they hope to eliminate problems. This could include implementing a Total Quality Management (TQM), Six Sigma, or Continuous Improvement quality program—or implementing either a Best Practices or Scorecard initiative.

- Taking actions *faster* is often seen as an effective problem response. Accelerating a cost-cutting or discounting program is typical. Speeding into the current quarter a product line reduction that was intended to be implemented across a year might be tried. Or a new supply chain or IT project is announced that is supposed to speed results obtainment.

- By far the favorite problem fix is finding a way to be *cheaper.* Without making any changes to the Success Formula, nor addressing a change to the Lock-ins, decisions are made to cut costs. Perhaps lower-cost parts are substituted, or new, low-cost vendors are procured (often from offshore). Or headcount is cut, leaving employees to get more work done. "Belt tightening" is seen as an effective answer for the problem.

These approaches are almost always ineffective at providing long-term solutions. Benefits are short term as competitors keep hammering away and market changes keep eroding the old Success Formula's value.

No matter how much D&E managers want to cut costs, over time costs always go up. True cost-based strategies do not rely on moving further down a known cost curve but, in fact, rely on creating an entirely new, lower-cost curve. New competitors that create price problems aren't simply more effective at doing what the business does. They deliver results entirely differently and thus have an entirely different cost curve. Short-term cost-cutting actions can make a Success Formula appear better for only the shortest time because soon enough costs will go up. Cost-reduction programs are not an effective tool to deal with competitive intrusion—they merely avoid addressing competitive challenges for a brief time.

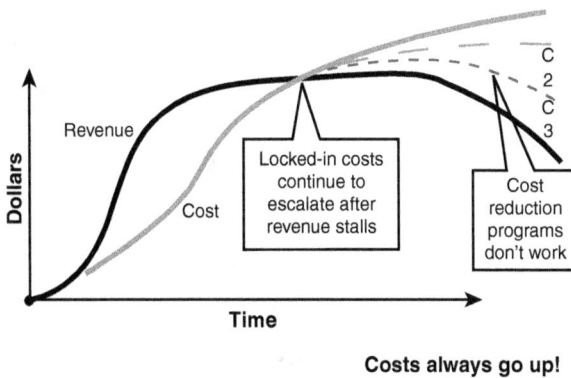

Costs always go up!

Figure 4.4 Costs always go up!

It is only rising revenues that can address a cost problem—or else finding an entirely new cost curve!

With each of these D&E responses there is usually a short-term benefit. Problems are abated for a quarter—maybe two. The improvement may be small, may be delayed, and may be overshadowed by other problems, but D&E managers will apply confirmation bias as they talk about improvements. The mere size and pain of their actions is seen as indicating success. The medicine tasted bad, so it must work, right? Market challenges are ignored or given lip service as focus remains on defending and extending both the Success Formula and how it is Locked-in.

TYPICAL D&E REACTIONS TO SERIOUS PROBLEMS

- Implement a "Back to Basics" program
- Merge or acquire a competitor
- Hire a "heroic" leader who will refocus and save the company
- Restate earnings
- Announce a reorganization that requires taking a huge one-time charge to earnings
- Install a new ERP system to improve execution
- Outsource major functions in a cost-cutting announcement
- Announce an across-the-board headcount reduction
- Sell off high-growth but small product lines
- Close down small subsidiaries or spin them off to management
- Obsess about execution while announcing a new quality program
- Announce a move to sell more in an offshore market—usually China
- Open an offshore facility in India or China and announce work will be transferred
- Announce new product variations are being rapidly released to market, while cutting back on total product lines
- Implement a "customer circle" focused on the largest customers, while raising prices to smaller customers

Unfortunately, these actions are mere stop-gap improvements to a challenged Success Formula. They are disturbances to the way things were done, but they do not affect the actual Success Formula itself. They will not, in fact *cannot*, have lasting competitive impact because they do not address the market challenges that created the problem. D&E actions merely create the illusion of addressing challenges while misallocating resources at a critical time and result in a sense of complacency on the part of management as to the business' potential downfall.

WHACKING THE CHICKEN COOP

In an agrarian economy, most families lived on farms, and almost all had laying hens. Egg production would occasionally decline, usually due to weather changes. The farmer would often react by using a stick to whack the chicken coop. Thinking the chickens were becoming lazy, the farmer expected a good, threatening whack would get them energized to lay again.

But whacking the chicken coop simply led to a lot of upset chickens. Short term, production rates declined further. Farmers reacted by slaughtering poorer-laying hens and eating them. Eventually the weather would change, and the chickens would return to earlier production rates. The farmer would declare victory, claiming his coop whacking got the chickens over their poor-laying ways. Although total egg production declined due to fewer chickens, he would point out that his cost of chicken feed declined as well—so all was good.

D&E downsizings are whacks at the business chicken coop. Problems are created by external events. They are not altered by layoffs or outsourcing. Nonetheless, D&E managers will claim costs declined by X%—so declare victory! Never mind that productivity is the same, or lower, and competitive viability has been reduced. Management may assert that profit margin percentages are up, even though revenue is down, so victory is claimed.

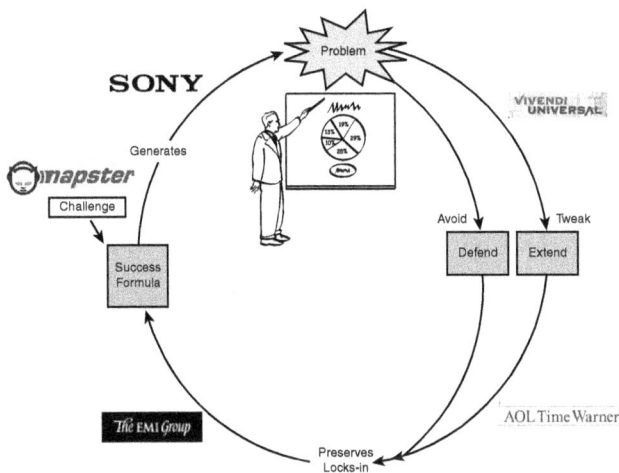

Figure 4.5 The music industry problem

Music companies entered the 1990s with decades of growth under their belts. They would place several musicians on long-term recording contracts. They produced an album for each and charged all costs to the musician's account. The recording company released CDs, and if the CD made money, the producers held the musicians to their contract to make more CDs—at the cost previously agreed to when the musician was unknown. It only took one in ten good-selling CDs to have success, and if the recording company found one Michael Jackson, Madonna, or George Strait every few years, they could exceed expectations.

But in the mid-1990s MP3 technology became available. This allowed enterprising listeners to digitize music from CDs and not only listen to it on their computers, but send the songs to anyone who had an Internet connection. Suddenly, CD sales weren't growing like they had, and profits weren't growing either. MP3 technology was a significant technology challenge to the music industry's Success Formula and all its participants.

Did the competitors react to this challenge by adopting MP3 and figuring out how to maximize growth? Hardly.

At first recording companies blamed musicians for making bad music. Poor sales were attributed to poor musical artists. Second, large companies tried buying up smaller companies, hoping that consolidation would somehow reduce competition. Then they identified top web sites used for music transfers, such as Napster, and sued them into oblivion for copyright infringement. They capped this off by suing customers ("downloaders") who used these sites.

Recording companies also blamed retailers for doing a terrible job of marketing CDs. They told analysts their growth problem was short term—revenue would jump soon as better musicians came along and as soon as the courts began enforcing copyright laws. They defended their product by reassuring analysts and distributors that CDs provided a higher quality music experience and thus would reestablish itself as the primary music distribution source over MP3s. And they began cutting prices on CDs to promote volume. All they asked for was more time so growth could return.

All through this period the market for recorded music did not decline. Consumption of music skyrocketed as digital files made recordings cheaper and easier to access—not to mention the flexibility of acquiring songs individually rather than purchasing an entire album collection via CD.

Interestingly, Sony had access to both MP3 technology and substantial music content. Sony was not only a leader in personal electronics, with ample access to electronic distributors, but it had millions of songs in its archive. Rather than aggressively promote the shift to digital music, Sony released a proprietary digital standard, attempting to control digital sales while defending CD sales. Sony, all by itself, could have led the transition to digital music and been the foremost market leader. But fear of CD cannibalization, along with hopes of recapturing past CD profits, kept Sony working hard, along with competitors, to defend and extend CD sales.

Meanwhile, Apple Computer was struggling to halt its market share decline in PCs. Amidst its computer sales woes, Apple's leadership recognized the technology transition happening in recorded music and launched both the iPod and iTunes. From a position of noncompetitor, Apple rapidly rose to the leadership position in digital music sales and quickly captured the profit lead among music companies—without signing a single musician!

The market for retail music did not decline. But the Defend & Extend Management practices of all the major recording industry players caused them to be late participating in this market shift. And each saw revenue falter as profits dropped dramatically.

Most prominent market challenges build up over time. MP3 technology existed for more than a decade before it made a difference to music companies. Although there were many observations of the challenge, inwardly focused D&E recording managers did not recognize these challenges until they created a serious problem. For them, reinforcing the Success Formula was so culturally powerful that challenges were not recognized. Even when "market sensing" systems brought new competitors to the attention of D&E managers, these pioneers were seen as pests to overcome rather than a threat to business viability—or a potential growth enhancement.

The New Definition of Business Success

For D&E managers, success really isn't about achieving results. Success becomes defending the Success Formula from market attacks. The goal becomes operating within Lock-ins and behaving predictably regardless of the results. D&E managers stop reacting to the market and instead manage a Success Formula and maintain Lock-in.

It is often more threatening and considered more of a failure to change the Success Formula than to miss results. Executives will say, "If that's what we have to do to succeed, someone else will have to do it," admitting the importance of Success Formulas to behavior and decisions. Never forget that Success Formulas exist not only at the company level, but also within individuals. For executives, Success Formula alignment between their personal one and the business' is very high. Many executives have their personal identities, as well as the identity of their organizations, tied to the Success Formula.

Within the Success Formula pyramid the economy, industry, company, business unit, functional unit, and individual Success Formulas operate in nested integration. Reacting to challenges is not as simple as changing the company Success Formula. Effective response requires changing all the Success Formulas inherited at and above the level of the challenge. If the principle change occurred in the economy, all Success Formulas have to change. Companies that are industry leaders may be forced to change the industry Success Formula in order to achieve desired rates of return. It is a daunting task to effectively address a market challenge across all the Success Formulas of the pyramid, even when looking merely at those above the company level, much less those of even greater magnitude.

Computer Sciences Corporation (CSC) has been a successful multi-billion dollar services firm. An early leader in IT services, the company had a very successful commercial IT consulting business with more than $1 billion in reported revenue in 2000. This business was built over many years by leaders steeped in the Success Formula they Locked-in during the rapid IT services growth in the 1980s and 1990s. This Success Formula included a proprietary development approach, as well as local offices that employed consultants to service local clients.

By 2002, the market for commercial IT services had changed dramatically. Between 2000 and 2002, all large American IT consulting competitors hit growth stalls, and all shifted from the Rapids to the Flats. Offshore vendors entered the market, abandoning proprietary development approaches in favor of new standards developed at Carnegie Mellon University (the CMM standards). These newly emerging suppliers offered services at dramatically lower prices, promising extremely highly educated technologists working offshore overnight and delivering results across the global Internet. These upstarts made dramatic inroads into most large corporations as they promised delivery while initially cutting market prices as much as 90%.

But CSC's commercial consulting business leaders continued to defend the business's traditional Success Formula. Management even extended it by reopening closed U.S. offices previously deemed uneconomic and maintaining staff at local sites in an effort to promote client-site consultants—even though these decisions created dramatically higher costs and frequently lower productivity. Every year commercial business unit leaders reaffirmed their commitment to the Success Formula, as traditional revenue declined more than 70% in less than a decade. Most employees were laid off or left to work in other businesses—including offshore competitors building revenue from their customers previously served by CSC.

Information Transparency Affects Everyone

One of the biggest operational impacts of the information economy is information transparency. Nearly all business information is now available immediately to practically anyone. Before networks and computers made instantaneous information access normal, business leaders could expect decisions would have several weeks, months, or even years to create value. But today everything a business does is known by customers, competitors, and vendors almost instantaneously. Competitors have so much information on each other that attempts by businesses to defend and extend are often thwarted before the defensive tactics can be undertaken! Information transparency makes D&E Management not only problematic, but obsolete.

D&E Management worked in the industrial economy. The slow speed, compared to today, of competitive reaction created relative stability. But with competitors today ready and able to react within minutes of a decision, D&E managers have no chance of taking action without immediate competitive reaction. As competition has become more dynamic and the nature of competition has shifted from assets to information, D&E Management has become too competitively obvious to produce growth or high returns.

Today's newspaper industry is drifting into obsolescence. After a century of continuous ad revenue growth, in the last few years web sites have grabbed enough ad dollars to make a significant dent in sales. Simultaneously, newspaper subscribers are canceling delivery as news is faster and more instantaneous online. especially those subscribers under age 40.

Despite this market shift, newspapers have not redefined their Success Formulas. In cutting costs and reorganizing operations, they have been unable to fend off onslaught by new competitors, led by Google, as they keep applying D&E techniques. Every year newspapers see revenue and profits decline further. Instead of defining their success based upon total news readership (regardless of media) and total market ad revenue (including the web), they use traditional measures such as local subscriptions and local newspaper ad sales to gauge competitiveness. Rather than shifting spending to compete against online news sites, they continue spending on projects intended to maintain departing subscribers and advertisers. Newspaper D&E managers claim success, looking at out-of-date metrics, in the face of rapidly declining returns as they become the newest "buggy whip" business.

Flying to the moon required a new engineering approach, one that embraced *dynamism* (using Einstein's view of physics) over *statism* (Newton's views of physics). In today's highly dynamic and interconnected business markets, we need a new approach to business management that can replace Defend & Extend.

PART II

Reinventing Success

The Phoenix Principle for Managing in an Uncertain World

If Defend & Extend Management doesn't produce long-term above average results, what does? What is The Phoenix Principle, and how is it applied to achieve improved or even breakthrough results?

There Is a Better Approach to Management

The Defend & Extend Management story might seem all too familiar—as if it's not new. As mentioned at the beginning of this book, for over 70 years, economists and the occasional management guru have discussed the poor results of individual businesses. Yet even though this story appears familiar, very few managers have changed their behavior even when they have recognized the problem.

It's like middle-age weight gain suffered by so many managers. Each passing year, especially over age 40, the struggle to avoid gaining weight becomes more difficult. Some people resort to diet supplements, hoping technology will grant a solution. Others seek a physician's help, often receiving the diagnosis, "You eat too much and don't exercise enough." Just knowing the cause does not solve the problem, as year after year the struggle goes on, and waistlines continue expanding.

Achieving goals requires we reinvent "success." Old definitions are mired in Defend & Extend Management objectives, and D&E "success" revolves around short-term tactics intended to support and reinforce the Success Formula. Daily, weekly, monthly, and quarterly D&E metrics are not tied to results, but instead to how well management maintains

Lock-in to the old Success Formula. When D&E efforts don't produce desired results, managers do not brand their organizations, work teams, or themselves as failures. Rather D&E managers declare ongoing success, telling investors and employees they should lower expectations. D&E Management, by continuing past behaviors, considers itself successful, even if it doesn't achieve a single goal!

At its core Defend & Extend Management overlooks the reality that organizations compete in dynamic markets. Defend & Extend produces Success Formula enhancement *only as long as the environment does not change.* D&E relies on static markets. But we know markets and competitors are not static. Stuff happens.

Competitive "game changers" were not envisioned by old management theories which promoted market consolidation and focused organizations. The goal of early management theory was reaching market maturity where the few remaining competitors could leverage "scale" in an oligopolistic and competitively friendly "follow-the-leader" stand-off. Early management theory developers believed businesses flourished in mature markets, throwing off cash for investors. Upon reaching maturity a business would become what the Boston Consulting Group called a "Cash Cow," requiring little or no investment while producing cash for dividends or new markets.

We now know that markets and competition are very dynamic. Mature markets produce multiple competitors that drive down returns. Although we like to think mature organizations are less risky investments and employers, they are not. We know that the shift from an industrial to an information economy has dramatically changed competition. Global access to resources, rapid adoption of new technology, and commoditized Internet access leveraging distribution channels allows new entrants with different strategies and cost models to enter markets regardless of where they are in the lifecycle.

To be successful businesses need to remain in the Rapids. It's no fun to be in the Flats, Swamp, or Whirlpool. Above-average returns will not be earned there. In dynamic markets it is critical to constantly grow. It's not possible to erect entry barriers that will protect returns when a business hits the Flats. Even patents are of only marginal value in low-growth businesses. The only way to make enough money to reinvest is to grow.

Success Today Is About Keeping a Success Formula Evergreen–Rather Than Defending & Extending It

The new definition of "success" is constantly adapting to challenges—no matter their source. Success requires the ability to redefine Success Formulas to stay competitive and earn good returns. Successful managers must modify their businesses, rather than just maintaining Lock-in. Success requires adaptability to market dynamism and changing competitors.

All Success Formulas become obsolete, and all Lock-ins eventually no longer serve their original purpose. Managing a Success Formula is a critical skill. Managers must change their "focus" from defending and extending the past to adapting to environmental and competitive changes. Long-term success requires organizational competency to manage the Success Formula.

The route to effective Success Formula management lies in Disrupting Lock-ins. Disruptions create opportunities for White Space—a place in which businesses can develop new Success Formulas toward which leaders can migrate their organizations. Those companies that demonstrate long-term superior performance and avoid Schumpeter's grip are those that become good at Disruptions and White Space management. These companies stay clear of the Whirlpool, and largely the Swamp, by intentionally throwing themselves back into the Rapids. They don't just desire to be in the Rapids but design their organizations to push them that direction as they near the Flats. As a result, they avoid the Reinvention Gap altogether.

Disrupting Lock-ins and utilizing White Space is The Phoenix Principle. The Phoenix Principle, like the mythic bird from which it is named, is not just about rebirth. The phoenix does not achieve merely a one-time "turnaround" that may have a short two to five year duration. Rather, the phoenix is capable of unceasing rebirth. Those that follow The Phoenix Principle can achieve an evergreen business model. And these organizations maintain a culture of vitality and success, making them great places to work as well as invest or partner with as a customer or vendor.

THE PHOENIX

"A mythical bird that never dies, the phoenix flies far ahead to the front, always scanning the landscape and distant space. It has the capacity for vision, for collecting sensory information about our environment and the events unfolding within it. The phoenix, with its great beauty, creates intense excitement and deathless inspiration."

—*The Feng Shui Handbook*, feng shui Master Lam Kam Chuen. New York: Henry Holt and Company, LLC, 1996.

"The phoenix is a bird with beautiful gold and red plumage. At the end of its life-cycle the phoenix builds itself a nest of cinnamon twigs that it then ignites; both nest and bird burn fiercely and are reduced to ashes, from which a new, young phoenix arises. The new phoenix is destined to live, usually, as long as the old one. The bird was also said to regenerate when hurt or wounded by a foe, thus being almost immortal and invincible."

—Wikipedia

Although The Phoenix Principle is not conceptually complex, it counters conventional wisdom. It contradicts long-held notions about how to succeed as a business and as a leader. The Phoenix Principle conflicts with popular goal-setting activities and compensation practices. The Phoenix Principle is *not about controlling results* but instead is about organizational behavior which promotes adapting to those things the marketplace rewards with above-average results.

Achieving above-average, long-term results is a *management* issue. Success Formulas and Lock-in are good when applied in the Rapids. They aid rapid growth. They are essential for moving from the Wellspring into the Rapids. But if managers are to avoid the Flats—and worse, the Swamp and Whirlpool—they must *manage* their Lock-ins and Success Formulas. Only by acknowledging Success Formulas and Lock-in can leaders begin *managing* them.

For example, when a dietician tells us to eat less and exercise more, it rarely makes any difference. We continue eating too much and exercising too little, even though we know our behavior produces the opposite of our desired goal. To achieve weight reduction, we have to change our Success Formula—which accommodates too little exercise and too many calories. We start by recognizing that our Success Formula

Identity is tied to being successful in business and part of a family, whereas our Strategies and Tactics are geared toward working hard at the office and family activities. We should identify our Lock-in as working long hours and enjoying "family style" daily dining. Working past 6:00 p.m. and family dinner can become sacred cows.

As we all know, buying yet another new wardrobe to cover a growing girth can pose a significant challenge—as would be learning we've developed potentially life-threatening high cholesterol or blood pressure. Or worse, a heart attack or diabetes tells us we are in real danger. We have to do something, but our eating behaviors are Locked-in!

Once we recognize our Success Formulas and Lock-ins, we can begin managing the challenges. We can modify our Identity to recognize the importance of other close associations such as social clubs or religious affiliations, making us less dependent on work and the traditional nuclear family. Strategies for work can focus on meeting expectations rather than just working long hours, and spending time with family can include entertainment events or sharing hobbies, rather than just eating. Communications can be augmented at work with conference calls and email, and with family more cell phone calls and less dining. When long work hours and family dining Lock-ins are exposed for what they are, we can start modifying them.

Even with insight into our Success Formulas, we will need extensive Lock-in Disruption to achieve our weight management goals. We need to reorganize our work schedules and change the number of meetings we have on our calendars. We should change when we eat, moving to early-day eating while reducing late-day calories. Standing meetings and formal dinner times might be abandoned entirely, creating more exercise time. Dinner menus could be dramatically altered to favor lower-calorie foods, even though these are less "tasty." As we Disrupt our work and eating patterns, we can experiment with new approaches to communication and meals. We go back into the Rapids, seeking a new Success Formula that better suits our needs as we try to shrink waistlines and improve our health.

Weight loss works when our lifestyle is changed. Success doesn't come by focusing on dieting (which is goal-driven behavior), but by changing how we live. Experimenting with new approaches to our daily lives and Disrupting old patterns eventually leads to an entirely new Success Formula—with better weight control. It is very frequent to hear a successful dieter say, "My diet worked when I quit dieting and realized

I had to change my life. It's now easy to live healthier without really thinking about it."

By recognizing our Success Formulas and how we Lock–in, we start the journey toward better results. It is only by Disrupting Lock-in that we can react to challenges. By managing Lock-in, we give ourselves the opportunity to create White Space in which we can design new Success Formulas as we reenter the Rapids.

Four Steps to Achieving Sustained Success in a Dynamic World

1. Stop Defend & Extend mentality and behavior.
2. Attack competitors' Lock-in.
3. Implement Disruptions that overturn Lock-in.
4. Implement White Space to create a new Success Formula.

Stop Defend & Extend Mentality and Behavior

Step 1 is obvious yet is often ignored. Simply stop defending and extending. Widespread real-time communication and information transparency allows things to happen faster than they did 20, 10, or even 5 years ago. We will never return to that competitive pace. According to one popular phrase, "This is the new normal." We cannot hope to succeed using D&E behaviors, so we must stop relying on them.

When Einstein discovered relativity, it made no sense for engineers to ignore the new physics. It was no longer sufficient to rely exclusively on static, Newtonian approaches after realizing we could flee gravity's constraints. In business we now have no choice but to recognize that dynamic markets create faster cycle times. It is impossible to succeed for longer than the briefest period by defending and extending a Success Formula constantly at risk of competitive obsolescence. We must flee D&E's bonds and effectively manage change.

Managers can no longer luxuriate in confirmation bias and exclude options. Recognizing that businesses compete in a dynamic world yet exist with Lock-ins requires leaders to put in place tools to help them identify and carefully consider new options.

Attack Competitors' Lock-in

Step 2 is to study and attack competitors' Lock-in. Every business has Lock-in. Companies decline because competitors make their Success Formulas obsolete, and they *fail to react* due to Lock-in. Focusing on competitors' Lock-in tells us how to put them at risk. Simultaneously, it surfaces our own Lock-ins and starts the process of managing them. What's hard to see in ourselves is often obvious in others, and we can use that insight as a point of competitive attack as well as self-study.

Steps 1 and 2 can provide immediate performance improvement and are often the starting points for successful turnarounds. If facing a crisis, implementing these two steps can "stop the bleeding" and identify new solutions. By recognizing the importance of Success Formulas and Lock-in and then using that information to alter immediate behavior, dramatic—even breakthrough—performance can be ignited.

Motorola hit a growth stall in 2000 and was in weak condition by 2003. After its stock declined 87%, the Board of Directors hired a new CEO. Ed Zander, former Sun Microsystems executive, was hired and acted quickly. He knocked down traditional executive offices and made executives lunch with him in the corporate cafeteria. He cut funding for overly grand technology "big bets" that could take years to reach fruition while partnering with other companies on joint product development. He rapidly pushed new products out the lethargic pipeline in both cell phones and digital video recorders. And he began investing heavily in acquisitions to give Motorola a position in the rapidly growing mobile data market, competing with Research-In-Motion.

By stopping old behaviors and attacking competitors' Lock-in, Motorola made a dramatic burst forward and gained share. Unfortunately, this burst was too short-lived. Lacking more fundamental change, Motorola again stalled in 2007, placing the organization and its leaders at risk.

Implement Disruptions That Overturn Lock-in

Step 3 is to implement Disruptions that attack Lock-in, which opens the door to more long-lived success. Attacking selected Lock-ins is the critical key to creating an environment open to Success Formula management.

It is not possible to change a Success Formula directly. It is not possible to somehow pluck out an old Success Formula and install a new one. Many strategy consultants and management gurus would like to do so, as they demonstrate by recommending that companies merely need to change strategy to succeed, but implementing a new strategy is not easy. Amid a plethora of data and charts, these advocates recommend a new vision or new markets where they would like the business to head. But then the projects stall. That's why consultants have a reputation for producing great PowerPoints but not much in the way of enhanced client returns.

Organizations are designed to implement Success Formulas, not change them. Locking-in behaviors is a structural design requirement. Success Formulas are wholly resistant to data onslaught, no matter how powerful the logic, and are so Locked-in, by design, that it's not possible to change them by direct assault.

All adaptation starts by attacking Lock-ins. Disrupting Lock-ins creates the opportunity for migration to new behavior.

Implement White Space to Create a New Success Formula

Step 4 is implementing White Space, where a new Success Formula can be developed. Success Formulas producing above average results are created in the crucible of market competition during the Rapids. Rather than designing a new Success Formula, leaders need to establish White Space where teams can create new Success Formulas as a result of marketplace competition.

White Space teams need permission to violate old Lock-ins (thus the requirement to first Disrupt) as well as resources to develop a new Success Formula. The old organization can then migrate toward the new Success Formula. It is by using White Space that any organization can become evergreen.

Organizations of Any Age or Size Can Utilize The Phoenix Principle to Achieve Breakthrough Performance

Management books are reluctant to offer much hope for Locked-in organizations—as they should be, given that traditional change management approaches have proven largely ineffective. These approaches usually require someone, outside or internal, to develop a future vision and then push it onto the organization. This person or group will promote "alignment," meaning, "You need to do what we're telling you to do." Practitioners find organizations less than malleable, with people unwilling to align to necessary changes and falling short of goals as Lock-in thwarts their efforts.

Many change leaders claim that personal reluctance to change thwarts organizational improvement. They recommend replacing key individuals to increase change acceptance, implying employees undermine change projects. This implies that somehow managers and employees want to fail. Yet we know that most people, in fact, want to succeed, and most enjoy change. Almost everyone enjoys dining in a new restaurant or visiting a new city. If we did not accept change, none of us would get married or have children!

Change approaches founded in re-engineering utilize exhaustive workflow- and decision-mapping to start the effort. Teams then remap work, hoping to create different behaviors, reach different decisions, and improve results. These mapping projects can go on for months or years—like trying to unwind all the spaghetti in a bowl and repackage it while everyone continues to eat it! Success is rare even after extensively mapping and remapping data flows and transactions.

Highly adaptive organizations do not rely on a vision or extensive mapping to succeed. There is no Chief Neuron in the human brain, yet we are able to recognize a dangerous neighborhood and drive carefully—without developing a new vision of our future. Herd animals on the Serengeti are able to recognize threats, identify opportunities for food and water, and cover great distances—altering their paths every year—without any predesigned mapping activity at all. Mental processes, as well as group behaviors, do not utilize modern change management tools. And they are more adaptive and far more successful.

Competition and practice are the best tools for making management decisions. Although we may like to think brilliant MBA graduates can eliminate risk, risk reduction efforts are pure D&E Management. In dynamic markets no one has a crystal ball that can predict competitive behavior. Good Success Formula development comes from marketplace participation.

Small companies need to adapt as well. But small companies rarely have full-time strategy or planning resources. In small and medium-sized businesses Lock-in allows lots of work to be done by relatively few people. But fewer people does not mean Lock-in is any less in effect. In fact, its influence might be greater because there are no people available for brainstorming or otherwise discussing market challenges and because many small business CEOs, vice-presidents, and directors wear multiple hats. Small business Lock-in can be just as strong or stronger than in big companies with greater access to outside information.

Statistically, small companies have higher failure rates than large companies and frequently Lock-in to a Success Formula and wait too late to adjust. When raising funds entrepreneurs create business plans and Lock-in those plans while still in the Wellspring. Markets then shift, and they fail. Although resources might seem scarce, successful small companies Disrupt themselves and keep White Space active. It's critical that young companies vigilantly attack Lock-ins, not yet justified by the Rapids, to avoid premature Success Formula commitment. Small companies that become large excel at White Space management in their early days.

For large, Locked-in organizations the struggle is no greater than for smaller competitors. The business must identify and attack its Lock-ins, and adjusting to market challenges requires a place to experiment. No business is so old or bureaucratic that it cannot undertake these tasks. Large companies are not too ossified to succeed. Most just lack the motivation to Disrupt and willingness to implement White Space.

Several of America's most successful companies, such as GE and Cisco, are quite large. But they have internal Disruption mechanisms which keep White Space alive. Large companies have vast cash resources and assets that can easily become cash, and they have bright and capable people eager to create a successful future. It's Lock-in that keeps large organizations from achieving more of their potential. Stopping D&E while disrupting Lock-in and implementing White Space can create success in even the oldest and largest business.

Despite popular myth, large corporations are full of innovations. The largest R&D budgets are in big businesses. And huge amounts of university funding are supplied by big business. Every year the vast bulk of new patents are granted to large corporations. These companies don't lack innovation or the desire to produce long-lived above-average returns, but Lock-in stands in their way of achieving breakout performance. By overcoming D&E management proclivities, the people and ideas in any organization can be unleashed to improve long-term results.

After completely missing the PC wave, IBM crash-landed in its traditional computer business. But then IBM was reborn as a different and far more viable long-term company that provides services. Size is neither an advantage nor an obstacle to long-term success. Any organization that wants to rejuvenate itself, that wants to be successful long-term, can do so. All it takes is the willingness to abandon D&E Management and instead follow The Phoenix Principle.

5

Don't Defend & Extend

What is the first step to becoming a Phoenix Principle company? How does a business stop Defend & Extend Management and start planning for future market needs?

Recognize the Problem

Isaac Asimov was a famous biochemist, college professor, Vice President of Mensa, scientific author, and science-fiction novelist. In the 1990s he said, "It is change, continuing change, inevitable change that is the dominant factor in our society today. No sensible decision can be made any longer without taking into account not only the world as it is, *but the world as it will be.*"

Perhaps the better phrase came from Wayne Gretzky, professional hockey player, "I skate to where the puck *will be.*"

If Defend & Extend Management existed to protect old Success Formulas, what is needed is a new management approach designed to develop new Success Formulas. This approach should help organizations evolve to future needs, positioning businesses to succeed by preparing for new competition—rather than remaining stuck analyzing history and current decisions.

In a dynamic world, leaders must realize that changing markets define competition. Those who succeed will make their organizations dynamic, mirroring dynamic markets.

Management cannot fixate on what they do and have done. Business leaders must eschew discussing past competencies; instead they should invest more time determining where customers and markets are headed. Successful leaders must learn how to reach new competitive positions before others beat them to the puck.

It is no longer sufficient for managers to understand their strengths and weaknesses. Nor is it sufficient to understand existing markets and customers. A business cannot hope to extend its longevity by understanding existing competitors. Mapping past and current capabilities and competitors will not create or maintain success in dynamic markets. To manage for constant change, leaders must focus on where markets, customers, and competitors will be *in the future*.

According to an old proverb, "Upon finding yourself in a hole, the first rule is *stop digging*." This requires two deliberate actions. First, recognize you are in a hole. Second, realize that continued digging will not get you out of the hole. You have to do something else. As much as we enjoy the dig, the more we do it, the deeper we get. Defending & Extending (D&E) a Success Formula digs us into a hole. Doing more D&E is more digging.

Success Formulas, Lock-in, and Defend & Extend Management provide a nomenclature—a language—for talking about how industries, businesses, functional units, work teams, and individuals end up with seemingly insurmountable problems. The first step toward a solution is recognizing a problem and developing a way to talk about it. Discussing Success Formulas and Lock-ins allows managers to identify issues and offer alternatives.

Understanding that we have Success Formulas allows managers to be explicit about them. Leaders can fully specify Identity, Strategy, and Tactics. They can discuss how these were developed and what purpose they served. Their existence can be connected to initial conditions at origination. By understanding them it is possible to recognize them, even measure them, and start changing them.

More importantly, leaders can discuss how the Success Formula was Locked-in. Lock-ins, whether behavioral or structural, which were previously implicit can be made explicit—and linked to how they support the Success Formula. Being explicit about Lock-in allows us to change from *reacting* as always to *intentionally changing* what we will do. The language of Defend & Extend Management creates a different conversation about problems. Whether a leader is in the Rapids, working to define a Success Formula and install Lock-ins, or in the Flats, Swamp, or Whirlpool needing to attack Lock-ins and redefine the Success Formula, explicit discussion applies everyone's best thinking toward market challenges and new solutions.

Books on "change management" begin with the premise that managers can plan their futures and then map routes to better results. As if management is as simple as a Mapquest query! These Defend & Extend approaches intend to *force* people to change by convincing them a better future awaits—as if the only change impediments are vision, education, and planning. And they use psychology tools trying to persuade people to change. By ignoring Lock-in, these efforts often end up replacing people—and still aren't successful.

Most people know what the business problems are and can frequently describe them in detail. It's not data or logic which keeps people from functioning differently—it's Lock-in. Old approaches to change are as outdated as the D&E theories that sprouted them.

Improving Organizational Performance Starts by Changing Lock-in

Discussions about "culture" or "business legacy" are of no value. Nor are exercises intended to define a future vision. Change comes from altering behavioral Lock-ins (such as hierarchical relationships or sacred cows), modifying structural Lock-ins (such as strategy development or decision-making systems), or altering the cost relationships (such as selling major assets, eliminating supply chains, or adopting new technology). The Phoenix Principle allows managers to move beyond the "culture" discussion, which is amorphous, vague, and causes eyes to glaze over—and rarely improves performance. Instead, leaders can proactively evolve their business along with markets by altering Lock-ins that created Defend & Extend behavior.

TEACHING DYNAMIC BEHAVIOR

When children are first learning soccer, everyone chases the ball. The objective is simply to find the ball and kick it. Beginning coaching lessons teach them to spread out, create open space, and pass the ball to each other. Players learn to kick the ball to teammates until someone can kick it in the goal.

But in a game, competitors don't stand still. Every time someone tries to kick the ball to a teammate, a competitor runs by interrupting the play. So coaches teach players to keep moving. Rather than passing the ball to a standing player, allowing a competitor watching that player to steal the ball, the pass should go to an open piece of grass, and the teammate should run to where the ball *will be*. Players are taught to be dynamic and to counteract constantly moving competitors.

Most coaches find this takes four to six years. Even in high school, getting players to move on the field—a known key to winning—is difficult. If it's so hard to teach athletes who are focused on one sport how to play dynamically, is it any wonder why it's so hard to teach complex business organizations to do the same?

Plan for the Future Rather Than the Past

Stopping Defending & Extending behavior is easier said than done. Lock-in keeps us doing what we did. If we only had to say, "Stop," while describing likely future outcomes of not stopping, all of us would be thin and free of tobacco, alcohol, and addictive drugs. Stopping requires taking *alternative actions to replace what we've always done*. We have to say, "Instead of doing that, do this."

Begin stopping D&E by changing the approach to planning. Most strategy and planning processes are designed to operate from the inside out, rather than from the outside in. They are intended to help organizations defend and extend the past, rather than change a Success Formula. But overcoming momentum and Lock-in requires *planning* to do so.

The first task in planning has traditionally been generating charts showing performance for the last few quarters or years. History has been the "jumping off point" for planning. But this provides no benefit to planning other than D&E planning. It either reinforces Lock-in to past actions or highlights the Lock-ins' consequences. It does not help leaders plan for a dynamic, different future.

If revenue went from 100 to 108, traditional planning would state, "Revenue is up 8%, which is more than the market." But to invest in new technologies, far more cash might be needed. For long-term viability, planning should start with, "Revenue gains of 8% are only 30% of what's needed to maintain competitiveness." The first statement is about the past. The second statement is about the future. A pat on the back might feel good, but it has nothing to do with future success.

The second most common planning activity is describing existing markets. This can include describing existing customers or customer segments and their preferences. It might include competitor descriptions, noting capabilities and recent market successes. But these merely describe what we already know about the past, through the lens of Lock-in. This either encourages Defend & Extend behavior or points out its risks. Missing are the best *future* opportunities, which might have nothing to do with past customers, markets, products, or competitors.

Apple Computer was a revolutionary industry, instrumental to the growth of desktop computing. Over time Apple moved further up the Rapids, becoming quite Locked-in to its "computing" Success Formula and the Macintosh. John Scully championed launching the first personal digital assistant (PDA), called the Newton. Extensively advertised, it overcame early glitches (such as its problematic handwriting interface) and sold over 375,000 units.

But the Newton was not on the Macintosh product path. The Macintosh, with millions of unit sales, dominated planner and executive attention. Members of Scully's executive team went to Apple's Board of Directors and requested Scully be fired and then quickly eliminated the Newton "diversion" as the company regained "focus" on the Mac, which was under intense competition from Windows-based personal computers.

Unfortunately Apple was not able to slow the market shift toward Wintel as corporations en masse standardized on Windows. Despite significant technical and advertising investments, Apple floundered.

Apple knew when it cancelled the Newton that Windows PCs were rapidly dropping in price and that corporate customers were standardizing with Windows. But the planning process was focused on defending and extending the Macintosh, so the PDA market, later developed with great success by PALM, was ignored.

By 2004 Apple introduced iPod and iTunes—products far removed from the Macintosh—and the company once again found firm footing. By 2007 Apple's iPhone put it in the high-growth cellular handset market. None of these products had anything to do with personal computer technology nor its historically entrenched computer marketplace. Apple's planning had to shift away from the Macintosh, toward entirely different products and markets, to resurrect Apple from a near fatal demise.

Planning is problematic when it begins by describing today or the past. While leaders might wish to "think outside the box," such brainstorming becomes less likely the more the box is described and defined. Looking at history tightens planning boundaries; it does not loosen them.

Should planning begin by describing where you start? Or should it begin by determining the destination? Lewis Carroll, author of *Alice's Adventures in Wonderland*, wrote, "If you don't know where you're going, any road will take you there." Planning should not be about where you start, but instead where you want to go. Knowing where you start might make you feel good, but what good is it for describing the future? Fixating on where you start presumes you have a map, which is not the case when maneuvering through dynamic markets that have no clear roads. It's more important to know where you want to be and then be willing to find a route.

Businesses do not have the luxury of well-defined routes to success. Like making sausage, business is rather messy. Customers and competitors constantly make unpredictable moves. Technology, financing, products, and cost factors relentlessly change, making forward progress more like hacking a route through the wilderness than selecting roads. Leaders have to be more like wagon train scouts than modern travel planners. Planning has to be about finding clues pointing the right direction rather than deciding which road might go from A to B.

No successful company can "plan" its way to success by looking at its history. Could Larry Page and Sergey Brin have projected with any statistical accuracy Google's revenue 24 months after founding the company? Could Jeff Bezos use projections from his first four quarters to estimate Amazon's size after three years? When Pierre Omidyar founded eBay as a place to exchange Pez dispensers, was it his history as a collector that projected a multi-billion dollar business? Could Dell's investors use his first year homemade PC sales to generate forecasts of multi-billion dollar annual revenues?

Why do managers think historical data is of any value when planning? If entrepreneurs do not rely on history when making plans, why should managers of existing businesses? Does historical data availability imply the planning is better? Or does data merely make us more comfortable, without aiding the process at all?

Successful planning must be about the future. Leaders must displace historical analysis with views of future growth—and not limited views of growth in historical markets. Growth can come from anywhere. Casting a very wide net is critical.

News Corporation started as a small Australian newspaper company. Only by looking for growth, no matter where it originated, could News Corp. move beyond defending and extending newspaper sales in "the land down under." Today News Corp. has a broad and growing presence in not only newspapers but television news, broadcast television, television production, cable television ownership, direct broadcast satellite, filmmaking, magazines, inserts, books, and the Internet. News Corp. reaches customers across the globe.

For over 100 years, Singer meant sewing machines. By the 1960s sewing machine competition was intense, and Singer's profits were weak. Asian manufacturers had entered the market, capturing market share from Singer. Executives recognized competing in sewing machines as they had done was a lousy business prospect. Rather than defend and extend by focusing on their historical markets and capabilities, Singer executives looked as broadly as possible. Realizing that Vietnam created growing demand, Singer set its sites on the rapidly growing defense market, leading to transformation. By the 1980s Ronald Reagan's military build-up led Singer to sell all its sewing machine assets, including rights to use the Singer name on sewing machines, to an offshore competitor. The company invested the proceeds in additional defense businesses, rapidly finalizing its conversion to defense contractor.

Successful planning requires having the widest possible field of view for growth opportunities. Why compete in a low-growth and competitively intense market when you don't have to? It's only notions about defending existing products, markets, or competencies that leads to such thinking.

"Reality-based planning" is merely a euphemism for limiting options to business extensions and defending old Success Formulas.

Planners should use the scientific method we learned in middle school. Develop a hypothesis about the future (a future Success Formula) and then set up tests that will provide insight for reaching that future. Don't focus on the unlikelihood of that future; instead define what is needed to get there. Identify the tools and technology and other resources needed to answer key questions. Design the development projects—tests—to acquire required capability, whether it is currently a capability or not. This method works very well in R&D and engineering for developing breakthrough technologies and products, and there is no reason not to apply it to business planning.

By the 1990s AT&T knew that wireless telephony would eclipse land-line growth. But AT&T's planning process did not start by imagining an America with no landlines thus no landline long distance service and then creating a plan for wireless success. Had this scenario served as the core of AT&T's planning exercise, the company could have escaped the grip of defending and extending its dying long distance business. Instead, despite its huge investment in AT&T Wireless, AT&T did not succeed in mobile telephony. As it declined, AT&T was gobbled up by SBC.

Kodak was awarded more patents in digital photography than any other company. The company's management knew digital photography's capabilities, including the likelihood that digital photography would surpass film cameras for capturing amateur photos, before anyone else. But within, Kodak planning started by reviewing film sales and margins and then developing projects to defend film. As a result Kodak marketed its digital cameras very late and lost market leadership.

Had Kodak started its planning with, "Digital photography will one day dominate amateur photography, so what must the winner do to succeed?" the company could have leveraged its early digital innovations. If planning had focused on future markets, rather than evaluating the current situation, Kodak could have avoided worrying about margin cannibalization leading to delayed market entry. Kodak could have addressed the challenge posed by digital photography much earlier, rather than waiting until the problem was so great it could no longer be avoided.

Future scenario development is where planning should start, rather than with historical analysis.

Break Down Barriers to Alternative Option Consideration

Most planning exercises are undertaken within a headquarters conference room or at an offsite meeting held in a nearby hotel. After the current situation review, a facilitator (possibly the leader) will say, "OK, now let's try to think outside the box." Is it surprising few new ideas surface?

Today all businesses must adjust to global competition. Lots of work formerly done in America and Europe is now done in India or China; Russia or Hungary; or (especially in agriculture) Brazil, Mexico, or Argentina. It's clear offshore competitors are doing things differently than domestic competitors. But most planning teams have limited knowledge about how these competitors behave and thus plan as if these competitors are much like themselves. Because the planners don't know what they don't know, they plan by extending what they do know.

Why not have planning meetings in Chennai, Hyderabad, Beijing, Hangzhou, Saint Petersburg, or Brasilia? Why not contact local companies in advance and set up meetings with tours? Listening to how these competitors think about their businesses and seeing what they do can provide missing insight. After starting planning sessions, intermix meetings with local managers. At the end of a week, the planning output will be far different from what would happen within headquarter's walls—or the resort hotel a few miles away. If the cost seems high, compare it to the cost of failure.

Don't Try to Think Outside the Box—Get Outside the Box, Then Think!

One of America's largest newspaper companies was under intense pressure to cut costs when advertising revenue was lost to Internet competitors. After years of traditional cost cutting, leaders asked themselves if there might be a better solution. They organized a trip to India where they met with the country's largest publisher and many suppliers of various services. They met with academics from leading Indian universities. The offshore planning output was quite different than previously planned. Within weeks the company began executing cutting-edge outsourcing to better meet customer needs and change its cost curve.

Plan for What You Don't Know Rather Than What You Do

Great opportunities are typically not wildly visible or screaming to be recognized. As leaders look globally for new ideas and markets, no stone is left unturned. It is not known opportunities which possess the greatest potential, but unknown opportunities, which Locked-in competitors fail to see.

Many organizations take great pride in knowing their best customers. They frequently invite large customers to participate in planning exercises, asking what can be done to improve satisfaction. Unfortunately, this is yet another Defend & Extend practice.

Big customers are tied to the same Lock-ins as the business. They largely mirror the practices of your business—after all that is why they are big customers. Their insights are rarely anything more than small extensions to the existing Success Formula. As large customers they share the same market knowledge, and blinders, as you.

Similarly, modern day Customer Resource Management (CRM) systems do a marvelous job creating customer profiles according to their value. Platinum, Gold, and Silver customer levels are based on revenue or margin, and participants are treated according to level. These systems also frequently identify a large block of customers which are costly to serve and provide little profitability, leading to tactical plans for moving these customers out of the portfolio—unless they suddenly accept your Success Formula.

The customers most valuable to future planning are not current good customers (especially large ones); they are the ones that have defected. Departed customers know something about competitors or substitutes which caused them to switch. Their insight led them to decide someone else's Success Formula was more attractive. Lost customers represent opportunities to better understand market shifts and emerging challenges. Ignoring them is extremely dangerous to future revenue.

Often customers of greatest value to planning are those the CRM system finds least attractive. Only by asking, "Why aren't these customers larger or more profitable? Does anyone serve them profitably? How could they generate more revenue and more profits?" can we learn more about market challenges. The existing Success Formula serves the needs of Platinum and Gold customers, so the most interesting customers are those that don't fit these categories. Weaker customers are the ones most likely to provide insight into market changes and emerging competitive threats.

Taking a large customer golfing might well encourage his or her continued loyalty, but it won't result in discovering what challenges are likely to steal them away. Large customers will appear happy right up until the day they switch. They want the Locked-in relationship benefits until they decide to change. It's smarter to spend time listening to lost customers and those that have not yet grown into large, profitable relationships to learn about competitive evolution. These customers are much more likely to tell you what you don't know because they are less likely to share your Lock-in.

While macro trends might be known by traditional planners, the odds are very high they have not explored *how* those trends will affect the business. Trends are discussed when they reinforce a Success Formula and widely ignored when they indicate an emerging problem. Planners focus on extending past actions with tactical changes yielding incremental improvements.

Gordon Moore, Intel's cofounder, is credited with predicting in 1965 that computer power would double every 24 months. Called Moore's Law, this rule of doubling meant it would not take long for computers to be extremely powerful and cheap. Yet, for the next 25 years, very few businesses used computer technology as a competitive tool. Not even early computer experts and data center managers planned for the impact powerful, cheap computers would have on competitiveness. All through the 1970s, as computers became faster and cheaper, and more people learned how to use them, the potential value of computer technology was largely ignored. As a result, most IT professionals and business leaders over-invested in mainframes, minicomputers, and their supporting technology, while simultaneously missing opportunities to improve their competitiveness. It wasn't until the 1990s that business leaders started thinking about applying computer technology as a game-changer, and many businesses still have not addressed information technology strategically.

MACRO TRENDS

- Average American life expectancy will soon be 90 years.
- The top 25% of Indian high school students is larger than *all* American high school students.
- If 100% of all U.S. manufacturing jobs were sent to China, the country would still have a labor surplus.
- Two thousand movies can be simultaneously streamed down a single glass fiber.
- The U.S. is not in the top 15 countries of the world with broadband penetration to the home.
- The human genome has been mapped.
- Livestock have been successfully cloned.
- Islam is the world's fastest growing major religion.
- Small changes in the earth's atmospheric temperature the past 40 years guarantees wider variability in weather patterns globally for the foreseeable future.
- There are more text messages each day than there are people on the planet.

What competitive challenges do these trends portend?

Most planners develop strategies based on what is known at the time. But knowing today can create blinders about the future. If an investor were evaluating company plans in 1905, he might well have known that there were only 144 miles of paved road and 8,000 automobiles. This could have kept him investing in horse feed and livery stables, rather than the soon to explode auto industry. If he had simultaneously known in 1905 that 95% of births took place in the home, and 90% of U.S. physicians had no college education, would he have been likely to invest in hospitals or medical insurance companies? It is critical that planners base their efforts not on the world as it is, but as it is likely to be.

THE WORLD IN 1905

- Average life expectancy in the U.S. was 47 years.

- Only 14% of homes had a working bathtub.

- Only 8% of homes had a telephone, and a three minute call from Denver to New York cost $11.00 at a time when the average wage was 22¢/hour.

- California, with only 1.4 million residents, was the twenty-first most populous state, trailing Alabama, Mississippi, and Tennessee, for example.

- The world's tallest structure was the Eiffel Tower and considered to have no practical use.

- Most women washed their hair only once per month and used borax or egg yolk as the cleanser.

- The population of Las Vegas was 30.

- Only 6% of Americans had graduated from high school.

- Marijuana, heroin, and morphine were available at the corner drug store.

- Eighteen percent of U.S. households had at least one full-time servant.

In the 1970s most businesses rented computer time from a large data center through a service called "time sharing." Boeing Computer Services (BCS) was one of the world's largest time sharing suppliers. Toward the decade's end, BCS's top executive was asked his opinion of small computers built with microprocessors. He responded that he could not imagine a need for such machines, and he dismissed them as hobbyist toys. Of course, Steve Jobs, Steve Wozniak, and Bill Gates had a different opinion.

It is critical organizations utilize scenario development when planning. No one has a crystal ball—not even those with deep insight to a technology or market. So it's important to develop multiple scenarios about the future and then monitor progress of those scenarios. Scenarios as investment guides are more likely to generate above-average returns than basing future investments on past results. Scenario planning leads to developing routes toward potential outcomes. Instead of committing to one plan, multiple opportunities are tracked and developed.

In the 1970s IBM, RCA, and GE were competing in the mainframe computer business. IBM had a substantial lead. RCA and GE were battling for second place and not making a lot of money. GE used scenarios to look at the future and realized it was impractical to compete with IBM's growing near monopoly. Competing with RCA would require significant investment, which was unlikely to yield a satisfactory return. GE sold its computer business to RCA, creating a profit for GE. RCA eventually wrote off its losses when exiting the mainframe market, and GE went on to significant success in other markets.

The Singer story highlights how a company used scenarios to redirect itself. D&E planning would have kept Singer competing in sewing machines long after its competitive advantage had been lost. Trying to find opportunities by exploring internal "core competencies" would have led to low-return options in subcontract manufacturing. But scenario planning showed that the U.S. defense budget was exploding and yielded a high growth market. Scenarios based on becoming a defense supplier showed opportunities for high returns.

Planning processes involve the organization's top management. At times lower level managers may be invited to participate. But how often are people from outside the company and industry involved? Even when consultants are involved, they are screened to assure they are well-versed, even experts, in the organization's business. If everyone in the room has the same background and the same experiences, how are challenges to be identified and new insights developed? Where are "outside the box" ideas to originate?

Despite the availability of very high-probability forecasts, few of these expectations are incorporated into traditional planning. Infusing macro trends and likely future outcomes almost always require someone from outside to bring leading trends to the discussion. Outsiders, lacking Lock-in blinders, are able to see opportunities for applying new trends in technology, business practice, globalization, or other areas to a business. It is critical that outsiders, true outsiders—people who may know nothing about the business—are involved.

The CEO of a large corporation was certain his best investment option was expanding the sales force. The head of Marketing was concerned that a larger sales force would raise cost but achieve few additional sales. Desperate, the Marketing leader asked a college student to demonstrate how competitors were using the Internet to reach existing customers. Even though the CEO was skeptical, when he learned that a 19-year-old could easily find competitive products at great prices, obtain a vendor number, and place an order, he became convinced he needed to consider alternative sales channels.

Most businesses are located fairly close to a university. Yet few businesses leverage universities for their benefit. While everyone knows that advances in nanotechnology and bio-engineering are happening rapidly, very few managers know what these technologies are, and even fewer have a clue how they can be applied—so they are ignored. Likewise, operating a location-independent global business model is widely studied by business school professors and simultaneously far from understood by the vast majority of U.S. business leaders having rarely worked in more than one or two countries. Why don't businesses take advantage of local university professors and leading graduate students as part of their planning?

No business in the next 20 years will escape macro trends of globalization, nanotechnology, and bio-engineering. But it is a rare business that is holding nanotech workshops for its senior leaders, even though the technology has been applied for more than a decade. And it's a rarer business yet that is asking for opportunities to apply nanotechnology or biotechnology to alter traditional competition. And almost no businesses are asking what investments they should be making in what could well be the next high-growth technologies. Adding expertise in far flung technologies to planning, whether from academia or consultants, opens the door to breakthrough opportunities.

NOT-SO-FAR-OUT PROJECTIONS

How could these innovations affect your business if they are developed?

- Stem cells able to regrow limbs, organs, or other organic tissue
- At-home laser eye surgery machines
- Personal nuclear generators at an average cost of $10,000
- A sugar-cube-sized supercomputer that can store everything ever published

- Clothing that detects airborne toxins, biological weapons, and secretes blocking agents
- Anti-freeze proteins preventing damage to human organs at sub-freezing temperatures
- Home floor tiles that consume dirt
- Network computers implanted in the ear and globally interconnected 24x7x365 for free

If these sound far out, how wild would the following have sounded to a business leader 40 years ago?

- Cell phones
- 24-hour television in over 100 channels
- First-run movies available for unlimited viewing in your home for a one time price of $4.99, using equipment that costs under $30
- All the information in the entire *Encyclopedia Britannica* (or an entire library) available instantaneously to everyone in their homes for free
- Unlimited long-distance usage for free
- A $30 oven that can bake a potato in five minutes
- Doctors threading a needle into a leg artery and then pushing it through the heart and into the brain, hooking into a blood clot and removing it, thus reversing a stroke
- Automobiles that go 80 miles per hour that achieve over 30 miles per gallon while operating an air conditioner
- People meeting each other, intending to marry, by connecting two computers

It is easy to hear about and discuss innovations and trends but then ignore them completely when planning. Lock-in makes trends invisible to planning processes.

At the beginning of this Information Revolution, we can anticipate that future success will be built on different technologies and business approaches than what worked in the Industrial Revolution. It's time to educate ourselves on these expected advancements.

This expertise can be found at an extremely affordable price. Professors are famous for affordability, especially those lacking a scientific prize or popular book authorship. Beyond professors, many U.S. universities house Small Business Development Centers (SBDCs) where businesses hire students to develop business plans. These affordable centers allow for competitive insight from someone not suffering from your Lock-in. In many colleges, professors are delighted to have businesses bring real-world problems to them, which students then can study and recommend solutions. Small grants have a long reach when applied to academic institutions and bring insights a business is unlikely to receive elsewhere.

How about doing an Internet search to find a small consultancy in a foreign country? A firm in India might well bring an entirely different point of view to the application of new innovations. And the price is likely to be very affordable.

In the late 1990s, during the early Internet boom, very few executives had any Internet knowledge. They had not entered the executive suite as email users and certainly not as web surfers. Few had PCs in their offices. As they heard about emerging Internet opportunities to lower cost or increase revenues, they lacked understanding and most often dismissed Internet investments.

To engage his company with an Internet opportunity, one enterprising CIO set up an Internet demonstration for his executive team, including the CEO, using four high school students. These students knew, more than anyone in the company, how to surf web sites, place orders, dig out arcane information, and link sites to their friends via email. After the 30-minute demo, followed by another 30-minute Q & A session, the executives quickly approved a web site investment and began using web technology, seeking competitive advantage. High school students brought much needed external information to this company's planning.

Many businesses have a negative opinion about consultants. Scott McNeely at Sun Microsystems used to ask any manager who wanted approval to hire a consultant, "If I hire him, why do I need you?" This implies that everything which needs to be known is known within the company. But managers are internally responsible for running the Success Formula and operating within Lock-ins. Expecting them to have external insights is wildly unrealistic given the intended goals of their positions.

A robust network of external consultants greatly increases the external knowledge available to any organization. Consultants not Locked-in to the Success Formula can study opportunities in their earliest stages and develop application approaches. Outside the business Lock-in, consultants can explore the strengths and weaknesses of an innovation, technology, or business practice and then become experts in how it can be applied. They can describe how that opportunity enhances a business, even when it violates a Lock-in. As a mechanism to open the doors for growth, consultants are an important tool for moving beyond D&E when planning.

Most businesses participate in their industry conferences. They may submit papers to the conference, have their leaders give speeches, and host a booth. Perhaps this has value as a customer event, but little new information will be learned by attending your own industry conference. Managers already know most, if not all, of what will be said.

On the other hand, attending industry conferences in which you don't participate can be very insightful. Listening to how others plan for macro trends can create new views which can be applied in your industry. Developments in industries in which you don't participate can be educational and produce new ideas for products, services, or customers. Attending conferences of other industries promotes *lateral thinking* about what you could do differently. But few commercial companies will attend a conference on military procurement or weaponry, even though there might be many opportunities. Few automobile suppliers will attend a conference on bakery equipment, even though some of these might be better customers than the big three U.S. auto manufacturers. Few real estate developers will attend conferences on nanotechnology, even though new nanotech materials might make their buildings of greater value.

The goal of these activities should be learning about what we don't know so new insights can be incorporated into planning—not just to know something new, but to apply it to the business. Leaders must seek opportunities for managers and employees to break free from Lock-in and explore new Success Formulas. Looking at the Success Formulas of other industries and companies creates opportunities to compete in new places and in new ways. Making these insights *central* to the planning process can improve planning.

Engineers at the University of Illinois Supercomputer Center developed Mosaic as an ARPAnet interface tool. (ARPAnet was a network forerunner of the commercial Internet.) Subsequently some of these engineers started two companies, Spyglass and Netscape, with browsers for new network users. In the midst of this early "browser war," Microsoft launched Internet Explorer (IE). Netscape decided to defend its browser business and undertook head-to-head competition with the software behemoth. Years later a struggling Netscape was acquired by AOL and virtually disappeared from the market.

After Microsoft announced IE, Spyglass took a very different course. Its leaders recognized that fighting Microsoft, which could bundle IE with the operating system at time of computer sale, was unlikely to lead to success. Spyglass began exploring *ubiquitous access*, a term referring to the potential for people anywhere, any place to have network access. To Spyglass this meant the Internet would be accessible on other platforms besides the PC. Continued investigation identified network access requirements for televisions, PDAs, and telephones—all technologies far removed from Spyglass's beginnings.

Nonetheless, Spyglass pursued developing browser capability for these alternative network access platforms. Although it had to climb significant technology learning curves, Spyglass quickly began developing prototypes and products. Within a few years, Spyglass was purchased by OpenTV for over $2.3 billion, a considerably higher valuation than when it was producing and selling computer technology. Spyglass changed its planning process from "How do I implement computer browsers better, faster, cheaper?" (the Netscape response) to pursuing an unknown future, based on nothing more than scenarios about ubiquitous access.

It's Not Hard to Stop Defending & Extending if You Change Your Planning Approach

It is possible to stop the Defend & Extend cycle. The first step is changing the approach to strategy and planning. Most strategy and planning work is designed to find ways for protecting an old Success Formula or extending it modestly. By changing the approach to this vital function, organizations can discover new opportunities for modifying their Success Formulas and improving returns.

Specific actions a leader can take include the following:

- Identify and write down your Success Formula and Lock-ins. Be explicit about them and why they exist.

- Use the language of Success Formula, Lock-in, and Defend & Extend to change the discussion and approach to market challenges and problems.
- Avoid using historical data for future planning.
- Focus planning activities on the future, not the present or the past.
- Plan from the future backward, rather than from the present forward.
- Look for growth markets, no matter where they are. Don't put limits on what opportunities can be considered.
- Undertake planning exercises in eye-opening locations.
- Utilize lost or low-volume customers to gain insight on market changes.
- Involve outsiders in the planning effort, including academics, students, and consultants.
- Research technologies and business developments that appear to have no link to your business but are emerging as important.
- Apply macro trends to your business, even when on the surface they appear to have minimal short-term impact.
- Utilize scenario planning to develop new insights and business opportunities.
- Attend conferences outside your industry.
- Encourage the use of younger workers, inside and outside the organization, to develop new strategic decisions.

6

Attack Competitors' Lock-in

How can I quickly take advantage of The Phoenix Principle? What can I do to leverage my knowledge about Defend & Extend for rapid improvement?

It's Easier to See Problems in Others' Success Formulas Than in Your Own

We need to understand our Success Formulas and Lock-ins—but that is hard to do. Self-analysis, even when aided by an outsider, is incredibly difficult. Lock-in removes options and focuses thinking into limited viewpoints while creating assumptions about the world built into the given Success Formula.

Lock-in configures decision-making processes so that many factors are taken for granted. We speed decision making by using assumptions we no longer review. Assumptions allow managers to quickly solve problems while developing more detailed tactics, defending and extending the Success Formula. In the Rapids, assumptions improve productivity by letting us do more—better, faster, and cheaper. Leaders act quickly because so much can be taken for granted.

Remember the Indian cab driver who could not comprehend my ideas for controlling cattle movements from Chapter 3, "The Power of Lock-in"? He assumed cattle should freely roam. As a result, he was blind to other options for managing the traffic/cow interface. Because I was neither Indian nor Hindu, it was easy for me to see other options. For him, it was very hard. He would need to surface his assumptions to even consider my idea.

The president of Addressograph Multigraph (AM) grew up in a military family, attended West Point, and spent many years as an Army officer before taking his position as president. His behavior was regimented; he would arrive for work daily at 6:30 a.m., eat lunch in the company cafeteria at 11:30, and depart promptly at 5:00 p.m. He always wore blue suits, white shirts, and a plain necktie.

In the early 1990s AM's managers requested a dress code change to allow for "casual Friday." Rather than business suits, they wanted to be able to wear business casual attire to work one day each week. The president told them, "I cannot imagine how this request would improve productivity, and I don't understand why you would ask for something like this. I think it's a bad idea, and we shouldn't do it." The dress standards did not change.

As its productivity improvement efforts progressed, AM management decided to institute a manufacturing plant reorganization, including shift times and workflow changes. After multiple meetings between AM's president and the manufacturing teams, the president commented to his executive team, "The manufacturing employees are very resistant to the shift change. They say they don't see any benefit. I don't understand why they simply can't give these changes a try and see if productivity improves."

The CFO was first to chuckle. He was soon accompanied by the head of marketing and then the manufacturing V.P. As laughter swelled, the AM president looked around the table, and with wide eyes asked, "What's so funny? Why are you laughing? All I said was that I can't understand how the manufacturing folks can be so rigid." The room fell into hysterical laughter. What was so apparent to others, the president completely missed in himself.

Lock-in to doing what we've always done makes us unaware of our own assumptions as well as the Lock-ins that guide our behavior and decisions. Before trying to change organizations, leaders must identify their Success Formulas and Lock-ins. This is far easier done by first looking at others rather than looking at ourselves.

By looking at competitors, managers can hope to escape their internal BIAS (Beliefs, Interpretations, Assumptions, and Strategies). They are more likely to recognize tactics competitors used to Lock-in behavior and decisions and tie those Lock-ins to strategies supporting competitors' Success Formulas. Analyzing competitors brings to the surface industry-wide commonalities. These common traits expose industry Success Formulas and Lock-ins, as well as individual competitor adaptations. Analyzing competitors creates an initial "baseline" Success Formula pyramid.

Once the first competitor's Success Formula and Lock-ins are defined, identifying them for other competitors is much easier. Then comparing yourself with competitors makes it easier to identify your own. Comparison against a standard, any standard, is much easier than trying to self-assess using a blank sheet of paper. Answering, "Do I have that Lock-in?" and "How do we accomplish the same goal?" is much easier than answering the more poorly defined, "What are my Lock-ins?" Once a business knows how its Lock-ins competitively compare, it can start making decisions to benefit itself at competitors' expense.

A 55-year-old U.S. high school football coach learned his skills in the upper Midwest. His favorite style mirrored the early National Football League central division, nicknamed "the black and blue" division for very physical ball running, blocking, and tackling. He would say he loved "smash-mouth football," a name for the hard-hitting style. His career win/loss record was good but not great.

After coaching for 30 years, late one season his team was undefeated. They were nationally ranked and had a chance to win the state title. Preparing for an upcoming game with his arch rival, the assistant coach asked questions about the other team's coach. An hour's discussion clearly exposed the opposing coach's style. He was very predictable. The "smash-mouth" coach suddenly realized not only his opponent's vulnerabilities, but by comparing himself with his rival, recognized his own predictability and the risks created.

The "smash-mouth" coach immediately changed his playbook. While defensively preparing for his competitor's most likely offense, he added several new plays to his own. In the game's second quarter he began using the new plays, surprising the other team. At half-time the coach had a sizable lead and won this critical game. His defense had prepared for the predictable competitor, and his offense confused the other team, creating opportunities for his team to make big plays.

Although business competition is far more complex than high school football, it is possible for leaders to study competitors and identify their patterns. Then managers can target competitors' vulnerabilities while developing new options for short-term wins.

Seek Out Alternative Competitive Tactics Rather Than Compete Head-to-Head

As previously described, most planning exercises defend or extend industry Lock-ins. These exercises look at relative competitor strength using parameters such as manufacturing cost, distribution coverage, or product features. These exercises then try to identify improvements on these attributes. Most books on business strategy and execution, such as those previously mentioned by Larry Bossidy and Jim Collins, are intended to guide managers in beating competitors head-to-head.

But head-to-head competition creates a war of attrition. Either everyone competes until there is only one competitor left standing, or competition leaves a small group of similar competitors unable to improve returns because they constantly battle using the same techniques. This kind of competition may raise testosterone levels, but it isn't very smart. From the outset it's clear all competitors will struggle, and most will not survive. At best, only one will ever earn long-term high rates of return. Thus the odds for any one competitor to succeed long-term is low.

There's a problem when applying sports analogies to business. Sports are designed as head-to-head competition yielding a single winner. Although thousands of competitors may start toward an Olympic gold medal, only one will reach the goal. The rules are designed for this competitive format—a single winner. In contrast, business offers an infinite variety of ways to compete. Unlike sports, there are relatively few rules in business. There are limitless opportunities to identify new competitive parameters and dominate them. Rather than competing head-to-head, businesses can constantly look for "game changers" in their quests to find more sources of revenue and greater returns.

Head-to-head competition is also expensive. It leads to investing in manufacturing plants, supply chains, distribution centers, R&D, and product development as competitors try to out-spend each other. It also leads to price wars as competitors strive to steal market share. Comparatively, finding alternative competitive options lowers the investment rate and allows a business to avoid price wars. Alternative competition seeks new ways to create value by either changing the cost curve in some new way or justifying higher prices through new forms of differentiation.

Compare Target and Kohl's discount stores with Wal-Mart. Wal-Mart has long been the industry Goliath. Wal-Mart is by far the largest, and undoubtedly the low-cost discount competitor. No one runs a lower-cost operation than Wal-Mart, nor does anyone offer lower prices to customers. Wal-Mart sought, and achieved, the low cost/price position. KMart discovered that competing head-to-head with Wal-Mart was disastrous and ended up bankrupt.

Target took a very different route. Instead of focusing solely on price, Target offered customers more fashionable soft goods. Target made its stores more pleasant and its advertising more avant-garde. Kohl's put its attention on clothing and built a reputation for offering near department store quality at discount prices. Both competitors have flourished, despite Wal-Mart's #1 position in size and cost. By finding other competitive variables, avoiding head-to-head price competition with Wal-Mart, both have grown faster and earned higher margins.

Defend & Extend strategists evaluate competitors by measuring performance along existing, known competitive parameters. They seek to be first on known variables, and tactics are intended to optimize performance on these parameters. Phoenix Principle strategists look at current competitive methods and then search for completely new ways to compete. Current parameters become a list of factors to avoid. Why enter a new business by striving to execute faster, better, or cheaper than existing players when you know they will be forced to respond to your every action? Seeing you coming, they will act quickly to defend their position.

Selling books was a hotly contested marketplace in the mid-1990s. There were many small booksellers struggling against the emerging new megastores such as Borders, Barnes & Noble, and Crown Books. Retailers either focused on niche segments or heavily promoted huge selection and big discounts, especially on best-sellers. Competition was cut-throat as margins declined, creating bankruptcies for many small retailers as well as Crown Books.

Competitors Locked-in to in-store browsing as a key success factor. They supported browsing by keeping lots of inventory on the shelves. They employed knowledgeable staff to help customers find books they would enjoy, and they kept best-seller lists and book reviews easily accessible for customers.

Despite high competitive intensity and industry Lock-in to browsing, Amazon entered the bookselling business. Jeff Bezos started Amazon with none of the traditional competitive strengths. He provided no salespeople with knowledge of books or opinions on which were good. He maintained almost no inventory. He did not even have a storefront. He did not offer books immediately but instead required buyers to wait for delivery. Customers could only buy on the Internet. And early on focus was not a vertical market nor best-sellers, but instead out-of-stock books that had to be ordered from publishers. Of course, Amazon became a huge success. By completely avoiding the traditional competitive factors, Amazon successfully entered bookselling.

E*Trade was similarly successful in stock brokerage, utilizing none of the traditional competitive tools such as personal brokers, analysts, or research reports. Merrill Lynch, Smith Barney, and other Wall Street firms had wide offerings and complete vertical integration. They were Locked-in to providing extensive research and knowledgeable customer service. They had huge research departments with proprietary opinions intended to improve investor returns, as well as a large broker staff supporting every customer question. These were large and enormously well-funded organizations that fought aggressively for investors.

E*Trade entered this market offering only links to publicly available research and low-price transactions. It completely ignored all the factors considered important to retail brokerage, and through its alternative competitive approach kept costs very low as it built an enormous client base.

Of course, doing the opposite of large competitors does not guarantee success. But there is no doubt that avoiding head-to-head competition dramatically lowers new participant entry cost. It is very hard to be an industry "game changer" if you enter a business doing what everyone else is doing. Experimenting with alternative approaches creates opportunities for industry restructuring, rapid growth, and above average returns.

Some might say Amazon and E*Trade were merely examples of the shift to Internet-based businesses. This underplays how both ventures completely disregarded traditional competitive methods. The Internet was just one of the entirely new competitive tools they used to gain early advantage and leverage in hotly contested and mature markets. Both later expanded to compete more broadly and changed the requirements for historical competitors to remain viable.

Do Not Overlook the Obvious When Defining Competitor Success Formulas

During the early 2000s real estate flourished. As interest rates plummeted to generational lows, monthly mortgage payments dropped. First-time homeowners jumped into the market, taking advantage of low rates, while existing homeowners traded up and began looking for second homes and investment properties. Nearly all these purchases required a new mortgage. Simultaneously homeowners by the millions refinanced real estate to access cash while lowering their monthly payments.

This mortgage activity created higher demand for property appraisals. However, in 2000 property appraisal was still largely a cottage industry, having changed little from the 1960s. A local appraiser would visit a property to check location, size, construction, and architecture. He or she would then compare the property with similar local properties. The appraiser subsequently estimated fair market value, providing a report to the lender. This process often took two weeks or longer as appraisers worked through growing lines of properties needing appraisals.

Some appraisers developed their own automated valuation models using the local assessor's office database. After keying into their PC valuation specifics and an address, the computer "guestimated" an initial value. But this still required verification by someone visiting the property. Even with this technical enhancement, appraisals still took a week—or longer.

An entrepreneur looking for new business in the real estate boom might recognize the arcane appraisal system as an opportunity. His starting point should be looking for Lock-in. Appraiser and mortgage company Lock-in starts with their belief that an appraiser needs to see the property. What appears like common sense, given how long the process has existed and differences in local real estate markets, slowed processing millions of mortgages annually.

Why should an appraiser physically view properties? In this era of satellite imagery, Google and Mapquest for example, does each building require a personal visit? Locking-in on site visits reinforced appraisers' Success Formula, but are they necessary?

Zaio, a start-up company in Calgary, Canada, identified this Lock-in and challenged it. Rather than highly inefficient appraisers visiting properties according to the incoming line of mortgage applications, Zaio decided to photograph every building in the top 250 North American standard metropolitan areas (SMAs). Building this image database would be more efficient than appraisers' random site visits, and it would be reusable.

Zaio hired available freelance commercial photographers to simply walk down their local streets and photograph every home, garage, and commercial building address by address. These were then uploaded to Zaio where the company combined the image with traditional home information such as size and architecture. Zaio brought in the assessors office information to establish initial property values. This allowed completing an appraisal online in most cases. Appraisal effort dropped, as did cost. And the time to complete an appraisal dropped from days or weeks to hours, allowing faster mortgage application processing.

The obvious Lock-in, visiting the building, held the key to finding an alternative competitive approach. Value was created by helping mortgage officers complete paperwork faster, putting their money to work as a mortgage more quickly and placing the home in applicants' hands sooner.

Zaio sold its database in zones of 10,000 buildings for $9,500. Enterprising small appraisers could rapidly expand their businesses, overtaking larger appraisal firms laden with high employee costs. But few appraisers initially bought. Although advantages were both immediate and long-term, traditional appraisers were reluctant. Zaio's product attacked their Lock-in and the assumptions in their Success Formula. Early customers were more typically large mortgage issuers that desired the benefits of Zaio and were not vested in the old Success Formula, further threatening traditional appraiser long-term viability.

Look at How Competitors Define Their Business

In the 1990s Aeroquip rightfully bragged it was the world's #1 hydraulic hose and fittings supplier. Though not a well-known consumer business, Aeroquip's products moved fluids in high pressure applications like brake lines, aircraft landing gear, industrial mills, and literally thousands of hydraulic applications. Aeroquip was very proud of its rich heritage as an industry founder and high quality manufacturer.

Cut-throat competition characterized hydraulic hose and fitting competition by the 1990s. Patents had expired years ago, so both domestic and international manufacturers made products identical to nearly all Aeroquip's catalog. Neither Aeroquip nor its competitors enjoyed a significant cost advantage. Offshore manufacturers were increasingly gaining share as they arbitraged lower labor costs and offered slightly lower prices. While Aeroquip claimed superior quality, most manufacturers met the American Society of Automotive Engineers standards for these products—and that was sufficient quality for most applications.

Looking for a way out of its price war, Aeroquip tried just about everything. But lacking product protection, Aeroquip struggled to find a competitive differentiator. As industry leader Aeroquip felt it was the lead boat to catch in the race, but the gap was closing. So management undertook a new approach when they decided to look at how competitors defined competition.

Aeroquip discovered the entire industry defined itself around products. Like many industrial businesses, engineers held high-ranking positions in pneumatic companies. Many executives had been in pneumatics their entire careers. In looking at competitors Aeroquip learned that everyone, literally everyone, defined themselves by the products they made. Every competitor said they were in the *hose and fittings business*.

Aeroquip's CEO launched a program to see how else Aeroquip could compete. Were product specs, price, and delivery the only factors that mattered? Aeroquip began interviewing customers that had recently given business to competitors. Some customers talked about receiving a slightly better price. But listening more closely, Aeroquip heard a different refrain. Some competitors were easier to do business with than Aeroquip.

Aeroquip realized every competitor could make hoses and fittings. It would be a low return battle competing strictly on quality and price. So management asked how Aeroquip could redefine competition, if not around the product. Although the answer was unclear, it was clear that competing heads-up against competitors would be rough sailing.

Revisiting customer interviews, Aeroquip realized most customers did not consider hoses and fittings as critical items. Manufacturing customers felt the products were cheap, and there wasn't much difference between suppliers. What really unnerved them were late or incomplete shipments. Because they operated just-in-time facilities, when a $1.50 hose or $5.00 fitting wasn't on the line when needed, it was infuriating. To compensate many overstocked these parts. Most maintained a "hose room" where employees put together subassemblies for the manufacturing line—as well as cross-referenced parts when the line was short what it needed.

Manufacturers didn't like their hose rooms. They didn't like the extra inventory, they didn't like the labor to build subassemblies, and they didn't like looking for solutions when a low-price part was not in stock—and Aeroquip's customers maintained hose rooms.

Aeroquip saw a new solution. Rather than competing on parts, they could compete by lowering customer operating costs. Aeroquip could be the industry's easiest company to do business with, cutting headaches and overhead. Aeroquip switched away from Lock-in on hoses to improving advance shipping notice accuracy and delivery dependability. Aeroquip studied customer schedules and prepared for purchase orders before receipt. The company agreed to take back inventory sitting on customer shelves if the customer would commit to more volume. Management placed customer inventory at local dealers while creating procedures for urgent material shipments if customer schedules changed.

Aeroquip installed a new website so manufacturers could track orders and deliveries. They made invoice reconciliation easier by moving it online. And they started talking with manufacturers about outsourcing their hose rooms. In a conversation with one customer, Aeroquip's vice-president of sales asked the manufacturing vice-president, "If you are so interested in all these services, why have you been beating us up on price for the last 10 years?" "Well," the manufacturer replied, "for the last 10 years you really haven't given me anything else to talk about. Now that you're bringing up my issues, this is a great conversation."

Once Aeroquip recognized that competitors defined their business around the product, Aeroquip began looking for an alternative. Aeroquip had been sharing the industry Lock-in. By focusing on competitors while continuing ruthlessly to meet product needs, Aeroquip saw it could change the game from product to service.

Identify Your Competitor's Advantage and Do Something Else

No business has higher failure rates than restaurants. Competition is intense between restaurateurs, and it's estimated that nine out of ten restaurants fail. Almost everywhere, restaurants are oversupplied in a marketplace where competition is considered mature and growth rarely exceeds the population increase. One of the most competitive restaurant segments is pizza. Every town in America has a pizzeria, and sometimes there's one on every block!

From inauspicious beginnings, Pizza Hut became a tremendous success. It was not founded in the Italian enclaves of New York or Chicago, but rather in Wichita, Kansas. Despite humble roots, Pizza Hut figured out how to break out of the pack and spread its franchise across not only the United States, but internationally. Pizza Hut became the largest and most successful pizza business, with restaurants in nearly every town having a few thousand or more people.

As Pizza Hut grew it advertised consistent quality. Pizza Hut offered a series of proprietary products, such as Deep Dish, as well as a host of toppings. By the 1980s Pizza Hut was North America's pizza standard. Even though debate could be raged over whose pizza is best, there's no doubt Pizza Hut's product was desired by more Americans than any other restaurant pizza.

As Pizza Hut thrived, Tom Monaghan struggled to keep his one pizza store alive. Despite his best efforts, he was not able to attract a consistent following. After a stint in the Marines, he partnered with his brother in suburban Detroit to open his pizzeria. But after many difficulties, his brother gave up. Tom Monaghan came close to failure several times. As a pizza purveyor, Tom simply wasn't able to make a product that kept customers coming back.

In the 1970s Tom realized he did have a loyal following from students at the University of Michigan. Although his pizza parlor remained relatively empty, students that had his pizza delivered were buying again and again. As he studied competitors, including Pizza Hut, it was clear they focused on quality. They talked about dough and topping freshness. Pizza Hut advertised in new and existing markets that its competitive advantage was product quality.

Years of competing on quality did Tom Monaghan little good. But as a delivery business, Monaghan realized his store had a much better future. Pursuing quality, Pizza Hut had decided not to deliver and showed little intention to do so. So Domino's, Tom Monaghan's pizza business, competitively positioned itself on delivery. While Pizza Hut bragged about how good its pizza was, Domino's began telling the world "30 minutes or free" without mentioning quality.

As Domino's grew, Pizza Hut evaluated the emerging competitor's success. Executives bought many pizzas and concluded they were far inferior to Pizza Hut. Although Pizza Hut made its dough fresh daily, Domino's utilized frozen pizza balls delivered to its stores. Where Pizza Hut utilized the best ingredients they could purchase, Domino's kept its ingredient costs much lower. In test after test, Pizza Hut found that customers greatly preferred its product to Domino's.

Not only did customers like Pizza Hut's product better, but customers identified positively with the trademarked "Red Roof" restaurants. These sit-down units were consistently clean and inviting. Comparatively, Domino's units were tiny and in low-rent locations where few would want to eat. Domino's units were not something an ad agency would photograph and represent as quality dining.

Pizza Hut's executives, focused on their quality metrics, were not concerned about Domino's. They expected customers would be quite willing to drive to the local Pizza Hut for a quality carry-out pizza.

Domino's leveraged how its largest competitor measured its competitive advantage. While Pizza Hut focused on quality, Domino's kept focusing on delivery. Doing so allowed Domino's to grow practically unchallenged by the world's leading pizza restaurant chain. In the 1980's Tom Monaghan was asked if he ever worried about Pizza Hut getting into delivery and slowing his growth. Mr. Monaghan replied that he had not seen Pizza Hut show much interest in delivery, and until he did he wasn't going to worry about it.

Pizza Hut was Locked-in to its Success Formula. Recognizing this, Domino's worried little about its much larger and better financed competitor. And Mr. Monaghan became a billionaire in a slow-growth and intensely competitive marketplace.

Have you ever looked at a high-end watch? A Rolex, Piaget, or Brietling? These watches are incredibly expensive, and if you ask the retailer, you will receive a lesson on the mechanical workings of high-end watches. Few people remember that mechanics were competitive differentiators for all watches well into the 1970s.

From the beginning of portable timekeeping, watch manufacturers competed on the quality of internal workings. Ads showed pictures of the mechanics and talked about gear precision. Switzerland was the home of many watch manufacturers, and the entire industry focused on watch mechanics. Even American manufacturers, primarily competing in lower price watches, promoted the quality of their mechanics. Popular 1960s watch ads featured John Cameron Swayze saying, "Timex—it takes a licking and keeps on ticking," referring to the robustness of that brand's mechanics.

In the 1970s Japanese manufacturers were using transistors and solid state technology in many new products. They figured out how to replace tubes in radios and televisions, improving output quality, reliability, and longevity. Looking for a new product, they identified the Swiss watch industry. Watchmakers were completely Locked-in to their mechanical workings.

Casio led other Japanese companies in figuring out how to combine the newly developed light emitting diode (LED) with solid state electronics to make a watch that had an easy-to-read digital face and incredible reliability. Utilizing electronics, these watches kept time within a minute a year, incredibly high reliability by standards of the day. Maintenance free, these watches never needed winding, instead only annual battery replacement. In large quantities these watches were cheaper to make than labor-intensive mechanical watches.

Completely ignoring electronic watch benefits, Swiss and American watch manufacturers blithely ignored new Japanese competitors. These companies were considered electronic firms, not watchmakers. Traditional manufacturers disregarded these electronic devices, convinced that they would never be popular with consumers.

Japanese manufacturers quickly geared up production. Utilizing high-volume manufacturing equipment previously developed for other electronics products, they rapidly reduced watch prices by 90%. Promoting extremely high reliability, no winding, and no maintenance, within a decade more than 80% of watch sales were electronic.

Not a single traditional manufacturer made the move to electronic watches. By recognizing that existing watch manufacturers measured their competitiveness via the mechanics, Casio and its brethren were able to take over the watch market with almost no competitive response.

When Competitors Lock-in to Differentiating Features, Use Standards

By the 1990s information technology (IT) services had become a multibillion dollar U.S. industry. As computers became fixtures in all companies, IT departments became very large. Almost all hired outside firms to assist with software development and installation. Growing demand for computers and applications led to growing demand for IT services.

Anderson Consulting, Deloitte Consulting, and Coopers & Lybrand Consulting each hired thousands of IT consultants. Additional thousands joined their ranks at Electronic Data Systems (EDS), Computer Sciences Corporation (CSC), IBM, and other consultancies. While a host of smaller competitors chipped away at the market, large firms dominated at big corporations and thereby dominated the industry.

These large firms used differentiation combined with customer Lock-in to grow their businesses. Each had its own proprietary software development and implementation methodology. Anderson Consulting's (renamed Accenture) approach was Method One. IT firms insured clients their consultants would be trained in and consistently apply the proprietary methodology. Clients were also trained in the methodology, further Locking-in the services provider.

Simultaneously, big service providers offered local staff to work on long-term engagements. Combining a well-developed and proprietary delivery methodology with trained local staff created consistency and long-term relationships. In many instances, after a services company supplied staff for 12 to 24 months, clients utilized that firm for almost 100% of its needs. Vendor change became increasingly unlikely, attributed to high switching costs.

IT services providers and their clients were mutually Locked-in. Although some executives might have argued that the consultant/client relationship was too cozy—leading to high consulting charges—most business leaders were very happy with these long-term relationships and the service consistency.

Infosys Technologies, Ltd., of Bangalore, India, was incorporated in 1981. From its start, Infosys supplied computer software engineering and consulting. Like almost all Indian companies at the time, Infosys began as a supplier to Indian companies. But in the early 1990s the Indian government created free trade zones, allowing IT services companies to sell offshore, thus earning much needed foreign exchange. Infosys moved quickly to do work for non-Indian companies.

Infosys was featured in Thomas Friedman's popular book *The World Is Flat*. Readers, as well as followers of rapidly growing Indian-based IT services companies, might be tempted to think Infosys and its brethren were simply benefactors of low labor costs combined with Internet access. But that belied the competitive hurdles created by U.S. services suppliers. Such a simplistic view would indicate that just being cheap and having market access was enough to succeed.

In fact, when Infosys entered the U.S. marketplace, no customers beat a path to its door. It was frequently rebuffed by U.S. customers much more concerned about service quality than low cost. If a software implementation was delayed due to weak methodology, loose implementation practices, or untrained staff, the costs of delay could rapidly swamp any savings from lower initial costs. Business interruption costs from a botched effort to implement a new manufacturing, sales force automation, or accounting project could be multiples of the installation charges. Derailed IT projects could cost the chief information officer (CIO) and his staff their jobs.

Thus risks were every bit as important as cost when selecting an IT services vendor. There were many reasons to work with Locked-in, trusted vendors. Corporate IT systems were complex amalgams of applications and databases that needed to share data. Long-term vendors had deep knowledge of the various systems and data flows, and methodology trained staff were prepared to migrate technologies.

Infosys and its Indian brethren *attacked* proprietary methodologies tying clients to local staff and justifying long-term relationships— existing competitors' critical Lock-in. Infosys adopted the Capability Maturity Model (CMM) developed by the Software Engineering Institute (SEI) at Carnegie Mellon University. Not only did CMM offer a model for software development and installation, it also provided a tool for assessing the maturity of implementing organizations.

CMM provided a standard for evaluating IT implementation. Rather than a proprietary method with no external validation or ability to gauge effectiveness, CMM was an open methodology available to everyone. It was not managed by vendors, with their vested interest in looking good, but rather by an independent institute at a noteworthy university. If SEI said a vendor company had reached level 4 maturity, then a customer had external vendor capability assurance.

Adopting CMM was a frontal assault on existing services providers' Lock-in. Heavily invested in their proprietary methods, these companies were not eager to stop supporting their "sacred cows." Recognizing that their proprietary offerings had historically provided differentiation and customer assurances for delivery, which protected their rates, these companies chose to defend and extend their methods rather than adopt a newly promoted industry standard.

As Infosys invested in its CMM capabilities, it rapidly came to prominence as the first IT services company to reach each of the five maturity levels. Infosys promoted the CMM process for software development and implementation and backed that with quality systems including Six Sigma, an approach developed by Bill Smith of Motorola in 1986, to eliminate defects. Focusing on IT quality and risk reduction through CMM and Six Sigma opened doors for Infosys. By attacking the industry Lock-in, Infosys developed opportunities to displace existing competitors—rather than merely arbitrage low-cost Indian-based engineers.

Although Infosys was incorporated in 1981, it wasn't until 1992 that it became a publicly traded company in India. Infosys started its U.S. market attack in 1993 by achieving International Organization for Standardization (ISO) 9001 certification. Infosys attained SEI CMM Level 4 certification in 1997. In 1999 Infosys achieved CMM Level 5 certification and was listed on the NASDAQ. It took Infosys 18 years to achieve its quality standards ranking and first achieve $100 million annual revenue.

Between 1999 and 2001, Infosys quadrupled revenue to $400 million. During the subsequent IT services market collapse, PriceWaterhouseCoopers (the old Coopers & Lybrand) lost more than 70% of its consultants and was taken over by IBM. Accenture closed its training college in St. Charles, Illinois. Both EDS and CSC shed thousands of consultants. From 2001 to 2004 Infosys grew its revenue more than 35% per year, reaching $1 billion annually. Within three years, by March, 2007, Infosys revenue again tripled to over $3 billion. In just seven years Infosys revenue had grown 30-fold!

Most large IT services providers moved up-market to outsourcing entire IT shops in their efforts to further Lock-in customers. Intense competition hurt margins, and EDS was almost forced to file for bankruptcy in the early 2000s as it cut price on outsourcing deals trying to compete. But this made little difference to Infosys. Building on its new position as the quality leader and continuing to promote standards rather than a proprietary solution, Infosys profits grew along with revenue. In 2007 return on equity remained a staggering 30.8%, return on assets a whopping 27.5%, while gross margin was 44.4%, and net income an incredible 27.5%. Infosys success was not a story of cheap labor with Internet access, but rather an example of *breaking competitor Lock-in through the calculated use of an industry standard.*

Stall Competitors Whenever Possible

As described earlier, growth stalls are deadly. To achieve above average performance, business leaders should stall competitors. When you discover their Lock-ins you can create alternative competitive approaches to stall them. Even in markets considered "mature" or filled with large and well-financed legacy players, it is possible to stall them and grow.

Businesses need not fear large markets with ostensibly limited growth prospects. Nor should they fear competitors that are well healed, thus capable of retribution. By attacking competitors' Lock-ins, there is a good likelihood of success. It is difficult to do what large competitors do better, but by attacking their Lock-in with alternative solutions, new competitors can "change the game."

Successful strategy does not optimize an existing Success Formula unless you are in the Rapids. For all other lifecycle stages, successful strategy requires identifying and attacking competitors' Lock-ins. Instead of applying Michael Porter's "5 Forces Model" of competition to Defend and Extend a Success Formula, you should use it to identify competitors' Lock-ins and attack them. Success comes from beating competitors rather than trying to protect your own business.

Write down competitors' Success Formulas. Explicitly define their Identity, Strategies, and Tactics until you clearly understand their Lock-ins. By trapping competitors in their Lock-ins, as we've seen, it is possible to change the rules of competition and leave competitors struggling to respond.

As you evaluate competitors, go through each of the Lock-in categories described in Chapter 4, "The Dark Side of Success—Defend & Extend Management." Examine how each competitor might implement Lock-in to defend and extend its business:

- Is their market definition tight or rigid?
- What sacred cows do they maintain in their product line, distribution channel, or technology base?
- Where do they focus product development? How much do they invest?
- What excuses have they recently given defending their Success Formula?
- How does their hierarchy keep them Defending and Extending?
- What assets do they focus on maintaining?

- What financial machinations have they recently implemented?
- What biases are visible in their strategy?
- What is predictable in their management personnel and hiring? What kinds of people are they consistently recruiting?
- What investments have they made in IT? What do you know about their systems and the impact on their operations?
- What large investments have they made in acquisitions, manufacturing plants, or supply chain partnerships? What do you know about their investment process and how it propagates consistent types of investments?
- Who hoards information in their organization? Who are the "experts?" The Status Quo Police?
- What is their cost model? What are their fixed and variable costs? What costs are Locked-in with investments or contracts?

For each Lock-in, determine the strength of that Lock-in. How powerfully is it Locked-in? How important is it to maintaining the Success Formula? Which Lock-in is most critical to defending and extending the Success Formula? What actions were recently taken to defend Lock-in and the Success Formula?

Which Lock-ins create vulnerabilities? Don't be afraid of any Lock-in. A competitor may claim to have a Porter-style entry barrier, supported with large investments. But the more invested in the so-called entry barrier, the more they are Locked-in. And the more Locked-in they are, the less they can respond to alternative challenges.

Most large American airlines were founded by ex-military personnel. They Locked-in at deregulation on their Success Formula:

- National or international coverage
- A hub-and-spoke system using a few major cities as central points for linking multiple destinations
- Confrontation with suppliers and employees to keep costs low
- Task routinization
- Own a ticket distribution system and link it to travel agents as salespeople
- Constantly invest in new airplane technology, pursuing lower cost and better yield
- Vary pricing to improve revenue per passenger per mile flown

Southwest attacked these Lock-ins. Founded by a New York lawyer, Southwest started flying only in Texas and slowly added new cities. It flew city-to-city rather than hubbing into a few locations. It collaborated with vendors and employees. It expanded employee roles, allowing them to do different tasks. It had no ticket distribution system and did not pay commissions to travel agents. Instead tickets were sold directly. Southwest used a single aircraft type, and all seats were priced the same for everyone on a flight.

After 30 years, Southwest made more profit than the entire rest of the airline industry. Yet not a single major airline changed its Lock-ins, much less copied Southwest. Books were written on Southwest's operations, and still United, American, Delta, Northwest, and other airlines faced bankruptcy while pursuing their old Success Formulas that were never consistently profitable.

Never underestimate competitors' willingness to remain Locked-in— even after they stall and their Lock-ins are proven ineffective at improving results. Attacking competitor Lock-ins is the fastest route to improved performance and gaining valuable insight about your own Lock-ins.

7

Disruptions Are Key to Becoming a Phoenix Principle Organization

How do I escape Lock-in? How do I get my organization out of its Defend & Extend rut? How do I begin evolving my Success Formula?

Disruptions Enable Long-Term Superior Performance

Until now, this book has explored performance improvement requiring only marginal behavioral change. The two previous chapters described reasonably easy activities to implement because they did not actually change Lock-in or attempt to change the Success Formula. Their prescriptions provide more Lock-in and Success Formula clarity but do not address changing either one. They treat the symptoms but don't provide a long-term cure.

Phoenix Principle organizations that achieve breakthrough performance change their Success Formulas. Developing long-term superior performance requires evolving Success Formulas after they're Locked-in to meet market challenges. Emulating the mythical phoenix demands constantly rejuvenating Success Formulas.

"Change" is the most dreaded word in management. It's popular to say, "People hate change." Managers hate being told they have to implement change. "Change is what you can do so I don't have to," is how a manager described his company's change effort. Yet companies that perform above average long-term are extremely good at change. They usually don't even talk about change or change management. They seem to, as the Nike slogan says, "Just Do It." But how?

Phoenix Principle companies don't focus on change. Instead, they use disruptions to attack Lock-in, and by counteracting Lock-in, they create the opportunity for evolution to happen. They don't focus on "Vision" or try to sell their organizations on forecasts or potential outcomes. Instead, they attack the Lock-in that is stopping them from reacting to market challenges. Disrupting Lock-in opens their organizations to finding ways out of the Swamp.

Visions, speeches, threats, and data make little difference to a Locked-in Success Formula. Even those convinced are still Locked-in. Leaders, managers, and employees at Polaroid, Montgomery Ward, Digital Equipment Corporation, and Brach's Candy all knew they needed new solutions. But communications and data did not change their behavioral, structural, or cost Lock-ins. Organizations don't need more convincing; they need a way to overcome Lock-in.

Lock-ins designed to protect a Success Formula are intertwined and connected—a tangled web of behaviors and processes. Using analytical efforts to change a Success Formula is like asking a meteorologist to stop a tornado with weather computers. He or she can explain the cause and what *could* change the pattern, but data and desire do not do much about the situation. Anyone who has found themselves mired in a year-long business process reengineering project or a four-year ERP implementation knows analytical impracticality.

There *are* organizations that transition toward more effective, updated Success Formulas. For example, Apple Computer transitioned from a Macintosh-wedded Success Formula to a company that distributes songs and sells music players. More recently Apple even began moving into the mobile telephone marketplace with a marketing splash, if not a large business. Clearly Apple is no longer simply a "computer" company.

What's the "secret sauce?" *The key to Success Formula evolution is the effective use of Disruptions.* Managing Disruptions is a critical Phoenix Principle skill and provides the foundation for creating and sustaining above-average performance.

It's Not Possible to Change a Success Formula Directly

Before defining a Disruption and describing implementation, it's worth answering the questions, "Why don't we just design a new Success Formula and then implement it?" "Can't we launch a new Success Formula just like we would launch a new benefits plan or open a manufacturing plant?" or "Why can't we plan it and implement?"

Efficiency and productivity are powerful concepts, but there are some problems where what appears to be the most efficient solution can be ineffective. When early construction experts tried to build the Panama Canal, their efforts were stymied by problems having nothing to do with canal construction. Although the project was straightforward, malaria-carrying mosquitoes and swamp bogs completely halted progress well short of success more than once. A new engineer approached the project by first focusing on draining the swamp. Only after eliminating the swamp did he turn to building the canal.

Similarly, Success Formulas cannot evolve by simply recommending changes. Lock-in acts like mosquitoes and bogs swamping the project. Because Success Formulas are Locked-in, they cannot be modified directly. Instead, *initial focus must be placed on attacking and modifying Lock-in*. When changing a Success Formula, Lock-in keeps us stuck in the swamp, fighting mosquitoes that grind progress to a halt. These swamps must be drained to find firm footing for the next steps.

Remember, Success Formulas that produce above-average performance are formed in the crucible of the Rapids. It is when competition meets customer expectations that Success Formulas find their market value. It is in the Rapids that productive Lock-ins are developed and put in place. Leaders needing a new Success Formula must *find a way back into the Rapids*. Doing this requires overcoming Lock-in that has pushed the organization into the Flats or further into the Swamp.

Disruptions Are Not Well Understood nor Taught

Disruptions are "pattern interrupts" to existing Lock-ins.

- Disruptions are internally generated—not external events.
- Disruptions focus on Lock-in—not the Success Formula.
- Disruptions cause the organization to stop and reassess.

To understand Disruptions, we first need to recognize what Disruptions are *not*. Too often leaders think their organization is Disrupted when it has only suffered a short-term disturbance. *Disruptions stop organizations by attacking one or more important Lock-in, forcing a re-evaluation of the Success Formula.* Disruptions jeopardize the Status Quo Police. Comparatively, disturbances change a tactic or alter strategy, while defending and extending the Success Formula, leaving the Status Quo Police in power.

Executives will say that a revenue or margin decline or large customer defection are Disruptions. They are not Disruptions. They are *problems created by market challenges*. Similarly, a dramatic market price reduction, competitor plant closing, or industry-wide demand drop are not Disruptions. They are external reactions to market challenges.

When reacting to problems, a business might undertake a significant lay-off, slash marketing and advertising budgets, or radically cut R&D and new product development spending. Frequently these are thought of as Disruptions. But, again, they are not. Although internally generated, they are Defend & Extend (D&E) behaviors that protect the old Success Formula undertaken to reduce short-term costs. There have been no changes to existing Lock-ins or diminution of Status Quo Police power.

Just because an organization is *affected* does not mean it is Disrupted. The aforementioned actions are disturbances which serve as stop-gap improvements intended to prop up the Success Formula. While the organization certainly saw something happen, and the pain felt was very real, the Success Formula was not Disrupted. The Lock-ins remained in place, and business was largely expected to go on as usual—hopefully with improved productivity.

WHACKING THE CHICKEN COOP–REVISITED

Remember the farmer who whacked his chicken coop when seeking more egg production? He Locked-in to thinking threats would improve productivity. While his whacking significantly disturbed the chickens, no disruption occurred in his farming approach. Short-term, his disturbance caused productivity to drop—and lacking a Success Formula Disruption, no long-term productivity improvement developed.

Alternatively, the farmer could have attacked his Lock-in to threats as a productivity improvement tactic. Instead of attacking the chicken coop, he could have attacked his assumptions about chicken motivation. Changing his approach, disrupting versus disturbing, would have allowed him to begin experimenting with feed, temperature, and lighting. These tests would have improved production as he altered environmental factors.

Disruptions are not generated from the outside but rather must come from within. External events are challenges, which become problems. External events do not create Disruptions. Disruptions require that we internally decide to change Lock-ins. We have to *deliberately* attack Lock-ins if we are to create evolutionary opportunities. Only by admitting we must leave our comfortable Success Formulas and their Lock-ins can we begin a new discovery process.

AMERICA'S AIRLINES CHALLENGED ON SEPTEMBER 11, 2001

On September 11, 2001, a pair of hijacked airplanes crashed into New York's World Trade Center towers. Many thought this created a Disruption for the American airlines. Rather, these events made apparent significant challenges confronting airline industry management. When American air travel was suspended for a week, an extraordinary opportunity was created for U.S. airline industry participants. As a group they had never produced an adequate rate of return for shareholders or high customer satisfaction. After these events, they could have Disrupted themselves and found new solutions to their many problems.

Instead, the industry reacted with several disturbances, none of which improved airline profitability or customer satisfaction. Focusing on rapidly returning to flying without attacking industry Lock-ins (described in the previous chapter), they missed an opportunity to implement significant Success Formula changes. The result was fewer

passengers the next year, higher security costs, and continued ineffective labor and supplier relations. Longer lines at U.S. airport security,
significant changes in passenger carry-on items, and additional cost
cuts contributed to even lower customer satisfaction ratings as old
approaches were extended at great inconvenience to customers.

The government mandated flight shutdown gave industry leaders a
rare opportunity to attack long-held Lock-ins which had stalled historical improvement efforts. Airlines could have changed their commitment to hub-and-spoke systems, which caused more passengers to
fly more flight legs and used more fuel. They could have altered pricing at a time when passengers were open to new approaches. Or they
could have attacked their never-ending dedication to cutting employee costs and instead sought new approaches to job descriptions and
work rules with unions. Because of the catastrophe, key people in government, suppliers, and customer representation were open to finding
new solutions to the travails of airlines and their passengers.

The events of September 11, 2001, were not a Disruption, but they
offered an industry struggling to improve profitability and customer
satisfaction a chance to implement Disruptions which could have
addressed challenges. By maintaining dedication to Lock-in, several
airlines soon found themselves in bankruptcy court with strained
union relationships and perpetually dissatisfied customers.

Disruptions—opening doors to new options—*must be created internally
by those responsible* for organizational Lock-in. Disruptions demonstrate
that Lock-in, which once served the organization well, is no longer
acceptable. The person responsible must demonstrate commitment to
overcoming Lock-in so the organization can recognize a need to move
forward. Because Status Quo Police are responsible for Lock-in
maintenance, Disruptions must curtail their power in an obvious and
recognizable way.

Both industry analysts and executives bemoan profit problems within
U.S. airlines. But as long as airline leaders refuse to admit internal
changes are necessary, no Disruption can occur. As long as they blame
weak performance on external problems such as fuel costs, regulations,

and labor unions, their own organizations cannot change. Steve Jobs, founder and returning CEO at Apple, quickly demonstrated commitment to a new Success Formula by directing product development funding into new areas and neutering those who formerly kept all investment dollars flowing primarily into Macintosh development. By admitting Apple had to change and attacking the Status Quo Police, he Disrupted things and allowed new solutions to develop.

It is critically important that Disruptions stop the organization. Consider the old adage, "You can't change cars on a moving train." Most leaders would prefer to somehow Disrupt while simultaneously maintaining business as usual. They want to reconfigure the business while at the same time operating the old Success Formula. They want to hold onto the past while trying to embrace the future. They try to claim the old Success Formula is in good shape, while trying to say it must change. This will not work. Computer Science Corporation's commercial consulting business (from Chapter 4, "The Dark Side of Success— Defend & Extend Management") said it would maintain loyalty to local offices and staff while achieving historical utilization and margin metrics. Remaining Locked-in while simultaneously seeking new solutions to offshore competitors guaranteed the business had no hope of turning around its fortunes.

Effective Disruptions cause people to stop and say, "Wow, we really have to do something very different." There is a sense of having lost a mooring as people recognize something very significant was removed that once simplified decision-making and monitored behavioral norms. It's a key attribute of Disruptions that they *stop* the organization and force it to reassess behaviors and decision-making processes. When almost everyone is saying, "Oh my gosh," a Disruption is likely to make a difference.

Good Leaders Are Good Disruptors

Too frequently Success Formula change is viewed as a personnel issue. Boards of Directors and executives believe too often that hiring the "right" manager, possibly a "superstar" with charisma or tremendous analytical skills, will change an organization. This approach is unlikely to improve a Success Formula. Many CEOs, as well as vice presidents and directors, have failed because of their belief that personal skill will beat

Lock-in, an all too common myth. Although business loves hero-worship, *heroes are not the key to long-term success.*

Any leader, regardless of background or style, will fail if he or she relies on goal definition or planning as the key to breakthrough performance. Likewise, any leader can improve long-term performance if he will Disrupt Lock-in and relentlessly push the organization back into the Rapids. "Superstars" aren't needed in Defend & Extend organizations. Rather, Disruptors—those willing to unleash internal capabilities—are needed. Using Disruptions to manage Lock-in is the distinguishing characteristic of managers that produce above-average results.

Xerox and Kodak had leaders who attempted to change their organizations with less-than-spectacular results. These leaders had a clear vision for their companies. They hired top strategists to produce new corporate strategies. They communicated their vision to employees and investors. But when they did not effectively attack Lock-in, their organizations could not move beyond defending and extending old markets and products.

The CEO

Metric Changer

Jack Welch, former CEO of General Electric, set a remarkable standard for both revenue and profit growth during his long tenure. GE's equity value soared dramatically, and Mr. Welch became one of the most envied CEOs of all time. The press nicknamed Jack Welch "Neutron Jack." He was well-known for constantly changing metrics, such as adding to traditional revenue and profit growth requirements by demanding businesses be first or second in their industries. Businesses that could not meet Mr. Welch's requirements were introduced to GE's powerful mergers and acquisitions group—which was as successful divesting businesses as it was acquiring them. "Neutron Jack" changed metrics and sold businesses that didn't meet new metrics. These Disruptions kept Lock-in from pushing GE into the Swamp.

When Internet commerce emerged in the mid-1990s, most business leaders had a rather tepid view of this new capability. Some hired consultants to offer implementation ideas, while others asked their internal IT managers for Internet ideas. Few businesses made much use of the web beyond extending their business marginally, if they did anything at all. Upstart competitors were given considerable time to create Information Economy advantages as traditional players remained Locked-in to old Success Formulas.

CEO Welch reacted to the Internet by demanding every GE business create a DestroyYourBusiness.com team, with the business unit carrying the cost. These teams reported to both business unit management and a corporate-based team with game-changing ideas that could be used by GE or its competitors. These teams were literally devoted to attacking Lock-in.

As globalization opened the door to well-trained offshore labor, most companies waited to see if it was worthwhile to venture into new lands. But CEO Welch started traveling to China and India long before it was popular. He mandated before 2000 that divisions plan and implement mission critical facilities in offshore markets. This led to a very successful order-to-cash management operation in India. Spun off as Genpact, in 2007 the business was valued at $530 million when initially publicly offered (IPOd) on the New York Stock Exchange.

Investment Shifter

As CEO, Steve Jobs has never been shy about Disrupting Lock-in. By championing Macintosh's first-ever graphical user interface (GUI), Mr. Jobs helped revolutionize computer usage. Obsessed about ease-of-use, he focused Apple's engineering funds on innovations like the Finder, bringing thousands of new users to personal computing—even though these innovations were widely derided as trivial by experts within the industry and his own company.

Mr. Jobs eventually agreed to share Apple's top job with former Pepsico executive John Scully. Within months Apple's Board considered Mr. Jobs too disruptive, and he was let go. He then founded NeXT. Although NeXT was a technology success, the company's products were not marketplace winners. Mr. Jobs had followed his personal Success Formula by creating computer products based on enhanced technology, but NeXT was not a big investor win.

Mr. Jobs purchased Pixar, originally founded to develop computer graphics hardware and software. But Pixar's future turned out to be limited as a technology company, partly because the computer graphics software market was small and partly because customers were pleased with the leading supplier, Silicon Graphics. Mr. Jobs Disrupted his own Lock-in to technology, as well as Pixar's, by converting the company into

a successful movie studio. Using its software, Pixar developed and
launched *Toy Story*. Transformed, Pixar began challenging Disney as a
world-class animator and successful film producer.

After Mr. Jobs' departure, Apple Locked-in on computers. Even
though the company was first to market with a PDA (the Newton),
championed by new CEO Scully, leadership was unwilling to pursue that
new market. Again fearing Disruption, the Board jettisoned Mr. Jobs'
replacement and dropped its investment in PDA technology, preferring
to Lock-in on ongoing Macintosh investments. Unfortunately, each
subsequent year saw declining Macintosh market share as lower priced
Windows-based computers improved capabilities and increased market
domination. By 2000 Apple was selling computers primarily to narrow
market niches and struggling to maintain viable R&D levels.

After a fifteen year absence, Mr. Jobs was brought back to Apple's top
position. He rapidly Disrupted by investing the R&D and new product
development budget into the iPod MP3-based music player and iTunes
music distribution web site. Of course, neither had anything to do with
Apple's Locked-in personal computer competition. In 2006 Mr. Jobs
agreed to jointly develop ROKR with mobile phone leader Motorola.
Although ROKR's success was limited, Apple independently launched
iPhone in 2007 to enthusiastic buyers. Apple had never previously
participated in telephony. Steve Jobs repeatedly demonstrated his
willingness to take Apple into new markets by attacking Lock-ins and
adopting new technologies and marketing approaches, even when Apple
had no experience or expertise.

Hierarchy Thwarter

Disruptive leader stories are not limited to rock-star personality CEOs.
Shortly after 2001 Whirlpool's long-tenured and mild-mannered CEO
David Whitwam recognized his business was becoming commoditized by
"big box" electronics retailers such as Best Buy. The distribution channel
was constantly promoting low price and reducing differences between, as
well as margin for, appliance manufacturers. Realizing he must introduce
new products to separate Whirlpool from competitors, he had to
overcome Whirlpool's innovation weaknesses.

Mr. Whitwam Disrupted Whirlpool by asking his entire organization
to send new ideas directly to him. This direct communication attacked
Whirlpool's hierarchy Lock-in. Company hierarchy was vetting all ideas,
resulting in too few reaching senior level consideration. While middle

managers were upset by the Disruption, taking this action unleashed multiple innovations for review and implementation.

Reaching out to the entire organization and bringing in consultants, as well as his commitment to innovation, signaled Mr. Whitwam's status as a change agent. His actions Disrupted Whirlpool's management team, causing them to ask, "What's going on around here? Why would our CEO do this?" Attacking hierarchy involved everyone in innovation unlike any previous initiative. Disruption caused Whirlpool's managers to realize hierarchy was less important than innovation.

One innovation from this Disruption seemed very small and likely would never have survived hierarchical vetting but made a big difference to Whirlpool. Someone recommended reintroducing front-loading washers, which use less water and produce a better wash but had not been sold for more than two decades. That was not the innovation. Introducing a slide-out drawer unit upon which the washer could sit, thus raising the washer door for easier access while providing storage and access for cleaning products, was. This was exactly the kind of innovation traditional managers would have vetted out and which made a significant difference when launched into the marketplace.

Whirlpool's hierarchy Disruption unleashed a series of improvements. Soon innovations developed not only into new products, but into new manufacturing processes and quality as managers globally utilized CEO access to promote ideas previously overlooked.

Sacred Cow Shooter

Carlos Gutierrez is known to most people as President George W. Bush's Secretary of Commerce. Prior to that position, he implemented Disruptions leading to dramatic change as Kellogg's CEO. When Mr. Gutierrez took the role, Kellogg was Locked-in to market share maintenance and keeping manufacturing plants busy. Promoting Locked-in legacy brands consumed nearly the entire marketing budget. Deadly price and coupon warring had evolved, seriously hurting margins. Kellogg's faltering stock price was linked to Wall Street analyst concerns about the future.

The 20-year Kellogg veteran quickly implemented several Disruptions. Launching a "Volume to Value" campaign, he changed all company reporting from weights to dollars. Weight-based reporting kept Kellogg's Locked-in to volume, no matter the margin. Changing reporting metrics Disrupted managers forcing discussions about volume versus margin. Rather than promoting products to the point of loss, managers were forced to discuss profitability and market share.

The founding manufacturing plant in Battle Creek, Michigan was a sacred cow, but Mr. Gutierrez converted the hometown facility into an R&D center and simultaneously increased R&D budgets while cutting product discount budgets. He focused on new product development in leadership meetings, disrupting historical agendas which had been dominated by sales and manufacturing (the Status Quo Police). Within months Kellogg's margins were up, and its stock price followed suit as analysts began writing positively about the company's projected fortunes.

Disruptions Are Not Limited to CEOs

Disruptions Should Be Institutionalized

One of Cisco Systems' stated objectives is to make its own products obsolete. This is an inherently disruptive objective. Most businesses like to think product lifecycles can be lengthened, defended, and extended to increase late lifecycle profitability. But Cisco obsoletes its own products, rather than allowing competitors to catch them. This disruptive objective keeps Cisco from falling into Defend & Extend Management behavior, no matter who sits in the CEO chair.

Managers Can Make a Huge Impact

Bill has managed business development for more than 20 years at a Midwestern industrial products company. His company traditionally competed in highly engineered products for moving fluids in chemical plants and refineries. Competition focused on product features, comparing engineering specifications, and price. In recent years, competition from offshore suppliers intensified, and customers moved facilities offshore, easing offshore supplier access and creating additional downward price pressure.

Like most industrial products companies, leadership at Bill's company loved talking about products and manufacturing expertise. Strategy discussions focused on extending product capabilities, finding new applications for existing products, seeking new geographic markets, and optimizing manufacturing. But recent market challenges had caused leadership to worry about how they would maintain sales and margins.

Bill could easily have spent his time defending and extending traditional products in traditional applications. Instead, Bill constantly chose to Disrupt his organization.

Bill visited Midwestern universities, learning what new technologies offered breakthrough product opportunities. He hosted regular meetings where marketers and engineers could receive technology updates and discuss new applications. He kept himself and his marketing peers, informed about Department of Energy investment programs and available product development grants. He read industry conference reports about cutting edge technologies and applied them to his company, distributing key readings to engineers, fellow marketers, and executives.

Although Bill wasn't a company vice-president, he decided his company should begin hosting its own industry conference. He encouraged a few top technologists and government officials to participate, and he acquired partial funding from a federal grant. Federal sponsorship encouraged cosponsors, who volunteered presentations and panel discussions. This pulled his own company into committing as conference host. Shortly, Bill's conference became a leading industry and regional technology application conference. A halo was created for his company, augmenting sales.

Bill regularly identified grants supporting new R&D initiatives between his company and local universities, thus Disrupting his engineering group so they kept their eyes on emerging technology applications. He explored joint ventures and partnerships with start-up companies, keeping the executive team disrupted and aware of new competitive products taking front-runner position with customers. He created partnerships with colleges through which he supplied a pipeline of new engineers with new skills, Disrupting human resources to recruit for new capabilities.

Bill did not have a large budget, nor did his position control lots of employees. But Bill's willingness to Disrupt Lock-in helped his company remain at the industry forefront.

Marketing Can Be Critical to Success

John was Marketing Director in an industrial products company. John spent more on distribution than promotion, and 90% of that went to legacy product brochures, price sheets, and catalogs. Marketing managers were organized by product line and spent most of their time developing pricing programs and reacting to competitors. John's department was Locked-in to defending and extending existing product sales.

Twice a year John's 12 managers argued over who would attend their industry conference. The three selected looked forward to a few days out of office, leisurely conversing with friends in other companies. This frustrated John because he felt little value was returned for the cost.

John chose a Disruptive alternative. He told his managers they all would go to the next conference. They would group into four teams of three. Upon returning from the conference, each team would have two weeks to develop a new business opportunity plan based on something learned at the conference. These plans would be presented to himself, the CEO, and the CFO—so they had to take these plans and presentations seriously.

One plan would be selected for implementation. That team would be dedicated to the effort, and their historical responsibilities would be spread among the other marketing managers. Budgets for marketing managers with traditional products would not increase; they would simply add new products. Budgets for transferred products would remain with the new opportunity development team. This way, John did not have to ask for additional funds. If the new team's plan did not succeed, there was no promise these managers would have a job. There was no plan to unwind changes to traditional product management.

This Disruption had an immediate impact. He successfully attacked Lock-in to product sacred cows as well as his product line organization. He also attacked traditional spending budgets, which had emphasized D&E sacred cows. Disruption forced his organization to develop new marketing approaches to old products, while the new team had a budget to develop new product and market opportunities.

A Marketing Manager's company was Locked-in to making marginal product improvements even though new competitors were gaining share. Leadership was influenced by customer interviews and surveys, which were focused on large accounts representing most revenue. But these customers were Locked-in to buying old products and knew little about new competitive offerings.

She Disrupted by engaging a student group from a nearby college to develop and implement focus groups with customers that had reduced purchases. Not Locked-in to the Success Formula, the students were unbiased when exploring why these customers' buying patterns changed. Although these focus groups were a class project with minimal cost, the results demonstrated that emerging competitors had far more influence on key buying criteria than previously realized. Even large customers were at risk of defecting.

IT Leaders Can Play a Critical Role

Functional leaders can use Disruptions as well. A CIO realized arguments between her staff and users over IT responsiveness seemed never-ending. While her team consistently met goals, users were not happy. Locked-in to traditional IT metrics tied to legacy system performance, reinforced with bonuses, her team was not responding to user requests.

So the CIO let users create metrics for evaluating IT. While she maintained classic IT metrics (such as system uptime) for internal team reviews, she allowed users to define their important IT metrics. Reinforced with reset bonus programs, her team quickly improved communication and alignment. Discussions about system upgrades and new software solutions took on greater urgency, and satisfaction improved.

An Information Technology Development Director found himself Locked-in to upgrading existing platforms. Although his team evaluated new technologies, rarely did they implement. It was always faster, easier, and cheaper to enhance existing platforms using old technologies.

So he mandated implementing one new technology annually into a mission critical system. This Disruption created hands-on technology experience rather than just analytical insight. Rapidly his team's new technology skills converted from analysis to implementation as they learned and then developed capability to test and use new technologies. Due to this Disruption his team was soon on the cutting-edge of many new technologies, enhancing their conversations with functional and business unit teams. The business quickly gained advantages by using leading technologies before competitors.

HR Leaders Can Be Important Disruptors

An HR director realized her team was Locked-in to traditional roles such as benefits and compensation. Although good at their jobs, her managers were adding insufficient value to business units looking for new competitive ideas in tough markets. She Disrupted her team by assigning every member a customer. Monthly, the HR managers reported to their peers customer status on revenues, margins, and satisfaction.

Narrow competency Lock-in broke down. HR contributions to job descriptions, organizational design, and flexible compensation increased, which aided hiring people more attuned to emerging market challenges.

An HR hiring manager realized his company's job descriptions forced recruits into the Locked-in mold of previous job holders, inhibiting progress toward meeting emerging market challenges. He Disrupted the recruiting process by posting openings on Monster.com and other online job boards. He received a wider set of profiles than previously gained from internal postings and recruiters. His attack on the Locked-in recruiting process and narrow job descriptions brought in new employees more aware of new competitors and with new competitive ideas.

These Disruptions worked because they attacked Lock-ins that had been impeding adaptation. Random Disruptions have no more value than disturbances. Managers must target Disruptions on Lock-ins that are keeping the Success Formula operating in the face of mounting challenges and weakening returns.

Avoiding Disruptions Creates Long-term Problems

Important as they are, Disruptions are the activity most avoided by leaders because they are not part of D&E Management. It takes courage to plan and initiate a Disruption.

For CEOs with access to significant resources, it's tempting to avoid Disruptions completely. They can direct resources into new markets or technologies without Disrupting. Unfortunately, organizations rapidly revert to their old Success Formulas soon after CEOs depart. Unless a Disruption is implemented, Success Formula evolution will be short-lived.

As General Motors Chairman in the 1980s, Roger Smith tried to change the future of what was then the world's largest automobile company. Demonstrating keen foresight, he took several actions considered controversial, but he minimized Disruptions as he attempted change.

Recognizing the growing importance of information technology, Mr. Smith purchased EDS, America's largest IT services company. Electronics use was skyrocketing, and Mr. Smith saw GM's need to compete in markets besides autos, so he acquired Hughes Electronics— beefing up GM's position in electronics and the rapidly growing aircraft market. Realizing Japanese companies approached auto competition very differently, Mr. Smith launched Saturn as a completely autonomous new business, free to build and sell cars unencumbered by GM's legacy.

These significant events were heralded as breakthroughs for GM. Most pundits considered them opportunities for GM to revitalize itself long-term in ways not yet discovered. GM had taken unprecedented action toward a new destiny.

But two decades later, it became clear these efforts did not yield the results Roger Smith desired. Neither EDS nor Hughes remained part of GM, as the company sold these assets, retrenching into traditional automobile and truck markets. Saturn, which built a cult following for its vehicles and dealers, became just another division forced to share parts and procurement methods, as well as most business processes, with monolithic GM.

In 2006 concern emerged that GM might be forced into bankruptcy. Its future was uncertain as it faced considerable competition from historical American, German, and Japanese carmakers as well as new Korean entrants. GM's market value at 2006's end was less than when Roger Smith led the charge for change. How GM would ever regain its lost value was far from clear.

What went wrong? Roger Smith never Disrupted GM. These corporate acquisitions were separated from traditional GM. Roger Smith never made GM's executives, directors, managers, employees, or suppliers *stop* and consider the challenges he saw looming. He did not attack Lock-ins that were keeping GM behaving the same, year after year, as competition grew more difficult, market share slowly declined, and returns diminished.

After Roger Smith retired, it was easy for the non-Disrupted automobile monolith to jettison EDS and Hughes Electronics, raising cash spent defending its old Success Formula. It was not difficult for leadership to remove Saturn's independence and push the division to adopt common procurement methods and parts—critically entrenched, traditional Lock-ins. Roger Smith's efforts to evolve GM's Success Formula were lost because he failed to Disrupt. The old Success Formula marched onward, despite weakening results, throwing out initiatives which could have helped GM become more successful.

Jack Greenberg, McDonald's Chairman in the 1990s, attempted to evolve his company's Success Formula. Mr. Greenberg purchased all or part of Chipotle's Grill, Donato's, Fazoli's, Pret a Manger, and Boston Market. Recognizing traditional McDonald's stores that were at or nearing global saturation, these acquisitions offered employees and franchisees new opportunities to grow.

But Mr. Greenberg made these acquisitions without Disrupting McDonald's. Making acquisitions from the corporate office, he did not force McDonald's management to stop and assess limited growth prospects nor weaknesses inherent in limited offerings tied to the Success Formula. He allowed the old Success Formula to continue operating unfettered while his acquisitions were largely ignored by the traditional organization. McDonald's leadership treated leaders in the acquired companies as inferior, even though their growth rates and margins were superior.

By 2007 McDonald's was well on its way to dismantling Mr. Greenberg's Success Formula evolution efforts. Fast-growing Chipotle's was spun off, raising cash used to improve McDonald's operating practices and buy back equity. McDonald's informed Boston Market's leaders a spin-off was likely to fund more share buybacks. After Mr. Greenberg's departure McDonald's "refocused" on hamburger units, selling higher growth businesses to defend and extend its increasingly out-of-date traditional Success Formula.

These two leaders had visions for their corporations. Facing Lock-in, they opted to avoid real Disruptions in their efforts to evolve. While this may have appeared clever, their initiatives did not successfully improve long-term health or viability. By avoiding Disruptions, their efforts were easily undone within just a few years. Without Disruptions, evolutionary efforts will be short-lived and often viewed later as distractions to the "core business."

Disruptions Produce Anxiety But Are Necessary

As discussed earlier, people fear the unknown more than they fear failure. Partly for this reason, leaders map out the future, hoping such mapping will reduce unknowns thus increasing manager and employee confidence. Because Disruptions increase unknowns short-term, leaders often avoid them. But without Disruptions, there can be no opportunity for change.

While Disruptions initially produce anxiety, people love working in the Rapids. The Rapids is where they are most creative, most resourceful, and have the most fun. By helping people realize that Disruptions unleash creativity, it is possible to make them motivated. Disruptions do not tell people what to do. Instead they interfere in the normal course of behavior. It is this *interference that creates the opportunity for future growth*. By Disrupting—attacking Lock-ins—it is possible to push people and organizations back into the Rapids. It's in the Rapids where developing new solutions is required and accepted. The Rapids is where managers define new solutions to challenges.

Now is an important time for Disruptions because many organizations have not evolved their Success Formulas from being based on an industrial economy to being rooted in the information economy. Without Disruptions, Industrial Era organizations will remain Locked-in and eventually fall victim to Schumpeter's predictions. As Kondratiev's long wave of change continues descending upon them, their vulnerabilities become more obvious, allowing new competitors to snatch away their value.

Evolving deeper into an information economy, it is clear we are learning about competitors' actions and decisions more quickly. Entry barriers are less valuable than before and diminishing quickly. Surviving, thriving businesses in the rapidly changing information economy *must* be able to Disrupt themselves regularly. Lock-in will have shorter lifecycle value, causing Success Formulas to produce high returns for shorter time periods. Only organizations skillful at Disruptions will maintain competitive longevity in what's been nicknamed the "hyper-competitive" information economy.

8

Develop New Success Formulas via White Space

How do I evolve my Success Formula? How do I design and implement new solutions? How do I return to the Rapids?

White Space Is Where Success Formulas Evolve or Are Created Anew

The last chapter provided a visual image of Disruptions by remarking, "You can't change cars on a moving train." "You can't change cars without two sets of tracks" helps put a visual to the role of White Space. Organizations beyond the Rapids have Locked-in Success Formulas. Locked-in organizations are stuck on their tracks, unable to create new Success Formulas. Another set of tracks is needed to do this kind of work. That second set of tracks is *White Space*.

White Space provides a location for new thinking, testing, and learning. General Motors managers likely perceive they have few decision alternatives due to their Lock-ins. Locked-in organizations are committed to Defending and Extending the old Success Formula. It's not possible for them to develop a new one while simultaneously optimizing value out of the tiring Success Formula. While Locked-in managers can intellectually envision other options and even contribute to designing them, they cannot implement them. Implementation requires White Space to try, learn, test, and evolve.

White Space is where organizations reenter the Rapids. Despite leadership's best efforts to design a new Success Formula, an idea on PowerPoint slides must be tested in the marketplace to determine if it produces positive results. Only through market competition can a new Success Formula prove its results-enhancing capability. No manager has a crystal ball, and Locked-in leadership teams typically have very cloudy ones from years of Defending and Extending. New business development plans must be tested through competition in the Rapids.

MEGAMISTAKES

Business leaders and strategists predict the future by extending past data. Unfortunately, most predictions aren't very accurate. Popular predictions from the 1950s to 1970s included

- By 1979 interstate highway vehicle separation would be automatically controlled by computerized cars. By 1990 unmanned vehicles would travel interstates controlled by highway substations programmed through a sort of passenger dial-a-destination.
- By 1978 newspapers were to be printed on home fax machines.
- By 1981 undersea mining and farming were to replace land-based commodity production.
- By 2000 farm tractors would be unmanned robots, and farm labor would be unavailable.
- By 2000 beef and pork would be so expensive that most protein would be nonanimal substitutes. Global food shortages would lead to dramatic growth in synthetic food consumption.
- Personal helicopters for urban commuting were to be commonplace by the 1990s.
- Due to land and labor shortages, factory constructed modular housing would replace traditional U.S. home construction by the 1980s.
- By the 1980s traditional lighting would be replaced by glowing wall paint, responding to widespread electricity shortages.

- By the 1970s clothes would be washed ultrasonically to save scarce, extremely expensive, water.

- Due to limited programming and little customer advantage, color TV penetration was not expected to exceed 10% of households.

- By 2000 *all* automobiles would be smaller, lighter, and without chrome.

- By the 1990s a hypersonic transport (HST) would fly at 17,000 miles per hour, completing a London to Sydney flight in 67 minutes.[1]

Forecasters tend to increase analytical complexity when trying to convince others of their prognostications. Unfortunately, there is no evidence that increased complexity improves forecast accuracy. Nor is there statistical evidence that industry standards are more accurate than guesses—or less subject to inaccuracies from marketplace shifts. Forecasting is simply not terribly helpful for figuring out a new Success Formula. Competition creates high-return Success Formulas. Competitors who remain in the Rapids are best able to avoid Schumpeter's prediction of failure, whereas many sophisticated forecasters find themselves on the rubble heap of failure.

Because forecasting is based on data projection, it should not surprise us that strategists and business leaders often make their worst forecasts when most struggling. Shifting market conditions cause forecast assumptions to lose validity, just as they cause results to deteriorate. Forecasting is least valuable when organizations are in the most trouble.

As described previously, scenario development is a powerful tool for developing new assumptions. Scenarios describe new potential outcomes that lead to new option development. But scenario planning is not Success Formula development. Scenarios highlight potential market shifts, Success Formula weaknesses, and risks from remaining devoted to existing Lock-in. Scenarios create a jumping-off point for White Space projects, in which market competition can create a valuable new Success Formula.

THE LAW OF UNINTENDED CONSEQUENCES

Predicting the future requires identifying and selecting from among multiple options. Predictions start with potential outcomes. Each of those outcomes then has another set of potential outcomes. Within short order, the number of possibilities explodes. It becomes impossible to think through them all. Worse, different outcomes intersect, leading to interactions which are impossible to predict, exponentially expanding options beyond what can be considered.

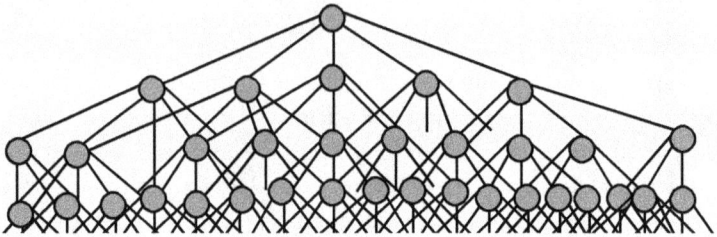

Figure 8.1 Exponential Option Growth

For example, modern medicine led to lengthening life spans. Predicting longer life spans did not predict dramatically rising costs for long-term care and extensive infirm or elderly medical services, which would challenge public and private insurance, which would lead to *de facto* care rationing via insurance and Medicare payout limits.

High gold prices led to increased mine openings, which led to increased mining in Brazil. Brazilian mining led to widespread deforestation, which created pollution problems in Brazil, which many people think contributed to global warming. Global warming fears are now leading to "carbon taxes" being applied to emissions, which is helping promote dramatic increases in ethanol production. Rapid ethanol growth has caused the price of corn, a primary ingredient for ethanol, to jump, raising the prices of agricultural land while also increasing the price of consumer products from cereal to tortillas.

The Soviet Union collapse created dramatic changes within newly independent eastern European countries. Furthermore, without the Soviet Union offering aid, weapons, and potential conflicts, China and India quickly aligned politically with the United States. This led to billions of underemployed people entering the global labor market, flattening inflation-adjusted incomes and decreasing job security for U.S. workers and middle-managers.

These results were unpredictable because so many potential outcomes, from so many interacting variables, made them far from obvious. Predictors have to weight all these circumstances, and all the possible outcomes, to arrive at a "most statistically likely" outcome. But it's not the most likely which create future problems. Instead, it's those overlooked. If even one future outcome is too lowly weighted because it seems too unlikely, and then that one occurs, the prediction can be completely wrong.

The Law of Unintended Consequences tells us it is impossible to predict the long-term consequences of any action taking place in a complicated, multivariable world. Unexpected things happen. Planners cannot know which variables will remain constant and which will change, as competition alters variables and their influence on outcomes.[2]

Success Formulas involve Identities, Strategies, and Tactics. Evolving a new Success Formula requires the latitude to change *all* these. Most organizational evolution focuses on tactical change. But evolving a Success Formula requires the option to redefine Identity as well as Strategy and Tactics. No Locked-in organization can redefine its Identity. Only in White Space can such openness exist.

White Space teams operate outside Lock-ins, even violate Lock-ins, developing new solutions to market challenges. *It is leadership's role to migrate the traditional organization toward a new Success Formula developed in White Space.* No one will enjoy long-term superior performance if they try bringing White Space back into the Locked-in organization. Lock-in violations will be instantly obvious, and Status Quo Police will move rapidly to kill the diversion. No matter how strong-willed the CEO, it is impossible for any leader to protect a new Success Formula thrown into an organization designed to defend and extend its past. Instead, by migrating an organization *toward* the new Success Formula (toward behaving like the White Space), businesses can have a long life and maintain above-average performance.

There Are Requirements for Effective White Space

White Space is a *dedicated* part of the organization which has

- *permission* to violate old Lock-ins and
- *sufficient resources* committed in advance to accomplish the goal.

White Space must be a dedicated workspace devoted to entering the Rapids and developing a new Success Formula. It cannot report to managers operating the old Success Formula, stuck in the Swamp. Defend & Extend (D&E) leaders must be committed to wringing as much value out of the old Success Formula as possible. They cannot simultaneously serve two opposite masters—optimization and adaptation. Such a desire is more than impractical; it is impossible. The first goal of D&E Management will always be meeting old Success Formula objectives. New initiatives will remain "on the back burner" as managers struggle with challenges to old Identities, Strategies, and Tactics. Although they may wish to change, Lock-in (even Disrupted Lock-in) stops them.

Managers inside the old Success Formula must operate according to Lock-ins. They cannot pick and choose which Lock-ins to abide by and which to ignore. The Status Quo Police won't tolerate such behavior. Embedded decision-making and workflow processes simply can't operate if someone tries ignoring Lock-ins. The only way someone can do something new is if they are given dedicated space in which to do it.

Even though Success Formulas grow tired, and their results dwindle, managers operating old Success Formulas never run out of investment ideas for marginal improvement. As discussed previously, these ideas rarely make a positive difference except in the very short term. Nonetheless, D&E Management constantly asks for money. White Space funding will rapidly evaporate, even when promised, if it must constantly compete with D&E managers. White Space's proverbial Peter will be robbed to pay the old Success Formula's Paul. Remember how GM and McDonald's sold high performing businesses to fund legacy improvements?

D&E managers are not well equipped to operate in more poorly defined White Space. Lock-in provides clear rules for decisions and behavior and usually clear performance metrics. White Space requires operating with fewer boundaries so new rules and metrics can be developed. Those measured by old metrics do not have similar, clear benchmarks for measuring Success Formula development performance. D&E Management tools are not designed for managing White Space.

But White Space is not a "skunk works." It's critically important that White Space projects receive high visibility. The entire organization is expected to someday migrate toward the new Success Formula developed in White Space. To understand this new Success Formula and gain commitment to its value, the older (and usually larger) organization must have consistent exposure to what is done in White Space and why.

Disruptions create anxiety about the future. Observing White Space, where ideas are tested and succeed in the marketplace, provides information, reducing unknowns. White Space also exposes the organization to challenges. It displays alternative Identity, Strategy, and Tactics. It throws off "lessons learned" from experiments. Thus, it is possible for leaders, managers, employees, suppliers, and investors to gain confidence in the new Success Formula and prepare themselves to leverage Disruptions into a migration path.

IBM's Florida-based development team created the modern-day PC using an Intel microprocessor plus a Microsoft operating system. They were able to develop customers for the new product, but they operated as an out-of-view skunk works. When traditional IBM finally decided to adopt the PC, the undisrupted computer organization simply rejected it. They felt the product was too cheap, offering little sales compensation, and was a distraction to traditional equipment and software sales. PC project leaders soon left IBM as the traditional organization absorbed and then killed the PC—like white corpuscles killing a potential infection.

IBM should have Disrupted its Lock-ins. And top leaders should have spent weeks or months apprising traditional business managers of PC group activities and successes via tools such as weekly highlights. They should have demonstrated how the project won customers, increased sales, improved margin, and grew. Then they should have developed additional Disruptions that would have fostered migration projects exploring how the traditional organization could compete more like the high-growth PC business.

Had they done this, IBM might have avoided the revenue problems created when customers switched from proprietary mainframes and minicomputers to servers on "open" architectures such as Unix. More than once IBM overinvested in sustaining its Success Formula too long, including developing proprietary server and desktop products well into the 1990s (AIX and PS2). After more than a decade of technology achievement and billions of invested dollars, but minimal market success, eventually IBM retrenched from most of these products—and created White Space to develop a new Services business.

Dedicated but highly visible White Space is central to developing a migration path. Disrupted, and realizing that Lock-ins must change to meet market challenges, White space becomes the lifeline for a moribund organization. White Space gives insight and focus to how an organization can overcome Lock-ins and adopt a new Success Formula. Because people are migrating toward something they can observe and understand, traditional hurdles to change become less of an obstacle. Remember, people do not reject change as much as they fear the unknown. Making White Space visible reduces unknowns and creates opportunities for people to design migration paths toward what they observe as successful.

When a significantly new product is introduced through a traditional sales force, it often does not succeed. Despite sales training, existing customers are more likely to buy traditional products, and salespeople receive more compensation from higher-revenue, traditional products. New products languish.

However, when new products are introduced via White Space, traditional salespeople can focus on what they have always sold—possibly even disparaging new products sold by counterparts in a new division. As new products prove their merit, and sales rise, it takes little time for salespeople to rapidly request transfers to the new division. Once they see a path to higher sales and commissions, it's far easier to figure out the migration route.

Recall AM (Addressograph-Multigraph) from Part 1, "Understanding How We Got Into This Mess." AM knew it had problems selling printing presses once copiers came on the scene. So AM's leadership launched a copier. But salespeople sold only a fraction of the goal. When salespeople tried selling copiers to traditional print shop customers, they weren't copier buyers. When salespeople tried selling copiers to office managers, printers were offended and threatened to buy presses, plate-makers, cutters, and supplies from competitors. Salespeople were obligated to maintain traditional sales as long as possible to preserve revenue and commissions, so they quickly retrenched to selling traditional products to traditional customers. New copier sales never developed.

AM should have launched a new White Space copier division. That division should have been given independence to figure out how to succeed in copiers. Although AM *believed* it knew how to succeed in copiers, its experience was all "BIS" (Butt-In-Seat) analysis rather than actual competition. Even though "leveraging" the sales force sounded appealing, it was naïve because no one in AM knew what was required to succeed against Xerox. Xerox didn't just sell copiers, it sold "clicks," referring to its per-page charge system. And whereas most printers had low-cost equipment that used high-cost supplies, copiers were just the opposite with extremely expensive equipment and almost no supplies. Significant purchasing differences eluded AM, including how copier customers budgeted and spent. Without a dedicated team operating outside Lock-ins, AM had no hope of attacking Xerox.

Managers usually object to two groups selling to the same customer. There is no doubt this approach lacks efficiency. But Xerox was stealing AM's customers. Only by competing with itself, as well as Xerox, could a new copier division learn, grow, and create a prosperous new Success Formula. It's Lock-in and the desire to keep an old Success Formula alive as long as possible that causes businesses to fear internal competition. Such competition is critical to learning and growing.

Permission

In addition to being dedicated, White Space must have explicit *permission to violate Lock-ins*. Few managers are trained in asking for, much less obtaining, such permission. Typically a manager might go to leadership saying

- Company revenues have declined due to inroads by lower-cost products (the problem).

- The company can source a lower-priced product from a third-party vendor.

- Because this new product requires no manufacturing investment, it will have a very high return on investment (ROI).

- The product will successfully leverage the company's new Internet site.

- The manager would like permission to introduce this new product.

And permission is given.

But this product is a big loser for distributors, who must tie up inventory and training in a low-priced, low-margin product. Our manager knows this, so he simply doesn't talk about it when asking permission for launch. He tells executives only what's necessary to get an okay to proceed. He knows the distributor organization is losing customers because it's high-cost and slow to react. Customers are moving toward lower-cost products delivered through just-in-time manufacturer delivery systems. He figures his product will be a beachhead for transitioning his company's distribution approach—an initiative championed by the COO.

Quickly new product sales exceed expectations. But within weeks of launch, the new product manager is fired, due to distributor complaints. "But sales are 300% of launch projections, and we have taken no discounts, so ROI is above forecast. And I had permission to sell the product on the web," the manager pleads. Although he exceeded expectations and proved the efficacy of online sales as promised, he was fired because he violated Lock-in to the distributors—and he did not explicitly ask for that permission. Results were irrelevant. Yes, he had permission to launch the product and sell on the web, but permission had not been granted to violate Lock-in.

Managers will ask, "What did the executives think would happen? Didn't they anticipate this distributor response?" The answer can be hard to accept. Without being explicit, there was no reason for executives to anticipate a Lock-in violation, so they ignored it just like the manager did. They assumed the old Success Formula would work as it always had while the new product rolled out. Until confronted with the Lock-in violation, there was no reason to expect it—and permission was not implicit.

Permission to do what's inside Lock-in is not White Space permission. It's Defend & Extend. White Space permission requires obtaining permission to violate a Lock-in. The marketing manager sold his idea but did not discuss the Lock-in he would violate. The only permission that matters in White Space is permission to violate Lock-in. That permission must be explicit, which reinforces the need for a Disruption. Once a Lock-in is attacked, it becomes clearer why permission must be granted to violate it. When creating White Space the objective cannot be finding a way to get a "yes." Rather, it must be honestly recognizing the Lock-ins which must be violated and getting permission for doing so.

Rather than asking for permission to sell a new product, the marketing manager should have asked for White Space. The revenue decline problem was a telltale sign of a much bigger challenge—in this case the emergence of lower-cost, primarily offshore, suppliers. Their success involved more than just low price. They had different distribution, were creating tiered product quality differentiation and were segmenting buyers into price versus quality groupings. The marketing manager could not help his company move forward without addressing the Success Formula—and that required White Space where he could address new challenges unencumbered by old Lock-ins.

Although the company's problem might have seemed as simple as price, to fix the problem, it must address the challenge and evolve its Success Formula. To develop a new Success Formula that can overcome challenges requires White Space. Company Identity might well have been tied to brand image and quality metrics or linked to desires for product leadership through development investments and thus above average gross margin requirements, or (as described) tied to distributor relationships and decades of mutual support. Oversimplifying challenges ignores the depth of the change required—and leads to approaches that fail as they are constrained by Lock-in. Managers end up spending more time in internal justification meetings than focusing on external market needs and creating new solutions. Working around Lock-ins dooms opportunities unable to evolve and grow.

Around 2000 Sears tried improving sales by launching new store concepts. One was Sears Hardware stores, leveraging the popular Craftsman tool brand to draw customers. Unlike traditional Sears stores, these hardware stores were smaller and located closer to competitors such as Ace, True Value, and Home Depot. These stores were successful at selling high-margin tools, grills, and other hardware items.

But leadership had not given the hardware store team permission to violate Sears' Lock-in to traditional general merchandise stores. As hardware store sales grew, leadership began questioning if these stores pulled customers away from traditional stores. In a freakish turn of logic, the more successful hardware stores became, the less desirable they were to executives who feared traditional store sales cannibalization. Although these new stores successfully attracted customers and achieved good retail metrics, they quickly lost management support. Expansion stopped, and eventually the stores were closed. Although Sears desperately needed a new Success Formula and was experimenting with new ideas, these were not

White Space projects because new ideas did not have permission to violate old Success Formula Lock-ins. Higher revenue and profits were not enough to keep Sears investing in successful new businesses once they violated Lock-in.

A low-growth fastener company hired a new business development manager, giving him permission to develop new opportunities. It took him little time to find a large, untapped opportunity in chemical gluing agents. For many applications users could replace nails or screws with adhesives, and more adhesives were being created weekly. The manager quickly prepared an executive opportunity assessment, which was even more quickly rejected. Leadership was happy to let him develop new products as long as they involved nails and screws. Obviously, his was not a White Space project but rather a D&E product extension initiative. Meanwhile, emerging competitors developed new adhesive sales.

All White Space leaders must ask themselves, "What Lock-ins must I violate to address market challenges and eventually earn high returns?" These leaders must then make sure they have explicit permission to violate those Lock-ins. If the requirement is not initially clear, the leaders must demand an open door to discuss Lock-in violation permission as needs appear. Without permission to violate Lock-ins, it's not White Space.

Resources

Insufficient funding is the most frequent reason White Space fails. The second is insufficient management attention. White Space projects strangle from lack of resources.

Resource systems are designed to feed old Success Formulas. That's why they were created—to funnel resources into areas critical for Success Formula operation. The goal of these systems is keeping the old Success Formula functioning, regardless of results. Resource allocation is not intended to be an openly competitive system, but rather a biased device to sort and fund Locked-in Success Formula options while limiting investments in everything else.

Sears' hardware stores requested funding to open new stores and acquire inventory. As sales rose, financial reviewers applied "cannibalization charges" to store P&Ls. Based on the notion that hardware store sales were not all incremental—thinking most of those sales would have been made at a traditional store anyway—P&L dollars were transferred from hardware to traditional stores. Further, reviewers determined traditional Sears store hardware customers bought additional items, and because hardware stores did not sell those other items, revenue was lost. So independent hardware stores were assigned a margin charge to compensate for traditional store lost revenue. These were blatant resource allocation efforts to keep funds flowing into the old Success Formula and traditional stores.

Pizza Hut behaved likewise when evaluating home delivery units competing with rapidly growing Domino's. As Pizza Hut's early home delivery stores opened, the resource allocation system decided many home delivered pizzas could have been sold as carry-outs from traditional sit-down Pizza Huts. So each newly opened home delivery store was assigned an overhead charge to compensate for lost revenue at traditional stores, while also being assessed a cannibalization charge for lost anticipated sales of other products, such as soda. These actions intentionally made traditional restaurants appear financially better and home delivery units appear financially worse, protecting traditional units tied to the old Success Formula. Not surprisingly, Pizza Hut home delivery stores failed to reach their market potential.

As financial resources were choked in both companies, management resources were also restricted. Opening new stores, whether hardware or pizza, required people to find sites, apply for and receive construction permits, purchase shelves and other equipment, fill them with inventory, hire staff, as well as create new store marketing and ongoing promotion programs. Both companies had robust management teams completing these tasks for traditional stores. Both organizations were unwilling to dedicate staff to these tasks for new store concepts, and when existing staff were asked to take on additional work, the managers complained they had no extra time to support new businesses and their unique needs.

D&E Management focuses on the "core business." Managers are judged first on how well they meet traditional requirements. In the panoply of metrics at annual review, the last discussed will be the one supporting White Space. As hierarchies review managerial assignments, each layer will support traditional business needs before considering White Space. And those who do the work will be hard-strapped to find time for working on anything not tied to D&E.

Any time a White Space project competes with an existing business for resources, financial allocation systems will starve White Space while feeding the traditional business. Many tricks are available to keep funds flowing into traditional investments, including

- Cannibalization charges
- "Risk adjusting" projections
- Applying higher rate of return requirements
- Forcing use of corporate resources
- Allocating hefty overhead charges from functional groups to the new business (such as big IT, marketing, HR, or R&D charges)

"Leveraging" existing managers, functional groups, and company processes to "help" White Space is guaranteed to keep traditional businesses resourced while sidelining White Space projects.

A 1990s consulting firm hired a new leader to build an Internet practice. Creating new client offerings, he recommended using low-cost Internet applications for email, telecommunications, accounting, and personnel tracking. But the firm's CFO balked at these requests, instead requiring the new partner "leverage" company investments in an enterprise email application, a corporate-wide mobile phone contract, and a newly installed ERP system. Quickly the Internet practice budget was overwhelmed with unexpected overhead charges allocated from these systems, the practice was deemed uneconomic by the management committee, and it was dropped.

Executive funding promises make little difference to old Success Formula biases. A CEO certain she wants to build a new business as part of her growth vision might promise to invest several million dollars in a White Space project. But unless those funds are set aside before the project begins, they will not find their way to White Space. Traditional businesses never run out of new investment ideas, and resource allocation systems are biased toward funding traditional businesses. Despite the CEO's goal, the quarterly project reviews and investment rankings will slowly raise D&E project standings while lowering White Space. Fairly soon, the project will find its financial resources gone.

It is imperative that White Space projects have money committed *in advance*. The amount must be whatever is forecasted to see the project through *to completion*. As soon as committed money runs out, leaders must expect the traditional organization will do whatever necessary to stop additional funds flowing into White Space. "Funding based on results" will inevitably lead to running out of money. The savvy D&E organization will create so many needs, while creating hurdles for White Space, that it will stop money flowing to White Space.

DuPont started its Electronic Imaging Division with a separate budget. But after the first year, DuPont's CFO recommended ranking all investments on similar criteria. As a result, DuPont's investments in new digital products were compared with incremental investments in decades-old chemical plants. Plant expansions, to meet assumed market growth, showed incremental returns well over 40%—some over 100%. But Electronic Imaging, with high new product obsolescence rates, had its margins hacked by evaluators challenging the likelihood of each new product's success. Adjusted ROIs declined precipitously, and new product funding dropped to almost nothing within three years after start-up.

Similarly, White Space teams must have their own management resources. Without them the traditional organization will suck up all available management time. Even though White Space resources may appear redundant, they are necessary for White Space to compete and create a new Success Formula that can overtake challenges and produce above-average returns. The only way to make sure resources are available is to make them dedicated—and hold them accountable for results.

White Space Management Must Be Accountable for Results

White Space managers cannot feel like they have a secure traditional job awaiting them if White Space does not succeed. White Space managers must be *committed* to project success. The role must have personal risk. Just as Success Formulas at risk from market shifts make jobs in traditional organizations subject to downsizing, outsourcing, and compensation freezes, White Space managers must accept the risk inherent with business in the Rapids. White Space employees must shoulder those risks while building a new Success Formula. For White Space to justify its own financial and management resources, those managers must be accountable for results.

White Space effectiveness can be seen at Illinois Tool Works, which has over 700 separate businesses. Each business has its own management staff, and businesses are not required to use common processes, common IT, or even common accounting applications. "Corporate" employees are not responsible for any functions. Each business has its own resources and its own P&L. While this may appear inefficient and chaotic to D&E

managers, ITW's consistent use of White Space and its demand that each business be responsible for its results, has produced over 20 years of growth in revenue and profits—a goal accomplished by few businesses.

White Space Is Not the Wellspring

Too many leaders confuse White Space projects with venture capital. Venture capital is Wellspring investing that has as its goal assisting small businesses find their way into the Rapids. Even most large venture investments target Wellspring businesses looking for the Rapids.

Unfortunately, even a portfolio of Wellspring ventures usually takes a long time to produce a group of Rapids opportunities. There is no way to predict what Wellspring ideas will become large nor any way to predict the timeline. This is not to say businesses should not invest in Wellspring projects or that a portfolio of Wellspring initiatives isn't a valuable growth tool. Given adequate time, usually measured in years, a venture portfolio can become large enough and varied enough to consistently feed White Space. Few companies in the Flats or Swamp have a well-developed venture collection because such risk-oriented investments do not mesh well with D&E Management.

White Space that relies on Wellspring projects is dangerous. These small investments are insufficient for attacking a large business growth stall. Most Wellspring projects will not produce enough impact fast enough to develop a sustainable new Success Formula. A Wellspring leader's goals and his or her plans for future markets are not a Success Formula. Businesses with tired Success Formulas need new ones to which they can migrate. When moving an organization out of the Swamp, it is important to get into the Rapids as fast as possible. That means White Space businesses must be in the early Rapids rather than the Wellspring.

GM's 1990s electric car was a Wellspring project. Hoping electric cars would create a breakthrough for GM, the company started a project with no defined market, no revenue, and no idea how to compete. Although GM invested billions of dollars, it made no difference because electric cars were unable to produce revenue quickly enough to make any difference. The Wellspring project took too long in its attempt to develop a marketplace large enough to create a new Success Formula toward which GM could migrate. It was nowhere near the Rapids. This lifecycle misunderstanding caused GM to overinvest early then abandon the project when it could not generate transformational capability quickly enough.

White Space projects must have enough revenue and market strength to demonstrate a new Success Formula, or they must be in markets large enough and growing fast enough to rapidly become Rapids opportunities. Whether originated internally or via acquisition, White Space must generate revenue fast enough to exhibit a Success Formula and attract the rest of the organization.

Toyota's hybrid car was an example of moving quickly into the Rapids. Rather than developing an electric car, Toyota set out to develop a high-mileage automobile. Rather than Locking-in on battery technology, Toyota adapted to market inputs as it combined batteries with generators and a traditional engine—which itself had modifications. And the styling, transmission, and other features were adapted to the hybrid approach. Hybrids rapidly found a significant following among buyers in the high-growth, high-mileage auto segment and continued to expand Toyota's growth at GM's expense.

Saturn was an organic White Space project. It was given ample funding and its own management team. It also quickly entered the large and fast growing small-car market. Thus, Saturn was White Space where a new Success Formula could be created and toward which GM could have migrated the rest of its auto business had old Lock-ins been Disrupted.

GM's Hughes Electronics acquisition was White Space. Hughes was large, profitable, and rapidly growing. Market growth rates and margins exceeded the automobile business. When acquired, Hughes was well-funded and had its own management team. As White Space, Hughes could show traditional GM how an alternative Success Formula produced superior results and toward which a Disrupted GM could have migrated.

Kellogg's successfully used White Space to turn around its fortunes. After Disrupting Kellogg's, CEO Gutierrez dedicated R&D, manufacturing, engineering, and marketing management to the new R&D program. The team was staffed with resources to not only innovate products but test them, figure out how to manufacture them, and launch them. R&D was given its own funding, independent of product division review, and permission to explore new products in any market using any combination of technologies. R&D reported to the CEO, and the group presented findings frequently to other division leaders. The R&D leader joined Kellogg's executive team and influenced company-wide product development. Independence coupled with permission to develop products and management resources for taking them to market, allowed this White Space to develop a new Success Formula with emphasis on new products and innovation.

The CEO acquired Keebler and placed it into a new Snack Foods Division reporting to him. Although Kellogg's used third-party food brokers as sales agents and delivered products through the traditional retail food distribution warehouse system, Keebler had its own salespeople and its own "store-door delivery" system trucking products from Keebler facilities to retail shelves. Putting Keebler inside a new division gave the business autonomy to utilize CEO permission for violating old sales and distribution Lock-ins. The new division had its own funding and management team. Snack Food executives were treated as equals with executives in traditional Kellogg's, and new Snack Food managers participated fully in company planning.

Traditional Kellogg's sold along product lines, so multiple salespeople called on each retailer even though products were not competitive. For decades this was not a problem. But by 2000 retailers were seeking simpler relationships with manufacturers. CEO Gutierrez created a White Space team targeted at selling all Kellogg's products to Wal-Mart, giving it immediate significant revenue. He appointed himself team leader, giving the team autonomy from business units, permission to develop new retailer-focused selling approaches, and CEO-directed funding. The team attracted many of Kellogg's best managers and rapidly developed a new Success Formula, combining its learning with the R&D and Snack Food projects.

These White Space projects were designed to help Kellogg's migrate its Success Formula. Operational independence was joined with active corporate goal-setting participation, joint planning, and frequent communications. Each project had defined product development, account development, sales, and margin goals. White Space leaders were expected to communicate their experiences with peers in the traditional business, whereas traditional business leaders were expected to build on Disruptions to identify ways they could migrate toward new Success Formula benefits.

Kellogg's rapidly

- Created a robust new product pipeline, adding substantial growth
- Developed a new approach to selling and servicing accounts, creating incremental revenue while lowering distribution costs

- Became more flexible in manufacturing and delivering products to meet market needs, lowering inventory and retailer out-of-stocks
- Became more successful growing sales in nontraditional grocery outlets such as discount stores

Kellogg's did not rely on one White Space project. Failure risk was lowered, and better outcomes resulted from implementing multiple projects. If one had failed, the business would not have been left without opportunity to improve. And multiple White Space projects shared learning, feeding each other's contribution toward a more robust, new Success Formula.

Kellogg's was not a high-tech company. Nor was Kellogg's in high-growth markets. Kellogg's was located in semirural central Michigan, not considered an innovation hotbed. Yet, Kellogg's evolved its Success Formula rather dramatically by effectively using White Space. Margins dramatically improved due to better sales practices, improved distribution, new products, and entry into new retail outlets—not from cost-cutting. Perceived as a moribund company with few opportunities for shareholder growth, Kellogg's quickly became favored by analysts. Investors cheered Success Formula evolution as much as employees and suppliers.

Old Success Formulas Must Migrate Toward White Space

As Kellogg's demonstrated, improved results come from migrating traditional businesses toward White Space. But more frequently, leaders use the opposite tactic. They create White Space projects and try "integrating" them back into the traditional organization. This always leads to disastrous results as the traditional business rapidly dismantles and eventually kills White Space.

Locked-in organizations have multiple tools for stopping investments and behavior outside Lock-in. Introducing a successful and rapidly growing new business into a Locked-in one does not change the Lock-in. Even if Disrupted, a Locked-in organization cannot simply adopt a new Success Formula. Organizations are designed to reject new ideas, and without a lot of work understanding new Success Formulas, Locked-in organizations will not develop migration paths.

Remember IBM's Florida skunk works that created the modern PC? In utilizing a new development approach incorporating hardware and software from multiple vendors, their product quite literally changed the nature of computer use. But when IBM tried integrating this successful operation into its traditional computer business, the result was failure. The PC team's Success Formula was radically different, and Lock-in simply would not allow a highly distributed vendor-supplied platform to receive ongoing funding from the traditional business.

Similarly, many acquisitions purchased for growth fail. Acquiring executives hope the high-growth business will provide leadership. And acquired executives are extremely hopeful that resources—finances, managerial staff, and often market access—will stimulate faster growth. But quickly both organizations feel let down as merger leads to discord. As the two Success Formulas smash into each other, the one controlling resources wins. Lock-in barriers control decisions, and resource allocation keeps money and talent flowing to traditional investments. Soon the acquirer blames acquired leadership for unwillingness to learn, while acquired leaders depart with anger toward the acquirer for promising but not delivering resources—while erecting enormous hurdles.

Success Formulas don't know how to negotiate or compromise. They merely exist, defended and extended by Lock-in. Whichever Success Formula controls resources will push them toward its defense. When confronted with a new Success Formula that tries operating outside Lock-in—perhaps even having its own Lock-in—the organization sees no option other than beating it into conformance. Even elaborate merger planning exercises fail because the resource-controlling Success Formula always wins.

For acquisitions to create growth, the parties must remain independent. They have to receive resources outside the Locked-in resource allocation system. There has to be extensive communication, post-Disruption, to the acquirer about the new Success Formula. Top executives have to constantly attack old Lock-ins, using those Disruptions as opportunities for migrating toward the new Success Formula. Only by migrating the old toward the new, deliberately using Disruptions and pushing resources toward the new Success Formula, will the organization transition.

The New York Stock Exchange (NYSE) is challenged by the growth of automated trading. Its veritable Specialist traders manning the posts find it harder to justify their positions as huge corporations, such as Microsoft and Cisco, successfully trade on the unmanned NASDAQ system. So the NYSE acquired Archipelago. New understanding about the automated system is allowing the NYSE to migrate toward a new Success Formula.

Unfortunately, too many White Space projects are spun off simply because leaders do not know how to migrate their Success Formulas. McDonald's nurtured Chipotle, but faced with Disrupting and migrating McDonald's traditional organization toward this new Success Formula, it was easier for leaders to sell the business, capture cash, and invest in D&E activities. Similarly, American Airlines invested in its extremely successful development of Travelocity, only to spin it off and use the cash for defending American's historical—and largely money-losing—airline. As a result too many organizations remain mired in the Swamp, unable to reenter the Rapids.

White Space uses learning to drive adaptation. D&E Management focuses on optimization so strongly that it loses tolerance for the vagaries of learning. Rapids businesses do not grow by linearly executing 100% accurate actions. Rather, tests are implemented, competitors react, some things work, and some don't, and results become information for future actions. Those who monitor White Space have to accept the learning process inherent in Rapids competition. White Space leaders must be held to expectations, but simultaneously company leaders must expect there will be problems and missed forecasts. Moving back into the Rapids requires finding out what works—which includes finding out what doesn't work. That's life in the Rapids.

White Space looks for fast-flowing tributaries that can carry a business out of the Swamp or the Flats. Prolonged success comes from repeatedly finding and following these tributaries. Traditional businesses must be attracted into these tributaries by implementing Disruptions, making leaders open to future potential. White Space finds fast water out of the mosquito-infested and problematic D&E Management Swamp.

Endnotes

1. Steven Schnaars, *Megamistakes* (The Free Press, 1989). Refer to this title for a more thorough discussion of forecasting risks.

2. James Gleick, *Chaos: Making a New Science* (Viking Press, 1987). Refer to this title for an easy-to-understand description of the butterfly effect. Pascale, Millman, and Gioja, *Surfing at the Edge of Chaos* (New York: Random House/Crown Publishing, 2000). Please review this title for application of the butterfly effect to business.

9

Maintain The Phoenix Principle for Long-Term Success

Once I evolve my Success Formula, what's next? How do I keep from falling into the Defend & Extend rut again? How do the best long-term performing organizations keep their Success Formulas "evergreen"?

Practice Makes Perfect

Too often strategy initiatives are considered events, something reviewed once a year. Change is addressed even less often. It's easy to think of Disruptions and establishing White Space as events and then return to Defend & Extend Management. That approach would be simple—and extremely short-sighted, depriving the organization of becoming a long-term above-average performer. *All* Success Formulas hit the Flats, so *all* need to be evolved. The Phoenix Principle must become a way of life.

Organizations improve via practice. The tenth marketing event is better than the fifth. The fourth product launch is better than the second. The third sourcing contract is better than the first. The same is true for Disruptions and White Space. Practicing makes the organization better at executing Disruptions, and more White Space projects lead to better results, faster while improving migration.

At General Electric CEO Welch created ongoing Disruptions. Although he implemented Disruptions, he expected fellow leaders to Disrupt as well.

GE built a skill set around Disruptions, and it is a company both quick to implement White Space and deft at managing it. Businesses enter, are managed, and exit GE continuously. GE is good at practicing and using Disruptions and White Space to improve long-term returns.

Illinois Tool Works (ITW) operates over 750 separate businesses. Constantly acquiring new businesses allows the company to continuously develop new market opportunities. Businesses are not forced into a single Success Formula or into a "core" market. Each business focuses on customers and how to evolve toward higher revenue and profits. After decades of practice, ITW does not look like a Disrupted organization as it refuses to allow Lock-in to pull it into D&E Management. Revenue and profits just keep growing.

GE and ITW have practiced Disruptions and White Space management so long they are now skilled at both. Neither company considers either activity events, but rather business as usual. Ironically, the word "execution" often means practicing D&E Management. But GE and ITW expertly "execute" Disruptions and White Space, keeping themselves out of the D&E rut.

The longer and more frequently Disruptions and White Space are practiced, the better an organization performs. No one thinks of Cisco as a Disruptive company, yet dedication to making their own products obsolete keeps Cisco constantly Disrupting its approach to markets, customers, products, and technologies. Cisco has maintained its enviable growth rate, whereas many other high tech companies have disappeared. Cisco is so adept at Disruptions and maintains such constant White Space, that employees, customers, suppliers, and investors find it normal.

Phoenix Principle Companies Are Often Hard to Define Traditionally

Organizational alignment with identity aids growth in the Rapids yet shallows the water, enhancing D&E Management, which leads to a drift into the Swamp. Wal-Mart closely identified with low-price retailing. Encyclopedia Britannica closely identified with static, printed information. Polaroid identified with "instant photography." These identities made the businesses easy to describe and easy for investors, employees, suppliers—and competitors—to understand. But they simultaneously restricted options.

We can often recognize Phoenix Principle companies by their unwillingness to be easily described. What business is Nike in? Early competitors Reebok and Adidas identified with shoes and apparel, Locked-in, and followed D&E Management, which lead to declining revenue growth and much lower margins. Early on Nike also identified with shoes and apparel, but when approaching the Flats chose a far more Disruptive path. Now Nike is much larger and more profitable, selling lots of products well beyond its initial markets. Disruptions and White Space lead organizations like Nike into new markets and new business practices. Evolving their Success Formulas, including their Identity, makes it harder to say what business they are in. They just grow and produce superior results.

Most people think of Starbucks as a "coffee company." But that gives short shrift to Starbucks' willingness to Disrupt and utilize White Space. Starbucks operates food establishments with both sit-down and carry-out service. It sells packaged coffee in traditional grocery stores. If this was all Starbucks did, the portfolio would be wider than McDonald's, Pizza Hut, or Proctor & Gamble have implemented with considerably more resources—and much more focus on its Success Formula.

But Starbucks does more. Starbucks is in liquor stores. In 2006 Starbucks produced and released the full-length feature movie, *Akeelah and the Bee*. Starbucks produces and distributes music, including the #1 CD in 2005 (*Ray Charles Greatest Hits*). In 2007 Starbucks' music agency represented former Beatles guitarist Paul McCartney, producing and distributing his album. They implement lots of White Space in anticipating the day when we have all the Starbucks stores the market can support. As long as the returning CEO doesn't drop the White Space, Starbucks can continue producing growth—but if he succumbs to D&E practices in search of short-term profits, then Starbucks can quickly pass right into the Swamp.

At first blush, 1-800-Flowers.com sounds like a narrowly defined business. But a deeper look reveals that in 2007, 1-800-Flowers also operated 1-800-Baskets, Bloom.net, Plow & Hearth, The Popcorn Factory, Ambrosia Wine Club, Hearth Song toys, Madison Place décor, Harry London candy, as well as Fannie Mae retail candy stores. While most dot-com businesses had failed by 2002, 1-800-Flowers demonstrated it could use Disruptions and White Space to break out of traditional markets and prosper.

Compare GM with Honda. GM bought EDS and Hughes Electronics to grow its technology base and markets but later sold both businesses, refocusing on cars. Honda started by selling small engines and then grew into manufacturing and selling snow blowers, electricity generators, lawn mowers, snowmobiles, lawn tractors, leaf blowers, motorcycles, automobiles, outboard boat motors (2 and 4-stroke), robots, and jet airplanes. Honda's products move through multiple distribution channels, including direct sales, dealers, and traditional retailers. Whereas GM remained Locked-in to its Success Formula, Honda used Disruptions to seek new markets and White Space to evolve its Success Formula.

What business is Honda in? What business is 1-800 Flowers or Starbucks in? What business is General Electric, Illinois Tool Works, or Apple in? Organizations that produce long-term superior performance defy easy definition. You could say *they are in the business of addressing market challenges by migrating toward customer demand and building Success Formulas that produce above average returns.* That would define them as Phoenix Principle organizations. And long-term performance, in fact long-term survivability, comes from Phoenix Principle implementation rather than maintaining an Identity.

Phoenix Principle Companies Are Willing to Fail

Lock-in to old metrics forces D&E Management to avoid small, short-term failures. Risk avoidance keeps organizations stuck with old technologies, products, and markets when altering direction would produce better results. AM kept marginally improving printing presses and plate-makers long after the market started shrinking. Because D&E Management lacks White Space and its learning outside Lock-in, it doesn't develop alternative investment options or the knowledge for effectively evaluating them.

Before Apple launched the wildly successful Macintosh, it launched the Lisa, which failed. As Macintosh's forerunner, the Lisa taught Apple what was needed for breakout performance. Before Pixar succeeded as a production company, NeXT failed as a technology venture. Failures are part of White Space. No one should plan for failure or desire to be part of one. But failures are part of learning. That is why they must be anticipated and utilized in White Space. Only by admitting that failure can happen is it possible to learn and make changes.

GM would not admit that its electric car objectives could not be met. So GM kept investing, trying to meet unrealistic objectives. GM not only overinvested in the electric car but kept other options, like hybrids, from developing. And investment money was diverted from other projects in the Rapids—such as Saturn and Hughes—that would have better used the resources.

Denying failure means denying market input, technological practicality, product limitations, and financial requirements for success. Sony had all the pieces to dominate digital music. It had deep expertise in consumer electronics and wide distribution access. Sony also had a recording company with its own music archive. The company did not ignore the opportunity digital music offered but invested in a proprietary solution rejected by consumers. Instead of admitting its failures in CD sales and proprietary technology, Sony kept trying to make its approach work—and gave the White Space competitor (Apple) an enormous market opportunity. Not admitting failure allowed Sony to Defend and Extend its poorly performing Success Formula rather than evolve it.

Southwest Airlines has led its industry for years. Most large competitors tried emulating Southwest. Delta launched Song, United launched Ted, and American launched Eagle. But these launches were not given White Space to fail and learn. They were forced to use company frequent flyer programs, reservation systems, aircraft, gates, and employees. Although they never came close to meeting Southwest's success, airlines kept investing. By not admitting failure, the airlines were unable to learn and unable to make the adjustments necessary in the Rapids when developing a new Success Formula.

An old entrepreneurial adage is "Fail early." Admitting failures early while investments are small provides funds for project retooling or recognizing a weak idea and investing elsewhere. Successfully applying marketplace learning in the Rapids reduces longer-term failure risk. Phoenix Principle organizations raise success odds long-term by admitting short-term failures and then *learning* from those failures.

Disruptions Only Appear Painful

People don't like to undertake Disruptions, but they are not nearly as painful as feared. Disruptions are like vaccinations. Although we don't look forward to a shot, it's only momentarily uncomfortable. Then it protects us from potentially far worse ailments. Disruptions provide the opportunity to get stronger and produce better results—for what is only perceived as pain. It's the fear of Disruptions within D&E Management that is the problem—not Disruptions themselves. Once organizations begin regularly Disrupting, the impression changes. Disruptions become normal. Could you imagine a physician not vaccinating a child because she was worried about the patient's fear of a shot?

Because D&E Management is Locked-in, *"success" becomes operating the Success Formula rather than producing results*. Managers aren't measured on market results, but rather how well they operate inside Lock-in, supporting the old Success Formula. Improving results requires altering how people are measured and reinforced. Disrupting refocuses behavior on market challenges—and on market results—and allows people to move away from painfully repetitive Lock-in and apply creativity toward improving market results.

Once Disrupted, individuals and organizations quickly respond positively to improved market results. Higher sales and margins lead to good things, rather than the lay-offs and other unpleasant actions taken after bad results. Once links between Disruptions and marketplace-driven behavior are reinforced, through White Space and migration plans, Disruption fear rapidly dissipates. Businesspeople recognize competitive requirements and respond positively to improved results.

Mid-1990s Microsoft was completely Locked-in to its traditional products. As the Internet changed PC usage, Bill Gates realized Microsoft was at risk. He rapidly Disrupted, changing company technology investments and implementing White Space projects to reposition Microsoft at the forefront of PC software. Managers at Microsoft did not leave because of Disruptions. Instead they recognized the company was developing a future migration path, quickly supported ongoing Disruptions, and participated in White Space, bringing to market new products like Internet Explorer.

When Carlos Gutierrez first Disrupted Kellogg's, the organization was uneasy. But his rapid implementation of White Space led to quickly focusing on Kellogg's migration path. Although people were first unsure how to proceed, rapid feedback on new projects gave insight into what steps they should take. As White Space developed, people at Kellogg's developed a migration path that moved the company from poor results to better ones—and leadership avoided draconian actions many anticipated.

As White Space projects are developed, employees and managers realize the Rapids is the most enjoyable location on the business lifecycle. White Space in the Rapids draws people to it. Like those in Kellogg's drawn to the Wal-Mart sales team or those drawn into the iPod and iTunes development teams at Apple, White Space is a magnet for managers looking to grow. When White Space quickly follows Disruptions, it becomes an attractive alternative to the painful disturbances expected from continued D&E Management.

Strategists Must Change Their Roles to Promote The Phoenix Principle

Some organizations expect their leadership team to be business strategists. Some companies have an internal strategist role or strategy group. Some hire consultants to develop strategy. Regardless of the source, businesses have people who create strategy. And the activities performed by these people need to change if we are to improve business performance and longevity.

Traditionally, strategy involved detailed analyses that sought new ways to Defend and Extend a Success Formula. Most strategy efforts were geared toward living within Lock-in, and frequently strategists became Status Quo Police. Strategic planning exercises can evolve into elaborate efforts, linked to financial planning, designed to identify marginal improvement, while making sure Success Formula risks are minimized.

Phoenix Principle companies utilize strategy very differently. Rather than accepting Lock-in, strategists identify BIASes and utilize data access as well as peer relationships to measure resources consumed in D&E activities compared to White Space investing. Phoenix Principle strategists highlight within operating unit and functional budgets resources dedicated to doing what's always been done. Pointing out resources consumed, both money and management, Defending & Extending versus White Space makes leaders aware that the business is not properly addressing market Challenges.

In Phoenix Principle organizations strategists highlight market challenges. Organizations and their leaders work within Lock-in designed only to deal with problems. Phoenix Principle strategists highlight what's causing problems and what these challenges imply for long-term performance. If an alternative technology, product, distribution method, or quality enhancement has slowed sales, margins, or customer growth, then strategists must highlight these factors and make them central to planning discussions.

A leading supplier in the automotive parts market recognized that customers were increasingly focusing on price, price, and price. Even when the company developed product improvements, the buyers would ask for enhanced products at the previous prices. Strategists made clear the company's bias for engineering and manufacturing and pointed out that although customers weren't willing to pay more for product improvements, the company continued offering them, hoping it could escape the price war—to no avail.

This company's market challenges were coming from product standardization, leading to more offshore competition. Product enhancements were rapidly copied because buyers would not purchase anything that wasn't industry standard. After pointing out the challenge, strategists were able to offer alternative competitive variables, such as more design assistance, faster delivery, and easier ordering, distinguishing the company from product-focused competitors.

Strategists can use portfolio techniques to highlight D&E investments. Whether evaluating acquisitions, new manufacturing plants, or outsourcing agreements, strategists should point out when an intended action will further Lock-in the organization or offer a Disruption and potential for White Space. Organizations are good at looking for D&E opportunities, and they dominate most internally developed investment options. By portraying where money and management time is spent, comparing D&E investments to Disruptive or White Space investments, a strategist can show leadership its likelihood of addressing market challenges—or its failure to do so.

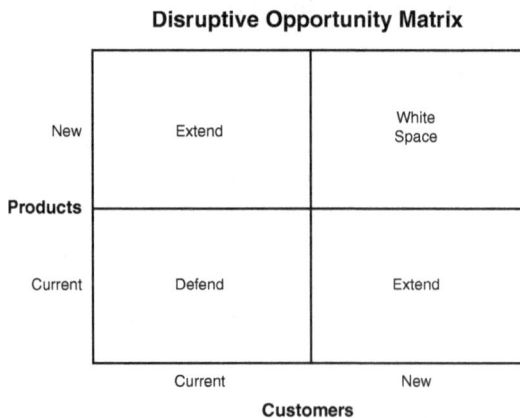

Disruptive Opportunity Matrix

	Current	New
New	Extend	White Space
Current	Defend	Extend

Products (vertical axis) / Customers (horizontal axis)

Figure 9.1 Disruptive Opportunity Matrix

An equipment manufacturing company strategist counted the number of meetings in which the team reviewed current product developments and sales. He also counted meetings where they reviewed new product opportunities, both organic and potentially acquired. Ninety percent of management time was spent defending and extending existing product sales, even though everyone admitted these products were nearing end of life from new technology. Highlighting time as well as money invested gave leadership important information about their need to change behavior to survive.

Strategists are also well positioned to introduce outsiders to leadership teams, bringing in alternative thinking. Lock-in closes off organizations to external stimuli. Only supportive input is collected. Phoenix Principle strategists can counter this bias by finding and introducing outside input that contradicts internally held beliefs and generates new discussions. Consultants, authors, professors, and college teams can introduce new practices and technologies. Don't forget Bill, the New Product Development Director, who utilized outsiders to keep his organization moving forward.

Strategists should also promote an aggressive exit program. Although most organizations remain on the alert for acquisition opportunities, far too few sell enough businesses. GE's M&A group is as good at selling businesses as buying them. Selling businesses helps GE avoid Lock-in and keeps management evaluating new markets. Selling businesses in the Defend or Extend boxes is an important Disruption tool and provides resources for White Space.

Although most business leaders talk a lot about competitive tactics, few define competitor Success Formulas. With running the daily business, operating managers have little time to do such external analysis. Phoenix Principle strategists develop competitive profiles and identify opportunities for exploiting competitor Lock-in by designing attacks. They also turn these profiles into benchmarks for helping management define its own Lock-ins and Success Formulas.

The London to New York flight route was dominated by British Airways. Virgin strategists looked at BA's market position and realized the company was so Locked-in, it could not react to a competitor. They noted BA had virtually ignored Freddie Laker and his failed airline, even though it had attracted thousands of passengers and filled its flights. Virgin, previously a music recording and distribution company, subsequently launched Virgin Atlantic, attracting hundreds of customers and an industry-leading return on investment. By constantly looking for Locked-in competitors, Virgin has successfully entered several new businesses, including mobile phones and recently U.S. air travel.

In Phoenix Principle companies, strategic planning processes help organizations Disrupt and implement White Space and monitor whether Disruptions target critical Lock-ins that are blinding the organization to market challenges. Additionally, strategic planning makes sure White Space initiatives are developed in advance of Disruptions so they are ready to be implemented. Then planning processes monitor White Space goal setting and performance. Finally, strategic planning assists Success Formula migration.

Managing White Space is where strategists take on a large value-adding role. Locked-in managers are too busy to manage White Space. Short-term goals require they primarily manage the existing business, even when implementing Disruptions. They need help defining, structuring, staffing, and monitoring White Space. They need help setting new metrics, allocating management time to review results, and assessing performance against goals for creating opportunities in the Rapids. Strategists must help them perform these tasks, track communications, and promote attractiveness for organization migration.

Whirlpool's CEO set up a separate strategy group to monitor White Space initiatives. While managers in the traditional business remained focused on intense current competition, others brought to market new opportunities required for next generation growth. The new organization not only had sales and margin targets, but communication requirements about results and challenges were addressed. Meanwhile, traditional business managers were required to develop migration plans.

Phoenix Principle Companies Help Customers Find and Use White Space

Most customers are as Locked-in to a business's Success Formula as the business itself. This creates a dilemma because large customers aren't looking to migrate. They often don't appreciate, or want, White Space. Phoenix Principle companies can't afford to remain Locked-in, nor can they afford to ignore market challenges. They must help customers migrate as well. Just like the Phoenix Principle organization needs White Space to develop a new Success Formula, it has to create White space for customers to experiment with new solutions.

The easiest product introductions don't change customer Lock-in. When new products fit inside customer Lock-in, adoption is easy. But frequently, new solutions violate old customer Lock-ins. The business is placed at risk by offering the new solution. It risks losing old customers before finding new ones. Revenues might fall as customers remain Locked-in and shift to traditional competitors.

In most instances, allowing the old business and White Space to compete will maximize revenue. As traditional customers enjoy Lock-in, the business continues to offer old solutions, meeting their expectations. Simultaneously, White Space offers customers new solutions and an opportunity to build a new Success Formula. Cisco's willingness to immediately launch new products, even when they compete with old products, exemplifies how well this approach can work.

But White Space teams still need to find and sell to new customers. The primary goal of business in the Rapids is finding new customers and demonstrating they will buy. So Phoenix Principle companies must create customer White Space through structured tests or pilots. Projects must be designed so that customers can experiment outside Lock-in. Just as businesses don't suddenly overcome Lock-in, customers don't either. White Space processes used internally have to be applied externally, helping customers migrate toward new solutions.

Agricultural companies supplying seed, fertilizer, and herbicides sell to notoriously risk-adverse farmers. Farmers invest in tillage, seed, and planting. Results depend on weather, bugs, birds, mold, and any number of other factors outside their control—over a multimonth time delay. If everything goes well, they make a razor thin margin. If factors turn bad, they can lose all their revenue. There's huge downside and limited upside. Prudence has proven a wise long-term approach.

Suppliers try to develop new seed, fertilizer, and herbicides which will produce superior results for farmers. If customers do not convert, eventually new entrants would steal them. So what should a major competitor, such as Pioneer, do? Designing tests on small land plots allowed customers to use new products and prove results before committing to large-scale adoption. Supplier companies had to create pilots, with limited risk, allowing farmers to learn new product benefits.

Not all customers are interested in testing, so Phoenix Principle companies must carefully identify and select targets. New solutions will fail if mass marketing concepts are tried. Phoenix Principle companies look for customers struggling with old solutions. Customers receiving declining value from old solutions are most willing to Disrupt and investigate new solutions, and they are most open to testing in White Space.

Only customers who Disrupt themselves will learn from White Space tests. One of the best Disruption tools is changing metrics. Before customers try a new solution, Phoenix Principle suppliers must create new metrics for customers to measure new solution benefits. Old metrics Defend and Extend Lock-in. New solutions providing new benefits require changing what's measured. Unless specified up-front, tests will not support new benefits. New metrics Disrupt how customers view old and new solutions, allowing pilot result acceptance, which leads to migration.

Most herbicide benefit comes from reduced tillage. Not running a tractor across fields saves fuel and maintenance. Secondly, less tillage means higher soil moisture, promoting rapid plant growth. Traditional metrics for herbicides did not include annual fuel savings or soil moisture conservation. Only by defining new herbicide payoff through fuel savings and ground moisture enhancement would increased value become clear.

A leading pump manufacturer realized many customers would save money by replacing old pumps with new ones. New pump energy savings would recover the investment within a few months. But when pump marketers asked customers if they would like to buy new energy-efficient pumps, customers said, "No, thanks."

Customers were interested in energy savings, but for years pumps had been purchased by plant maintenance. This department was measured on keeping maintenance costs low—not energy costs. Maintenance's annual budget, and the supervisor's bonus, were based on meeting plant uptime requirements and meeting budget. To maintenance, new pumps that paid for themselves with energy savings were an unnecessary, easily avoided cost.

Energy budgets were with plant managers. But pump salespeople didn't traditionally talk to plant manages. And they didn't want to upset relationships with maintenance supervisors by going higher in the organization. Nonetheless, emerging competitors were introducing new energy-efficient pumps, and they didn't have legacy relationships with maintenance supervisors hindering plant manager sales calls.

To overcome this dilemma, the pump new product manager identified plant managers who had either written articles on energy consumption or been interviewed on the topic. These customers were already aware of pump efficiency value. The new product manager targeted these plant managers, asking if they would consider a controlled test using one of the new pumps. If the pump didn't achieve the desired energy savings, it would be discounted to match old pump pricing. If it cut energy costs, the supplier wanted to share the savings and tell other customers about the benefits.

The pump manufacturer worked with the plant manager implementing the following actions to create White Space, test product performance, and demonstrate future value.

1. The plant manager met with operations and maintenance personnel, explaining the test.
2. The supplier helped rewrite operations and maintenance procedures to take advantage of new pump benefits.
3. New pumps were installed where their energy saving results could be measured.
4. The pump manufacturer and customer cooperated on installation and testing.
5. Energy-saving changes to maintenance procedures, flow rates, and operator actions were tested and logged.

Implementation quickly demonstrated energy savings, leading to rapid plant migration and communication to other potential customers.

Customers like buying from Phoenix Principle companies because they know these suppliers help them migrate to new solutions. Helping customers implement White Space allows Phoenix Principle companies to leverage their White Space skills, improving new product introduction success and longevity.

The Phoenix Principle Isn't Hard to Practice–It's Just Different

Following The Phoenix Principle isn't hard. Any organization can do it. Start by recognizing that above-average performance comes from Disruptions, followed by White Space—and the more you practice, the better you get.

Phoenix Principle organizations hire leaders and managers willing to Disrupt and implement White Space. Making Disruptions normal, rather than something to be avoided, is critical to success. Managers must be willing to Disrupt, unleashing internal ideas, and White Space skills must be added. This requires changing recruiting, job descriptions, interview practices, and promotion criteria to bring on and advance people demonstrating these skills. Boards of Directors should look for these skills in CEOs because, from the top downward, improving performance and longevity requires Disruptors. Instead of focusing on consistency, which leads to Defend & Extend practices, organizations have to focus on market challenges. Hirers must place the value of Disruptions above the value of Lock-in.

Leaders have to look past efficiency to commit White Space resources. Efficiency does not create long-term success. Long-term success takes dedicated resources—money and management—for new Success Formula creation.

Now Is the Time to Implement The Phoenix Principle

The Phoenix Principle focuses on the future. Recognizing market challenges and overcoming them with Disruptions and White Space keeps organizations in the Rapids. It *is* possible to adapt to Kondratiev's change cycles and overcome Schumpeter's claim that organizations cannot achieve the longevity of markets. Businesses can improve results and increase longevity. But leaders cannot rest; challenges will just keep coming.

Over the past two hundred years, there's no doubt the pace of technology development and adoption has accelerated. Compare how long it took to adopt ocean sailing, then train travel, then automobiles— or the adoption time for telephones, televisions, PCs, and then the Internet. Technological advances are arriving faster and being adopted faster. Education and globalization have increased our ability to more quickly integrate technology into society.

Technological advances impact the bottom of every Success Formula pyramid. When shifts happen lower in the pyramid, upper parts have to adjust. As our information economy continues unfolding—and we see new technologies emerging based not only on electronics but nanotechnology and biology—we have to expect ongoing changes at the base. This means more challenges putting more pressure faster on all Success Formulas as their half-life keeps shortening. The only defense from extinction will be our ability to rapidly deploy Disruptions and evolve new Success Formulas while adopting environmental changes.

Near-term market challenges are already apparent. America's demographics are changing markedly, and historical biases toward European ancestry are short-lived. Ubiquitous connectivity is practically here, providing instantaneous information to almost everyone on topics they find important. Nanotechnology is emerging as a powerful tool for developing new products and solutions. Globalization has unleashed hundreds of millions of new, skilled workers, both blue and white collar, onto the labor market, forever changing where and how we work. And security is redefined by necessary cross-border relationships.

We could choose to ignore these trends, or we could wait and react in the future, allowing D&E practices to continue making Schumpeter look like a genius. Or we can adopt trends quickly and modify Success Formulas to meet new challenges. Future innovations are a cornucopia of opportunities for the Phoenix Principle company!

Epilogue

Phoenix Principle People

EPILOGUE

Phoenix Principle
People

How do I use The Phoenix Principle in my life?

You Are the Top of the Pyramid

Success Formula performance is controlled from the bottom up. But Success Formula behaviors are controlled from the top down.

Success Formula results are determined by how well the pyramid aligns from the economy to the industry and upward. Poor alignment with the base yields poor results. Ongoing misalignment leads to deteriorating performance. But how a Success Formula is defined and implemented is controlled by individuals, work teams, and functional groups—from the top down. People are responsible for the Success Formula and how it is implemented. Only people can maintain Lock-in or choose to change a Success Formula.

Identity

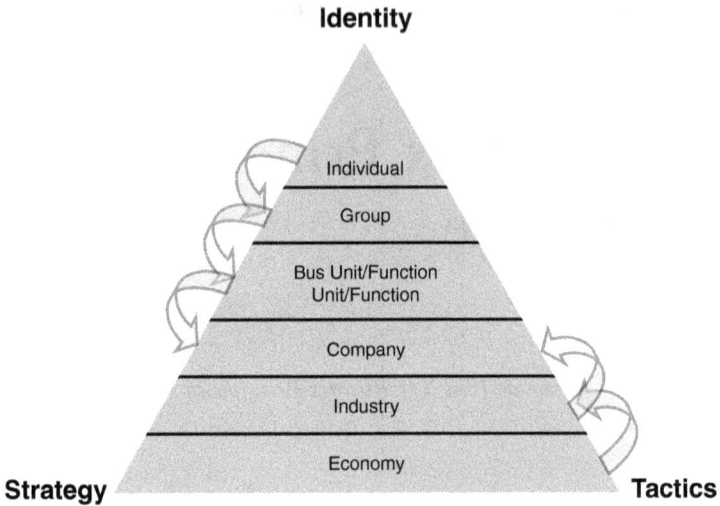

Strategy   **Tactics**

Figure E.1 Company Success Formulas are wedged between macro trends rolling up and micro Success Formulas rolling down.

Individual Success Formulas—those at the top of the Success Formula pyramid—are incredibly important to results. People Lock-in personal Success Formulas and then Defend and Extend them. Leadership roles imply direction setting and conformance maintenance, and leaders apply their individual Success Formulas to these roles. If a CEO's Success Formula does not reflect what is important in the economy, then his organization will not perform well. Peering down the hierarchy, any time a vice-president's, director's, or manager's individual Success Formula is not aligned with the base of the pyramid, performance risk is created.

It is possible for a single person to have a dramatic impact, negatively or positively, on an organization. A high-growth company can install a leader Locked-in to traditional Defend & Extend practices and falter quickly. When McDonald's replaced CEO Greenberg with the more conservative ex-controller, Mr. Cantalupo, the company turned away from growing its acquisitions and instead focused on shuttering restaurants, financial re-engineering through one-time charges and extending existing store sales. Quickly the new leader enforced his by-the-numbers Lock-in and refortified a Defend & Extend culture.

It is possible to identify a leader's Success Formula, and from that predict how his organization will behave. Have you heard someone say, "If Joe takes over that group, you know it will..."? The more consistently

Joe's Success Formula is observed across his leadership team, the easier it is to predict what his team will do. Leaders control resources and Lock-in tools such as hiring, promotions, IT applications, and process investments through which they push their Success Formulas onto groups and entire organizations.

Similarly, leaders who use Disruptions and White Space can quickly and dramatically impact a lagging business's performance. Remember the dramatic turnaround at Apple when Steve Jobs returned as CEO? Results are not about heroic behavior, but rather how leaders and managers apply their individual Success Formulas to finding growth markets and migrating an organization.

The importance of individual Success Formulas is not limited to CEOs. Functional leaders can quickly alter their group's behavior by changing critical metrics and rewards. In today's highly competitive marketplace, chief information officers have notably short tenure. Technology specialists, formerly the preferred background for CIOs, often struggle to achieve desired business goals. So organizations have begun hiring CIOs without traditional IT skills but who are willing to dramatically alter project priorities and funding to mobilize IT resources toward business needs.

Similarly, business unit leaders are finding their individual Success Formulas have a huge impact on unit performance. Traditionally, country heads in multinational corporations were chartered to apply the company Success Formula in foreign markets. But simple Extend behavior no longer achieves desired results in today's globally savvy and differentiated marketplace. Look no further than Wal-Mart's consistent failures to extend their Success Formula internationally.

Country leaders now have to overcome traditional Lock-ins and develop new Success Formulas tailored to local market needs. Through creating new Success Formulas, country managers can catalyze headquarters Disruptions, and their businesses can serve as White Space for evolving the multinational into a more powerful global competitor. Remember Kellogg's, where the international business head, Mr. Gutierez, took over the top post of a company needing change?

Directors and managers influence their work teams by their D&E versus Phoenix Principle actions. In the mid-1990s, a leading telecom company created an internal team dedicated to enhancing broadband sales. The nascent market was doubling in size quarterly as Internet use grew. The team leader spent his first three weeks confirming all team members could return to previous jobs upon project conclusion. The next four weeks were spent establishing parameters for recommendations, based on existing products, customer relationships, and systems. Not surprisingly, his team developed few new initiatives for broadband sales growth and was disbanded after only six months. While this company's broadband sales remained stagnant, the marketplace exploded.

A product manager willing to utilize external input can make an enormous difference. In *Leading the Revolution* Gary Hamel describes how a midlevel IBM programmer introduced web browsing to the laptop product manager. The product manager kept promoting Disruptions until granted a White Space project to promote IBM network solutions (a fledgling business) for sporting event information dissemination. This White Space project won the opportunity for IBM to manage data for the Olympics and led IBM's emergence as a marketplace leader in the fast-growing network computing market.

People critically affect organizational performance because everyone has a personal Success Formula that will align, or not, with marketplace requirements. Locked-in personal Success Formulas fall victim to market shifts, just like those in Locked-in companies. Keeping organizations attuned to market challenges requires leaders and managers maintain personal capacity for the Disruption and re-alignment of their individual Success Formulas.

Do You Disrupt Your Lock-in and Use Personal White Space

Just as assumptions and Lock-in make it hard for a business to recognize its Success Formula, it's hard for individuals to recognize their personal Success Formulas. Most managers simply recognize they have core beliefs about leading and managing, but few people think about their Identities, Strategies, and Tactics in a formal way. People rarely recognize how they Lock-in their Success Formula with daily behaviors or the structures used to make decisions.

All individuals have a Success Formula and Lock-in. Most managers' Success Formulas are defined between age 18 and 30. During these early adult years, future managers observe leaders in education, government, and their organizations—be they for-profit or not-for-profit. Simultaneously, most managers-in-training read newspapers, magazines, and books, and then in conjunction with their personal experiences, draw conclusions about how case stories and theories lead to results. After a few early experiments and reflecting on outcomes, individuals develop a strong commitment to their leadership Identities, Strategies that they believe are likely to produce the best results, and Tactics that mobilize resources in the desired direction.

Quickly their Success Formula is Locked-in by beliefs in hierarchy, sacred management cows, and industry norms. Further, most people develop their own biased decision-making processes, which incorporate personal preferences for

- *Data*. How much and what kind?
- *Metrics*. Which they prefer to watch closely, and which they don't.
- *People*. What sorts of people to trust, and which not.
- *Knowledge repositories for obtaining information*. Schools, industry, networking, or functional groups, for example.

The majority of management decisions soon become narrowly bounded by individual Success Formula Lock-ins.

PERSONAL LOCK-INS

Have you ever experienced a manager with absolute commitment to preset decisions, regardless of circumstances? Have you heard a manager say

- Never hire consultants.
- Employees should be in the office.
- Customer satisfaction is tied to price.
- The most effective work is done before noon.
- It's always best to be market share leader.
- You can't fail following industry best practices.
- Don't be first; try to be a fast second after you see what works.
- The boss is always right.
- Unions hurt business.
- Out-of-work job seekers are less desirable than currently employed candidates.
- Graduates from top MBA schools are arrogant.

- Creative people belong in marketing.
- R&D results can't be measured.
- Offshore suppliers produce lower quality.
- All decisions should be made through consensus building.
- It's the role of a leader to decide.
- Hierarchy is bad.
- Big corporations are wasteful.
- Small businesses are lean.
- Always negotiate the lowest possible price.
- No meeting should last more than 45 minutes.

These Lock-ins reflect personal Success Formulas and help managers make consistent, quick decisions.

Because we have Locked-in personal Success Formulas, we cannot grow unless we allow Disruptions in our personal lives. Only through Disruptions can we create White Space in which to develop new decision-making approaches and improve our performance.

For individuals, just like organizations, Disruptions are not disturbances. Being laid-off is a disturbance. Receiving a promotion, demotion, a weak review or moving locations are disturbances. Although these can substantially impact our lives, they don't really change how we make decisions or behave. And they don't lead us into White Space.

Individual Disruptions come from within, just like all other Disruptions. Individual Disruptions stop us and cause us to say, "I'm going to use this opportunity to lead me toward different decisions and behaviors."

PERSONAL DISRUPTIONS

Examples of personal Disruptions include

- Selling significant personal assets, like a house, to attack debt Lock-in
- Pursuing education in an entirely new field, such as an engineer taking classes in law or a marketer studying physics, attacking previous decision-making assumptions

- Taking a position in a completely different industry to attack assumptions about business models
- Joining a networking group far from your specialty, attacking Lock-in to data sources or decision-making processes
- Taking a position in a different function to attack functional Lock-in
- Moving to a foreign country, attacking Lock-ins to social norms

Personal Disruptions open the door to personal White Space. It is within personal White Space that we grow and create new Success Formulas as individuals. Unless we first Disrupt, we will enter new situations attempting to convert them into our old Success Formulas.

Howard Cosell was a famous sportscaster. Few people remember that he was first a lawyer. Only after dramatically lowering his cost of living was he able enter White Space, exploring his passion for sports. Had he not moved into a low-cost apartment, committed himself to mass transit, and told his family he was unwilling to practice law, he could not have created a new approach for success in broadcasting.

Personal White Space has the same requirements as organizational White Space. It's not White Space unless first there's a Disruption followed by *permission* to operate outside old Lock-ins and *resources* to actually implement it.

Permission requires we do more than commit to trying something new. We also must obtain permission from those close to us. If a spouse does not give permission, then it will be impossible to enter White Space. If a boss will not grant permission, then it's not possible to try something new on the job. It's not sufficient that we give ourselves permission (which itself often isn't easy) to enter White Space, it also requires that those we primarily interact with grant permission as well.

Steve graduated high school and became a dispatcher for the state police. Five years later he was married and had two children. Steve realized his income growth was limited, and his family would better prosper if he obtained an accounting degree. His bosses agreed Steve's economic prospects were better studying accounting, acknowledged he was bright, and encouraged him to increase his education. His wife agreed that additional income would benefit the family. So he enrolled in college.

Quickly Steve found he was unable to keep up work, family requirements, and college studies. Although verbally supportive, his work would not agree to customize his schedule to accommodate class attendance. Nor were his superiors willing to allow swapping shifts with co-workers or taking time off without pay. Further, college attendance radically shifted more family responsibilities onto his wife, who found herself unprepared for additional duties. Although she wanted higher family income, she did not feel she had signed up to being a single parent.

Neither his employer nor his family gave Steve permission to reduce work hours, short-term income, or family responsibilities. Fairly quickly he was forced to drop out of school. Lacking permission, he remained Locked-in to the job and family integral to his individual Success Formula. He attempted entering White Space without a Disruption and without permission to violate Lock-ins.

Similarly, Gloria, an R&D group middle manager, concluded her opportunities for corporate advancement would greatly improve if she had a graduate degree. Her employer agreed and said he would adjust her schedule to accommodate classes. Her spouse agreed and fully supported making changes so Gloria could spend time in class and studying. But, a quick review of her finances demonstrated that family living costs, including a substantial mortgage and two auto leases, left no resources for spending on education, much less taking a predictable income reduction to pursue classes. Although she had the desire and permission, Gloria did not have the resources to enter White Space.

We must recognize that many new personal Success Formula efforts fail because they lack permission or resources. Steve could have tried shift-trading with a colleague without asking his boss for permission. Or he might have hired a house cleaner or babysitter to assist his wife. But either, lacking a Disruption and explicit permission, would have ended up in disaster as his boss and family became discouraged that he was not fulfilling the Success Formula responsibilities *as they defined them*. Despite our lack of training in how to do it, obtaining permission for White Space is a requirement across the Success Formula pyramid.

Gloria might have sought a second mortgage or utilized high interest rate credit card debt, trying to maintain her lifestyle while incurring the extra cost of advanced education. But more debt would have applied extreme pressure on her family finances and put her educational goal in jeopardy. Without resources identified and committed in advance to see through her effort to completion, Gloria was unlikely to achieve her goal.

In both instances, Disruptions were needed to make personal White Space viable. Disruptions such as selling an automobile, or even the family home, could attack existing Lock-ins, alter permission, and free up resources to invest in White Space. Although the desire for White Space exists, without permission and resources—preceded by Disruption—White Space resources aren't really possible.

Applying Personal Disruptions and White Space to Work

There's a big difference between taking a job in a new industry where you intend to bring "new thinking" to your new employer and taking a new position to learn how that industry makes decisions. The former is using D&E Management to externally influence new workmates. The latter is using Disruption and White Space to alter your Success Formula. The outcome will differ markedly, given that the former is likely to fail while the latter has greater likelihood of personal and professional growth.

Ironically, most managers taking a new job and most management recruiters believe the objective should be bringing a new employer their history. But this leads to either (a) joining together common Success Formulas, producing only marginal improvement, or (b) a collision between inconsistent Success Formulas creating conflict and productivity declines. When managers make transitional moves, whether crossing industry, function, or geography, the greatest positive impact happens if the manager first Disrupts himself and then enters the new position as White Space. He should communicate his arrival as a Disruption to peers and subordinates and seek those willing to join him in White Space. By pulling everyone into White Space, a new Success Formula can be developed, likely producing better results.

When Ed Zander joined Motorola as CEO, analysts called for him to quickly cut headcount. Motorola had lost market share in several businesses and had already laid off thousands. Instead of continuing the bloodletting, Mr. Zander used his arrival as an opportunity to Disrupt Motorola. He attacked Lock-ins to hierarchy by changing physical office structures, bringing executives into the company cafeteria, and reducing both the time and style of executive meetings. He attacked Lock-ins to engineering by putting more focus on design and placing his own office near the design group. He also quickly partnered with Apple on a new mobile handset, attacking the not-invented-here mentality. Instead of shedding businesses, he began an acquisition program that addressed shortcomings in existing product lines. Quickly, Motorola sprouted multiple White Space projects, and its revenue and margins rapidly improved.

Unfortunately, he did not continue to Disrupt and implement White Space in the cell phone handset business. Instead, after the successful RAZR launch, Motorola tried traditional D&E tactics for growing share at the expense of profits, without stimulating innovation and new products. As a result, Mr. Zander left the CEO position in 2007 when Motorola handset revenues stalled. Failure to maintain Disruptions and White Space stalled Mr. Zander's initial turnaround success. Vigilance is the most important requirement for maintaining Phoenix Principle returns—and far too often we fall victim to the siren's call for Defending and Extending.

The stereotypical D&E turnaround manager is Al Dunlap. Mr. Dunlap took over Scott Paper Company, firing thousands of employees while closing several plants. He quickly sold Scott, generating cash for investors while employees and suppliers took it on the chin. Nicknamed Chainsaw Al for his aggressive cost-reduction practices, Mr. Dunlap took the same approach after taking the helm at Sunbeam-Oster. Unfortunately, he became another "one-hit wonder" when aggressive cost cutting backfired. He eliminated jobs and suppliers, but investors lost millions as Sunbeam's share price declined more than 75%. Mr. Dunlap was eventually held responsible for accounting irregularities, requiring he personally pay $15 million in settling a shareholder lawsuit.

Of course, organizations already have Success Formulas when hiring. It's not as if organizations are White Space. A Locked-in organization expects new hires will rapidly accept existing Lock-ins and conform to the Success Formula. So it's critical new employees quickly determine whether they have corporate permission and resources. If they don't have either, then they would be best served to adopt the existing employer Success Formula as fast as possible—or prepare to restart their job hunt. Because there *will* be Success Formula alignment.

Organizations Can Help Develop
Phoenix Principle People

One management development tool within GE is moving managers between several different positions. This helps GE leadership understand the manager's capacity to Disrupt himself and evolve his Success Formula. It also demonstrates the manager's ability to pull others into White Space with him, thus producing enhanced performance. Although GE is not perfect, this process helps GE advance individuals with great capacity for Disruption, personal growth, and White Space management. Likewise, this makes GE veterans highly desirable for leadership positions by other companies. And it contributes to GE's success as the longest lasting company on the original Dow Jones Industrial Average— after nearly a century.

A leading middle-market industrial parts supplier had a traditional strategy approach. But as the information economy brought out global competitors, these executives realized their strategy was insufficient. The CEO Disrupted his organization with a consultant-led project attacking Lock-in to product superiority. The project highlighted rapid competitor product copying, which, coupled with lower competitor prices, predicted market share losses. To find new competitive approaches, the CEO launched another project evaluating how IT could be more strategically used. This project had permission to explore new distribution arrangements and relationships with customers and was independently funded.

The CEO reached into operations for a director with company knowledge and a keen eye for competitors. Although he had no IT background, Rick was made the project lead. He was told if the project failed, he would fail—and likely the company as well. Rick was challenged to develop a new individual Success Formula as well as one for his company. He was given permission to obtain special skills from outsiders—skills he did not possess but would need to master. He was offered HR resources for counseling in his new role, accounting resources to develop and manage a budget, money to hire consultants, and his pick of company managers to staff his project.

Given permission and resources for White Space, Rick rapidly developed a new management approach. He created a different hierarchy and new metrics for reporting project progress. He built skills in

Internet competition. And he began using different software tools to obtain, organize, and display information for decision making. Rick built a new individual Success Formula and one for his White Space organization. Within months, his company began migrating toward his more competitive Success Formula, beating back offshore competitors.

Too many organizations complain they cannot keep their best managers. They complain pay packages for superior performers are impossible to obtain. Yet, when departing, these high-performing managers say their decision to move was based on issues beyond pay. They often discuss the lack of opportunity for personal growth.

Time and again top performers look for opportunities to Disrupt and lead White Space. Recognizing that ongoing optimization limits personal growth, they seek positions allowing them to try new things. When opportunities are not presented in their own organizations, they find them elsewhere. And organizations like GE, willing to Disrupt and implement White Space, attract these superior performers.

The Phoenix Principle Is Available to All of Us

Every day we hear about institutions in trouble. It's not just businesses failing, but non-profit organizations and government units seeing their value diminish. Locked-in to old ways, their Success Formulas atrophy. Similarly, we hear about occupations disappearing as market and technology changes make skills outdated. Friends lose their jobs, often forever. Depression would be easy, wondering if we all are destined to obsolescence and eventual demise.

We all can grow by realizing that Disruptions and White Space create opportunities for unending improvement. Individuals can awaken to new growth ideas and move into new careers. Although success is not guaranteed, White Space creates the excitement of opportunity and puts fun into life. To avoid being locked out, learn to attack Lock-in. To find long-term success, we all must recognize Lock-in, attack it, and then give ourselves permission to try new approaches while finding resources to keep White Space in our lives.

Index

N

O

P

Q–R

X–Z

www.ingramcontent.com/pod-product-compliance
Lightning Source LLC
Chambersburg PA
CBHW060249220326
41598CB00027B/4039